# Writing and Growing

# Writing and Growing

## Transforming High School Students into Writers

Timothy Horan

ROWMAN & LITTLEFIELD
Lanham • Boulder • New York • London

Published by Rowman & Littlefield

An imprint of The Rowman & Littlefield Publishing Group, Inc.
4501 Forbes Boulevard, Suite 200, Lanham, Maryland 20706
www.rowman.com

86-90 Paul Street, London EC2A 4NE, United Kingdom

Copyright © 2022 by Timothy Horan

*All rights reserved.* No part of this book may be reproduced in any form or by any electronic or mechanical means, unless specifically noted at the bottom of a page, including information storage and retrieval systems, without written permission from the publisher, except by a reviewer who may quote passages in a review.

British Library Cataloguing in Publication Information Available

**Library of Congress Cataloging-in-Publication Data**

Names: Horan, Timothy, author.
Title: Writing and growing: transforming high school students into writers / Timothy Horan.
Description: Lanham, Maryland: Rowman & Littlefield, [2022] | Includes bibliographical references and index. | Summary: "This book contains twenty original writing projects created specifically for high school students"—Provided by publisher.
Identifiers: LCCN 2022005585 (print) | LCCN 2022005586 (ebook) | ISBN 9781475850222 (Cloth) | ISBN 9781475850239 (Paperback) | ISBN 9781475850246 (ePub)
Subjects: LCSH: English language—Composition and exercises—Study and teaching (Secondary)
Classification: LCC LB1631 .H72 2022 (print) | LCC LB1631 (ebook) | DDC 808/.0420712—dc23/eng/20220223
LC record available at https://lccn.loc.gov/2022005585
LC ebook record available at https://lccn.loc.gov/2022005586

*To Lt. John B. Horan, FDNY*
*To Nurse Mary O. Horan, LPN*
*And to Michelle, who possesses the greatest of all gifts—*
*A heart filled with love*

# Contents

| | |
|---|---|
| Acknowledgments | xi |
| Introduction: High School Students and Their Finest Selves | 1 |
| Chapter 1: Grades Nine and Ten: First Writing Project: The Personal Argumentative Essay: "Television and Streaming Video" | 9 |
| Chapter 2: Grades Nine and Ten: Second Writing Project: The Informative Essay: "A Goal for the Future" | 21 |
| Chapter 3: Grades Nine and Ten: Third Writing Project: The Short Story: "You Attain Your Goal" | 29 |
| Chapter 4: Grades Nine and Ten: Fourth Writing Project: The Personal Reflective Essay: "Your Favorite Place" (First Draft) | 39 |
| Chapter 5: Grades Nine and Ten: Fifth Writing Project: The Personal Reflective Essay: "Your Favorite Place" (Second Draft: Revising and Editing) | 49 |
| Chapter 6: Grades Nine and Ten: Sixth Writing Project: The Personal Reflective Essay: "Your Favorite Place" (Third Draft: E-book) | 55 |
| Chapter 7: Grades Nine and Ten: Seventh Writing Project: The Literary Research Paper: "Dreams and Loneliness in Steinbeck's Novella *Of Mice and Men*" (First Draft: Literary Analysis) | 63 |
| Chapter 8: Grades Nine and Ten: Eighth Writing Project: The Literary Research Paper: "Dreams and Loneliness in Steinbeck's Novella *Of Mice and Men*" (Second Draft: Secondary Sources) | 73 |

Chapter 9: Grades Nine and Ten: Ninth Writing Project: The Literary Research Paper: "Dreams and Loneliness in Steinbeck's Novella *Of Mice and Men*" (Third Draft: Creative Coda)     83

Chapter 10: Grades Nine and Ten: Tenth Writing Project: The Reflective Essay: "Looking Back on a Year of Writing"     93

Chapter 11: Grades Eleven and Twelve: First Writing Project: The Argumentative Essay: "Are Cell Phones Good for High School Students?" (Part One)     103

Chapter 12: Grades Eleven and Twelve: Second Writing Project: The Informative Research Essay: "Cell Phone Addiction" (Part Two)     113

Chapter 13: Grades Eleven and Twelve: Third Writing Project: The Reflective Short Story: "A Day without My Cell Phone" (Part Three)     123

Chapter 14: Grades Eleven and Twelve: Fourth Writing Project: The Personal Research Essay: "My Ideal Career" (Part One)     133

Chapter 15: Grades Eleven and Twelve: Fifth Writing Project: The Creative Essay: "My Ideal Career: Workplace Log Entries" (Part Two)     143

Chapter 16: Grades Eleven and Twelve: Sixth Writing Project: The Informative Oral Presentation: "My Ideal Career" (Part Three)     153

Chapter 17: Grades Eleven and Twelve: Seventh Writing Project: The Informative Research Project: "The History behind *The Crucible*" (Part One)     163

Chapter 18: Grades Eleven and Twelve: Eighth Writing Project: Literary Analysis: "Interpreting *The Crucible*" (Part Two)     175

Chapter 19: Grades Eleven and Twelve: Ninth Writing Project: The Creative Project: "Unearthing *The Crucible*" (Part Three)     185

Chapter 20: Grades Eleven and Twelve: Tenth Writing Project: The Reflective Project: "Creating a Time Capsule"     195

| | |
|---|---|
| Conclusion: A Call for Change | 207 |
| Notes | 215 |
| References | 217 |
| Index | 221 |

# Acknowledgments

Composing this book was a journey of writing and growing, generously assisted by kindness and miracles. And now, I want to thank everyone who somehow helped along the way. To my mother, who bought me a toy typewriter and lots of books when I was very young. To my father, who taught me carpentry and helped me build a library in my house. To St. John's University (Queens, NY), for introducing me to the beauties of literature and writing. To Long Island University (NY), for gently propelling me into the world of teaching. To library friends Debbie Antolini and Shannon Brady. To former students who answered all my questions: Brandon; Denise; Jade; Jennifer; Olivia; and Reece. To all the wonderful people at Rowman & Littlefield, especially Tom Koerner, Carlie Wall, and RoseMary Ludt, for being so kind and professional. To departed friends Tycho and Oscar, for their unwavering love and loyalty. And to my beloved Michelle, whose laughter sounds like distant bells on a still and silent summer night.

# Introduction

## *High School Students and Their Finest Selves*

This book contains a four-year writing program specifically designed for high school students.[1] In these pages, you will find twenty writing assignments that are original, engaging, and quirky. I designed all of them to become welcome additions to the worlds of high school students and to the curriculum of the contemporary academy. As I developed this book, I remained very close to a pair of sibling objectives. First, I wanted to teach high school students how to write. This is of crucial importance, because, overwhelmingly, *our secondary students cannot write* (my twenty-plus years in education have confirmed this, over and over).

My second goal was to assist students as they grow toward adulthood and independence. During these formative years, they are discovering and creating their identities, maturing into young adults, and making choices that will reverberate throughout their lives. With this in mind, I designed a score of writing projects on subjects central to the lives and worlds of adolescents. This program will help students grow not just as writers, but as human beings.

As you read this book, you will find assignments about students' consumption of television (and streaming video), goals for the future, their favorite place in the world, their relationship with cell phones, recent historical events, and their ideal career. Along the way, students will write short stories, a diary entry, a centuries-old court transcript, and different forms of literary analysis. At the end of each year, students will compose reflective pieces in which they evaluate how much they have grown as writers, and as human beings.

## IS THIS BOOK ABOUT THE COMMON CORE?

The answer to that question is *yes and no*. In creating these writing assignments, I used the Common Core Writing Standards as organizational tools and general pedagogical guidelines to help create a coherent framework of learning. Before adopting the writing standards as a guiding schema, I studied them deeply and found them to be beautifully designed and truly excellent resources for teaching and learning how to write. And now, let's look at how the high school standards are organized.

There are ten writing standards for grades nine and ten, and another ten (similar) writing standards for grades eleven and twelve. Following this structure, I designed twenty writing assignments original to this book, and I present them here in twenty chapters. The standards are brief but intricate texts that suggest (but do not mandate) lessons and elements to offer students. Here, I'd like to dispel a myth that seems to surround the Common Core. The writing standards do *not* represent inviolable axioms that must be upheld word for word.

In fact, the Common Core organization enthusiastically encourages teachers to *interpret the standards*, stating that teachers who include the standards in their teaching "will continue to devise lesson plans and tailor instruction to the individual needs of the students in their classrooms" ("Myths vs. Facts"). The standards serve as *guidelines* for educators, who can teach them and differentiate them as they wish—and this is precisely what I did in this book.

In each chapter, I begin by providing the Common Core Writing Standard that sparked the writing assignment (I refer to this as the "Main Standard"). After that, I present a brief section called "Author's Notes." In these notes, I interpret the standard and describe how the chapter's writing assignment enacts and creatively embodies the principles contained in the main standard that inspired it.

As you read the "Author's Notes," you'll also find that many of them include the phrase "alternate topics." As you absorb and practice the methods and techniques of this writing program, I encourage you to interpret the standards and create your own original writing assignments based on the alternate topics I provide. As you do this, be sure to use the projects in this book as exemplars, and always utilize the structure and principles of this system. Creating your own writing assignments will allow you to differentiate writing projects for your own students and will help to avoid potential repetition between (and among) the grades.

Many of the standards also include additional information and qualifications, which I refer to as "sub-standards." I provide these as well, along with additional "Author's Notes" describing the connection between the writing assignment and the sub-standard. As you read the sub-standards, you will notice the occasional presence of *asterisks* (i.e., *Sub-standard A). These asterisks designate importance. In sub-standards marked with an asterisk, there is a valuable element that plays a prominent role in the writing assignment—and in the students' learning.

## OVERVIEW OF THIS WRITING PROGRAM

As students proceed through this program, they will complete ten writing projects each year. In terms of pacing, students will write, revise, and edit *one project each month*. Each writing assignment is highly choreographed because our students must learn the structure and organization of writing (academic as well as creative). Nonetheless, the assignments also allow room for *choice and creativity*, and these are purposeful designs included to harness and heighten engagement. As I developed these projects, I strove to incorporate a balance of structure and originality—a combination highly effective for the minds of fledgling writers.

As students move through the program, the writing projects will increase in length and complexity, successively building on each other and periodically repeating and reinforcing methods and techniques essential for writing proficiency. At the end of the program, students will be well-rounded and experienced writers ready for the rigors of writing in college and the workplace. They will also be better equipped to approach, interpret, and understand the complex worlds of college, career, and adulthood.

And now, let's talk about the *length* of projects. Students will undoubtedly ask, "How long does this have to be?" It's difficult to assign a strict factor to an organic process (i.e., *How tall does a tree have to be?*), but our students are fledgling writers, and they need structure and guidance. So, we'll begin the program with assignments of reasonable lengths (*about three pages long*), then have their projects grow a bit longer each year. Instruct students to write in twelve point, Times New Roman font, double-spaced, and give them these suggested (and approximate) lengths:

- Ninth Grade: At least three pages long
- Tenth Grade: Three-to-five pages long (five pages will be preferable by the end of the year)
- Eleventh Grade: At least five pages long (more than five pages will be preferable by the end of the year)
- Twelfth Grade: Five-to-eight pages long (more than eight pages will be preferable by the end of the year)

## THE FIVE-PART OUTLINE

Outlines are an indispensable ingredient in learning how to write and are wonderful tools for organizing ideas and essays. They create an organized writing plan that is clear, simple, and visible, and they help prevent writer's block. In this book, *every project* will germinate with a method I developed called the "Five-Part Outline"[2] (please understand that this is *not* the five-paragraph essay). The five-part outline is *extremely* effective in teaching students how to write and is one of the mainstays of this writing program.

When students are given an assignment and begin thinking about it, their ideas are a maelstrom of swirling confusion, and students often feel overwhelmed by the infinite panoply of textual possibilities. When we teach students the five-part outline and they plug ideas into it, their thoughts assume a visible, physical form, and students watch in gratified amazement as a clear plan begins to develop in front of them. It works beautifully, so let's take a closer look at it.

The five-part outline is based, in part, on what I term the "rule of three." The rule of three is a highly effective principle in which I assert that to examine anything in reasonable academic depth, it must be considered in at least *three elements*. This is because (I tell my students) "one is an example, two is a pair, three is a *pattern*" (Horan, *Create Your School Library Writing Center, Grades 7–12*, 53).

In the model of the five-part outline, I refer to these three elements as the three "subtopics." The subtopics are contained within (or relate to) the main topic of the assignment. They are central to the writing project (literally and figuratively), and they are quite flexible. Students can choose more than three subtopics if they wish (and possibly fewer than three, though this is not encouraged), and each subtopic can generate several paragraphs. (The rule of three also applies to the "organization" of subtopics, which can often be effectively discussed with *three relevant examples*.)

Let's look at an example of a five-part outline in which the student is writing an essay on his or her *ideal career* (which we'll see in chapter 14). With a personal research project of this nature, we'll start the process by choosing these three subtopics: *Describe the Career; Describe the Training Necessary for the Career; Describe Why You Want This Career.* When we have chosen our subtopics, we put an Introduction in front of them and a Conclusion after them. These function as rhetorical bookends that comment on the main subject and its three subtopics. For our sample *career* project, a simple five-part outline would look like this:

1. Introduction (Provide an overview of the topic. Write this last)

2. First Subtopic: *Describe Your Ideal Career*
3. Second Subtopic: *Describe the Training and Education Your Career Requires*
4. Third Subtopic: *Describe Why You Want This Particular Career*
5. Conclusion (restate career; emphasize its positive aspects; project enthusiasm)

See how that works? It's a clear and simple method that introduces students to the organization of the academic essay and produces a quality product. As you teach students the content of the five-part outline, also teach them the *order* in which to compose their essays, especially the wise exhortation to *write your introduction last*. Explain this as follows:

Skip the Introduction (for now), and write your subtopics *first*. This allows you to truly understand the subject of your essay. When you finish your subtopics, write your Conclusion. This way, you can conclude it properly, and with insight. Write your Introduction *last*, because you can't accurately introduce something that does not yet exist.

The five-part outline is extremely effective in teaching students how to write. Once again, I want to emphasize that this is not a rigid model but is highly flexible and designed to change and evolve with the student's learning and thinking. It can contract for fledgling writers, and it can expand into greater length and complexity as students become more confident and skilled at composition. Also instruct your students to provide a *title* for *everything they write*. The title should be simple, clear, and specific, and it should exactly describe what the piece is about. Like the five-part outline, the title will likely evolve as students compose their projects.

Each chapter in this book concludes with a one-page outline original to this work of scholarship. These documents correspond to the chapter's individual writing assignment, and are designed to be copied and given to each student. They assist with organizing information, developing ideas, and understanding the major concepts of each writing assignment. As you teach each writing project in this book, please make copies of these outlines and distribute them to *all* of your students. They are indispensable tools that will assist students as you unravel the mysteries of composition and transform your students into writers.

## THE ONE-STORY APPROACH

Throughout the assignments described in this book, our students will be writing several creative pieces, such as short stories. When instructing your students how to write a short story, you might begin by asking your students a difficult question: *How many stories are there in the world?* They'll probably say things like *"Millions!" "Too many to count!"* and *"I have no idea."*

Although there is some truth to all those answers, you'll surprise them by saying this: "There is only *one* story in the world." It's sort of a trick answer to a trick question, and it makes for a fun discussion. Although ultimately unprovable, there *is* a great deal of truth to the assertion that there *is* only one story in the world. And you'll explain it to them, discuss it with them, and ask them to take notes.

The monolithic story to which we're alluding is a story *structure* common to nearly all "conventional" stories to which our students (and we) have been exposed. It is simple in its geography, and, in its barest form, it's a narrative of solving a problem or attaining a goal. Let us refer to this as the "One-Story" approach (an original term). Here is an example, based on Arthurian lore:

> A knight goes out in quest of the Holy Grail. He learns that the Grail is locked up inside a castle. To make matters worse, the castle and Grail are actively guarded by a fire-spitting dragon. The knight either slays the dragon, or the dragon slays him.

If you look at the Arthurian tale above, you'll see that it is composed of three basic parts that, put together, create an archetypal plot. In simplest terms, here they are:

1. *Grail*: A person, or persons, *want* something.
2. *Conflict*: Someone (or something) works to prevent that person from attaining the desired goal.
3. *Resolution*: The person attains the goal (usually a happy ending) or does not attain the goal (usually an unhappy ending).

Although largely truthful and accurate, this three-step model of the One-Story has been streamlined for high school students. It is important that each student understands the structure of the story conveyed through this model, because *students will be using this model as they compose their short stories* (and, like *all* the projects in this book, these short stories will have a five-part structure, proceeding as follows: *Introduction*; *Grail*; *Conflict*; *Resolution*; *Conclusion*).

## HOW SHOULD YOU USE THIS BOOK?

Every piece of writing has a purpose and an audience (this is a bit of useful wisdom you might share with your students). The primary *audience* for this book is an educator who has the privilege and opportunity to teach high school students the art of writing. The primary *purpose* of this book is to show those educators a new and highly effective method for teaching these students how to write and grow.

However, this book has other audiences and other purposes also. This book is relevant for teachers on *all* levels (above and below high school) who want to employ *simplicity*, *clarity*, and *humanity* as they teach students how to write. These teachers can differentiate the writing projects and tailor them to their classes and their students—and have a terrific time doing it. This book can even be used in college and graduate school in programs that teach composition and education. Beyond that, this book will be very useful to students and writers on all levels, introducing them to an engaging and unique approach to the writing process.

However, whether you're a teacher, professor, student, writer, or person who's in love with the world and with words (as I am), I urge you to approach this book with an open mind and a sense of creativity and exploration. The writing program articulated in this book encourages freedom, fun, and choice among its students—and it encourages these values among its teachers. When it comes to implementing the projects described here, there are no firm or fustian rules (and I feel the same way about writing). But if there are no rules, how should you use this book?

As a teacher, you can, if you want, assign all writing projects exactly as indicated and this would work very well. Or you can implement *some* writing assignments as indicated, and differentiate others according to your whims. Or you can absorb the principles, knowledge, and spirit contained in this book and develop *your own* interesting and unique writing projects. All of that would work very well and be lots of fun.

However, no matter how you choose to use this book, I hope you read it with a smile on your face and your imagination ablaze. I also hope you consider this book a colorful and kaleidoscopic grab bag of ideas and activities that will energize your teaching and help your students to grow as writers and human beings. It is my utmost hope that this writing program will help students to reach their full potential. As writing teachers, let's confidently instruct our students as they grow toward a future filled with challenge and possibility. And let's hope they continue to utilize the lessons we teach them as they explore their identities through writing and proudly grow into their finest selves.

*Chapter 1*

# Grades Nine and Ten: First Writing Project

## *The Personal Argumentative Essay: "Television and Streaming Video"*

Main Standard 9–10.1:
Write arguments to support claims in an analysis of substantive topics or texts, using valid reasoning and relevant and sufficient evidence.

*Author's Notes: In this argumentative essay, students will evaluate the effect that streaming video has on their lives. Alternate topics for argumentative essays include* social media; video games; ways to deal with cyberbullying, *and* evaluating the link between technology and loneliness. *Students will write this in the first-person.*

*Sub-Standard A:
Introduce precise claim(s), distinguish the claim(s) from alternate or opposing claims, and create an organization that establishes clear relationships among claim(s), counterclaims, reasons, and evidence.

*Author's Notes: Students will begin their essays with a clear thesis statement. This essay will be organized by using the five-part outline.*

*Sub-Standard B:
Develop claim(s) and counterclaims fairly, supplying evidence for each while pointing out the strengths and limitations of both in a manner that anticipates the audience's knowledge level and concerns.

*Author's Notes:* Students will provide a section describing their major arguments. After that, they will describe at least one counterargument.

Sub-Standard C:
Use words, phrases, and clauses to link the major sections of the text; to create cohesion; and to clarify the relationships between claim(s) and reasons, between reasons and evidence, and between claim(s) and counterclaims.

*Author's Notes:* Students will use transitional words, phrases, and sentences, such as however; nevertheless; next; additionally; afterward; because of this; as a result; on the other hand; the next day; *et cetera*.

Sub-Standard D:
Establish and maintain a formal style and objective tone while attending to the norms and conventions of the discipline in which they are writing.

*Author's Notes:* Students will write this project in the first person. However, they will use a formal "academic" voice, refraining from using the slang and abbreviations common when sending text messages.

Sub-Standard E:
Provide a concluding statement or section that follows from and supports the argument presented.

*Author's Notes:* Students will provide a brief conclusion to this project (probably one paragraph long). The conclusion will include elements of summary and a final assertion that their point of view is the correct one.

## TEXT TYPES AND PURPOSES

As we embark on our adventure of writing in high school, we should note that the ten standards are broken into three groups of three standards each and a final "group" of one standard. The first group is called "Text Types and Purposes," and it offers us three very different types of writing assignments. These are the *argumentative essay*, the *informative essay*, and the *creative composition*. Let's look at the first one, because that's what we're doing here.

In this current project, we introduce our students to the argumentative essay, sometimes referred to as the "persuasive essay." This is a very important mode of writing, and our students will see it over and over as they write for high school (and college). The *purpose* of the argumentative essay (you'll explain to your students) is to convince your reader that *your* point of view is the correct one and that those who disagree with you are wrong. Because this is a *personal* argumentative essay, students will write it in the first person, and they will use their own knowledge and experience, rather than research from external sources. Let's look at the requirements of Standard One.

As students compose their argumentative essays, they need to define their claims clearly, include at least one counterclaim, and keep the essay organized. As they write, they will argue their claims logically and support their claims with evidence. Finally, they will incorporate smooth transitions, keep a formal tone, and wrap things up with a snappy conclusion. This is a tall order for our ninth and tenth graders. We cannot simply say to them, "Go and write an argumentative essay," because they don't know how to do it. We have to teach them each step of the way, and this is precisely what we're going to do.

## THE TOPIC

The topic of this essay is television and the various streaming video incarnations that our students consume. We are giving them this topic for two reasons. First, the students will find this interesting and engaging, as most of them enjoy video media, such as television and the internet. Our students consume these media voraciously, usually for entertainment, and occasionally to learn. Their natural interest in this topic will heighten engagement levels and increase their motivation to write about this subject.

More important, we are giving them this topic because it implicitly asks them to *evaluate* the media they consume, to consider their relationships with it, and to reflect on the effect it is having on their lives. This is a worthwhile and complex evaluation. The video media available to our students range from educational and artistic to shallow and mind-numbing, low-level entertainment. Too much of either (especially the latter) is not good for their minds or their bodies, and it's not a productive use of time. In this project, we are tacitly asking them to evaluate the choices they make.

## TEACHING THE ACADEMIC ARGUMENT

Before we introduce the topic, we must teach our students the structure of the academic argument. Like all assignments in this book, we will present it to students in the format of the five-part outline. This will keep students' writing and thoughts organized, and it will help them understand the components of the academic argument and how they are presented.

Begin this journey by telling your students that the academic argument is composed of four major ingredients: *thesis, definition of terms, evidence, counterarguments*. In their arguments, they must include all four elements, or their essays won't be effective. Let's start with the *thesis*.

## THESIS

A thesis is the major *idea* driving an essay. This idea—*the thesis*—will be expressed through a *thesis statement*. Thesis statements may seem simple, but they are notoriously difficult to understand, to learn, and to teach. Because we're teaching ninth and tenth graders (a developmental level ripe for learning), we'll present this component with great simplicity. First, tell your students that *they must have a thesis*. This is *the most important part* of any academic writing. It must be driven by a single major idea.

In terms of writing, the importance of this governing idea (the thesis) cannot be overstated. If students (or writers in general) don't understand what they're writing about, they will be plagued by writer's block, and the text they generate will be unfocused and lifeless (this is *extremely* common among high school students). Tell your students that all argumentative essays begin with an *essential question*. In this case, the question they'll be answering is a simple one and can be expressed as follows: *Are television and streaming media good for high school students or bad for high school students?*

This a basic "A or B" question. We are giving students the topic, and they must choose a side. Many of your students will undoubtedly respond that "it's both," and this is a good sign. They are seeing this issue in terms of complexity and in terms of nuance and degree. However (you'll tell them), *they must choose a side*. If they attempt to argue both sides, the essay will be insipid and dull, where it should be bold and vibrant. The "other side," you'll tell them, will be expressed through counterarguments (which you'll teach later). *But how do we write thesis statements? And, where should the thesis statement be placed?*

There are several good answers to these questions, but remember, we're dealing with young students, so we want to seize this grand teachable moment, and present things with clarity and simplicity. First, tell your students that a thesis statement should (ideally) be expressed in *one sentence*. That sentence should be simple, clear, and direct, and it should be *the first sentence in the essay* (which is to say, the thesis statement will be *the first sentence in the introduction*). Tell the reader immediately what the essay is about, and express it clearly and confidently.

Yes, there are other ways to write thesis statements, other places to put it, and other ways to teach it, but *first-sentence-placement* is the simplest and most effective method for fledgling writers. It is the easiest entrance through this particular gateway of knowledge. For this essay, students can choose from two basic thesis statements, and these might be expressed as follows:

- Television and streaming media are a positive force for high school students.
- High school students should avoid television and streaming media.

Those are two possible examples, and you should encourage your students to express their own thesis statements in their own individual manners.

## DEFINITION OF TERMS

Early in the essay (probably in the second paragraph), students will describe the argument in greater terms, which will require them to *define their terms*. Here, they will define and describe the items and ideas being discussed *as they are using them in the essay*. For example, what exactly do we mean by "streaming video?" This is a rather elastic term, filled with different types and brands, so students will need to describe exactly what they are talking about.

Let us consider some other possibilities. Is a student talking exclusively about *television*? If so, is the student discussing "free" television channels or well-known television packages that require monthly payments? Is the student referring to certain internet-based streaming websites? Is the student including *YouTube* in the argument? Will the student be discussing video that streams to the students' cell phones (often viewed late at night)? The term "streaming video" is rather fuzzy at the edges, and students must decide what they will be discussing in the essay and then clearly "define" the subject to the reader. Don't leave the reader guessing.

## EVIDENCE AND ANALYSIS

This is a very important component in the research essay, because this is where the writer will "prove" his or her thesis to the reader. Very often, the evidence discussed in the argumentative essay will be based in reliable research. However, this current essay will *not* be based in research. In this project, students will rely upon personal experience and knowledge derived from their own habits and interactions with their peers. They will use their observations and experience as evidence and discuss them as *examples* supporting the main thesis. (In this section, students are encouraged to discuss at least *three* supporting examples.)

And how will they present their evidence persuasively? Through the process of *summary and commentary*. To present each example, the *summary* portion will include descriptions of personal experience (this is the "evidence"). After that, the *commentary* portion will be used to persuasively argue those points, demonstrating how they reveal the validity of the thesis. In teaching our students the process of summary and commentary, we are gently and silently introducing them to the basis of all logical analysis, which may also be explained as *description and interpretation*. (We will see more of this process in the following chapter.)

For example, let's say that a student is arguing that streaming video is largely *beneficial* for high school students. In her discussion, she will supply several examples (*three* is always a good number) to support her main contention. She will describe each example (*summary*) and then show how it illustrates and supports the writer's main thesis (*commentary*). Employing the summary and commentary paradigm, one of her examples might look like the following:

> Streaming video can be very helpful for high school students. For example, I like to watch Netflix. This is a great source of educational videos. The other day, I watched a documentary movie on the solar system. This video was very helpful. I learned a lot from it, and it really helped with a project I'm doing in my science class.

That's a brief hypothetical example, but it works well. It restates the central thesis and then supports it effectively with an example that functions as strong illustrative "evidence." Share this example with students. It works well for a paper of this nature, makes perfect sense, and it would be hard to argue against the point being made.

## COUNTERARGUMENTS

Here, start by explaining to students the concept of counterarguments. Whenever evaluating debatable topics (whether in-school or out), we should consider both sides of every issue. Very few issues in the world are truly "black-and-white"; most controversial issues have gray areas, with good and bad points on both sides. Because of this, students must include at least one opposing argument in their essays (up to three), which will be expressed in a single paragraph. Here, they will once again employ the process of summary and commentary. After describing the counterargument (summary), they will show why it is not terribly important or why it doesn't negate the major thesis being argued (commentary).

This is difficult to learn, but done well, it will strengthen their essays—and their minds. For example, let us continue the earlier example, in which a student argued that streaming video is good for high school students. A counterargument in her essay might sound like this:

> Of course, there is a great deal of bad programming available to high school students. For example, there are sitcoms, dumb TV series, and lots of silly videos on the internet. These are available to students at any time, and some students watch them instead of doing their homework. But this doesn't mean that all streaming videos are bad for students. It means that students sometimes make bad choices. So, the solution is not to tell students to stop watching TV and video, but to *teach them* how to watch it, so that they stay healthy and learn good things.

Again, that hypothetical example would be very successful in this paper. The student validated the counterargument and then did something rather sophisticated: she applied *conditions* to the opposing point of view, weakening its power and strengthening her argument. To do this, she did not argue for students to have *unrestricted access to streaming video* (which would be a simple and unrealistic argument). She argued for continued access to streaming video, but in an informed and moderated format—which makes perfect sense.

This is called a "qualifying" argument, and it is a highly effective technique for persuasion. Share this passage with your students, explain it, and encourage them to include qualifying arguments in their essays (to the best of their abilities). We'll learn more about this topic in chapter 11.

## LET'S GET STARTED

To begin teaching this project—and the argumentative essay—give your students an overview in which you describe the nature of the argumentative essay and the subject of this assignment. Tell them that they will eventually have to choose a side *for* or *against* the various forms of streaming video they are consuming (and writing about). To get them thinking about the subject in greater depth and complexity, have a rollicking in-class discussion in which you offer your students questions such as the following (which they'll find quite engaging):

- What types of videos do you consume?
- On average, how many hours per day do you spend watching videos?

And now, transition to *evaluative* questions:

- Is this good for your brain and your mental health?
- Is this good for your body and your physical health?
- Are there more productive things that you could be doing?

After your students begin to understand this topic and think about it in greater complexity, give them an in-class free-write (of perhaps four minutes). Ask them to take out a pen and paper, to write their names on it, and to draw a "t-chart" on the paper. To do this, they will draw one vertical line down the middle of the paper and a horizontal line near the top of the paper (this chart will look like a lowercase letter "t").

Have them label the left column the "Good Points of TV and Streaming Video," and have them label the right column the "Bad Points of TV and Streaming Video."

Next, give them two minutes to write down their thoughts on the *good points* of streaming video, then another two minutes to write down their thoughts on the *bad points* of streaming video. Last, tell them to look at their findings and to choose a side they actually believe in. When they have made a choice, have them circle it and hand the worksheet to you. They have now taken a side on an important issue. This is the *thesis*, and it will focus and propel their essays.

## THE ARGUMENTATIVE ESSAY: FORMAT AND ORGANIZATION

After students choose a thesis for their projects, you will teach them the format and organization of the argumentative essay. To begin this process, hand each student a copy of *Outline 9–10.1* (located at the end of this chapter). Tell them they will organize their essays by using the five-part outline. This provides a friendly entry into the academic argument and makes structure and organization visible to nervous students. Here are the five major parts of this essay. As you describe each, encourage your students to write notes on the outline.

### 1. Introduction

Students will begin their essays by expressing their thesis statements in the form of a single, simple sentence. *This is the first sentence of the essay.* After that, they will write (perhaps) another three or four sentences in which they provide an overview of the essay. Instruct your students to *write their introductions last*. This is an *extremely* effective technique for writing compositions. The best way to accurately introduce an essay is *after it is written*. The introduction will likely be one paragraph long.

## 2. First Subtopic: *Definition of Terms*

Here, students will define their terms *as they are using them in their essays*. They will also describe the argument in greater detail so that readers can better follow the student's argument. This will likely be one paragraph long (but can be longer if necessary).

## 3. Second Subtopic: *The Main Argument*

This is the most important part of the essay. Here, students will provide their main arguments in favor of the central thesis driving the paper. The goal here is to provide evidence in the form of personal knowledge and experience. Encourage your students to include at least *three specific supportive examples* (and to present each example in its own paragraph). For each example, students should include a mixture of summary (describing the example) and interpretive commentary. In the commentary, they will explain how these examples argue in favor of the thesis.

## 4. Third Subtopic: *Counterarguments*

In this section, students should include at least one carefully chosen counterargument (and no more than three). They will describe the counterargument and validate its meaning. After that, they will show why it is not overwhelmingly important or why their point of view is more supportable. (They can also include *qualifying arguments*, if those will be helpful.) This is challenging and difficult to learn, but, handled properly, it will help strengthen students' essays, and help them to think in greater complexity. This will likely be one paragraph long (but can be longer if necessary).

## 5. Conclusion

Here, students will (literally) conclude their arguments. In it, students will restate the thesis statement, summarize their findings, and once again affirm that their point of view is the correct one. The conclusion will likely be one paragraph long and may be composed of four or five sentences. The students will write this second-to-last (just before they compose their introduction).

## FROM ARGUMENT TO ENLIGHTENMENT

In this project, we introduced students to the academic argument, and taught them the basics of organizing and presenting a convincing persuasive essay. This is certainly valuable learning, because they'll encounter this format repeatedly throughout their academic careers. It is not an intuitive writing model, and it must be taught and practiced. Nonetheless, there was other valuable learning occurring here also.

In asking students to evaluate the topic of *television and streaming video* and its impact on their lives, we are implicitly asking students to reflect on their actions and the result of their choices. Writing activities that involve self-reflection and evaluation always result in self-knowledge and enlightenment, which are extremely valuable assets on our students' journey toward growth and personal development.

Ninth and Tenth Grade, First Writing Project: *Outline 9–10.1*
The Personal Argumentative Essay: "Television and Streaming Video"
Name_____ Date_____
Title _____

For the title, state your position on the issue. Example: Streaming Media Are Very Good for High School Students

1. Introduction. Your first sentence is your thesis statement. After that, write three or four sentences describing what this essay is about. Tip: *Write your introduction last.*

2. First Subtopic: *Define Your Terms.* What types of streaming video will you be discussing? Explain them to your reader. Don't assume your reader knows what you're talking about.
   a. First type of streaming video (name it and describe it)
   b. Second type of streaming video (name it and describe it)
   c. Third type of streaming video (name it and describe it)

3. Second Subtopic: *Your Main Arguments.* Provide at least three specific examples that support your thesis. For each example, include a mixture of summary and commentary.
   a. First Example (summary and commentary)
   b. Second Example (summary and commentary)
   c. Third Example (summary and commentary)

4. Third Subtopic: *Counterarguments.* Think of at least one valid argument (and no more than three) *against* your position. Describe why *your* position is stronger than the counterargument.
   a. First Counterargument (this is necessary)
   b. Second Counterargument (helpful, but not necessary)
   c. Third Counterargument (helpful, but not necessary)

5. Conclusion: Restate your thesis statement, and summarize your essay. Close by affirming that your position is the correct one. Write the conclusion second-to-last.

*This page is permitted to copy.*

*Chapter 2*

# Grades Nine and Ten: Second Writing Project

## *The Informative Essay: "A Goal for the Future"*

Main Standard 9–10.2:
Write informative/explanatory texts to examine and convey complex ideas, concepts, and information clearly and accurately through the effective selection, organization, and analysis of content.

*Author's Notes: Students will write an informative essay in which they describe and discuss one of their primary goals for the future. Alternate topics for this essay include the following:* What are you proudest of? What's the most difficult thing you've ever done? What makes you happiest? *Students will write this in the first-person.*

\*Sub-Standard A:
Introduce a topic; organize complex ideas, concepts, and information to make important connections and distinctions; include formatting (e.g., headings), graphics (e.g., figures, tables), and multimedia when useful to aiding comprehension.

*Author's Notes: After choosing a topic, students will use the five-part outline to describe and discuss that topic. They will include headings for the subtopics and will include an illustration relevant to the topic.*

Sub-Standard B:
Develop the topic with well-chosen, relevant, and sufficient facts, extended definitions, concrete details, quotations, or other information and examples appropriate to the audience's knowledge of the topic.

*Author's Notes: Students will define and describe the topic for their readers. They will also develop and elucidate the topic through the use of specific examples.*

Sub-Standard C:
Use appropriate and varied transitions to link the major sections of the text, create cohesion, and clarify the relationships among complex ideas and concepts.

*Author's Notes: Once again, students will use transitional words, phrases, and sentences, such as* however; nevertheless; next; additionally; afterward; because of this; as a result; on the other hand; the next day; *et cetera.*

Sub-Standard D:
Use precise language and domain-specific vocabulary to manage the complexity of the topic.

*Author's Notes: When discussing aspects of the topic that are not common knowledge, students will provide appropriate definitions and explanations.*

Sub-Standard E:
Establish and maintain a formal style and objective tone while attending to the norms and conventions of the discipline in which they are writing.

*Author's Notes: Although writing in the first person, students will use a formal "academic" voice, refraining from using the slang and abbreviations often used when sending email and text messages.*

Sub-Standard F:
Provide a concluding statement or section that follows from and supports the information or explanation presented (e.g., articulating implications or the significance of the topic).

*Author's Notes: Students will provide a brief conclusion to this project that will include elements of summary and a final assertion that the goal described is worthwhile to pursue. This will likely be one paragraph long.*

## WHAT IS OUR GOAL?

In this project, students will write an informative personal essay on one of their major goals in life. The purpose of an informative essay is to teach (or *inform*) readers on a particular topic, so the writing must be clear, organized, and focused. Although informative essays often include *research*, this essay will not. Our students are still quite young, and we're introducing them slowly and gently to the world of academic writing. As this project is *personal* in nature, students will choose their own topics (and subtopics), write in a (formal) first-person voice, and draw their material from their memories, knowledge, and interests.

In their projects, students will also include *headings* and *graphics*. They will do this by giving each subtopic an explanatory heading (essentially a title within the text). To do this, students can use the general headings supplied on *Outline 9–10.2*, or they can (preferably) formulate their own specific headings. For the *graphic* component, students will include an illustration in the third subtopic. This can be a photo (taken from the internet) or a drawing done by the student. This illustration must relate to (and elucidate) the topic being discussed. Let's take a closer look at the requirements of this essay.

## SELECTION AND ORGANIZATION

The current standard asks students to write "explanatory" or "informative" essays on an unspecified topic. When students have chosen a main topic (an actual goal in their lives), they will present it carefully through a tripartite process of "selection, organization, and analysis." All three are extremely important to the writing process and to our students' development as writers. When students' goals are finalized, you will help them organize their essays by giving them the five-part outline (located at the end of this chapter) and helping them choose three subtopics for their essays (an extremely important part of writing an essay). As you can see, there is a great deal of choice built into this project for the purpose of increasing student engagement.

As you assist with the selection of subtopics, keep in mind that the choice and organization of subtopics should always be simple, logical, and intuitive. In this project, we will organize our subtopics according to the following broad schema:

- First Subtopic: The student's connection to the goal
- Second Subtopic: The goal described in greater detail
- Third Subtopic: The results of achieving the goal

If you look closely at those three, you'll find a basic chronological pattern suggesting *before*, *during*, and *after*. It is simple and intuitive, it works very well for informative essays, and it is the organizational backbone of this assignment. You'll explain all of this to our students, and they'll find it embodied on *Outline 9–10.2* also. That's selection and organization. Let's talk about analysis.

## ANALYSIS: SUMMARY AND COMMENTARY

The main standard requires students to perform "analysis." This is complex and challenging by nature, and it represents the most important new learning occurring in this project. As we teach the process of analysis, we're going to stick to the basics and keep things simple. We will teach students a foundational (but highly effective) analytical model called *summary and commentary*.

In the previous chapter, we introduced students to this process, but in a greatly simplified format that offered students a friendly introduction to basic interpretation. Now, we will build on that knowledge and teach students how to perform *analytical* summary and commentary. In this chapter, we will use this method to teach students how to insightfully *develop their ideas*. This is notoriously difficult for high school students, who, in many cases, can *present* ideas, but not *develop* them. Nonetheless, this is an extremely important skill for our students to learn, and it is also the heartbeat of this project. We will present it simply, in a two-part process:

1. *Summary*: Describe and discuss the thing being taught.
2. *Commentary*: Explain, interpret, and analyze the thing being taught.

Here is an example of this pedagogical paradigm in action. As you read it, note that it starts with summary and then transitions to commentary. (If you're looking for a line of demarcation between summary and commentary, the *summary* portion ends with the sentence, "I want to write books." Everything *after* that is *commentary*). The following paragraph would go in the first subtopic; note that I have included a *heading* (at the left margin) as a visual exemplar for this project. Please share this with students.

**My Connection to the Goal**

My highest goal in life is to be an author and to write books. I have wanted to do this for my entire life. I discovered this when I was five years old, in kindergarten. I opened the classroom copy of a children's book called the *Three Billy*

*Goats Gruff*, and I said to myself, "This is what I want to do with my life. I want to write books." That feeling has never left me, and it has guided many of the choices I have made. I want to be a writer for several reasons. First, I love being creative. When I write, I am creating something from nothing, and this is always a thrilling experience. I also love sharing my ideas and my work with others. When I think that my books and my writing will bring pleasure and knowledge to other people, I feel grateful and honored, and it gives my life meaning. If I could choose anything in the world to do, I would choose to be a writer.

If you read the above carefully, you'll notice that the summary and commentary modeled there flowered alchemically into *development of ideas*. As students absorb these principles, they will learn how to analyze ideas and discuss them with insight and meaning. This is a crucial component in their intellectual development, and it will constitute an enormous leap on their journey toward becoming skilled and perceptive writers.

## LET'S GET STARTED

After explaining the basics of this project, it's time to have your students choose a subject for the essay. Emphasize that they will be writing about one of their major goals in life. If students tell you they don't have a goal yet, they need to think of one. It's necessary for this essay—and for their lives. To help them brainstorm, offer them the following parameters: *Don't try to be funny, or treat this as a joke. Your goal must be positive in nature, and it must be authentic. It must help you, help others, or somehow help the world. It must be possible to attain. The teacher must approve the goal you're writing about.*

Next, suggest to them the following examples. The goal might be one of the following: *to attain a certain career; attend a certain university; play a sport in college; become a professional athlete; qualify for the Olympics; become an actor or actress; win a prestigious award; attain a specific achievement (such as a black belt in a martial art); write a book; learn a certain language; play a musical instrument; invent something marvelous; travel to another country, or simply to learn (or do) something wonderful.*

When your students understand the concept, ask them to take out a pen and some paper, and have them do a three-minute free-write on this subject. Tell them to list their interests and hobbies and to imagine where they might see themselves in ten years. *What would they like to be? What would they like to do?* As they brainstorm on paper, they can write lists or generate stream-of-consciousness word association. At the end of the three minutes, ask them to circle their top choices, to choose their favorite, and to get it approved by you. And a journey toward achievement has begun.

## THE STRUCTURE OF THIS ESSAY

When students' topics are chosen and approved, give each student a copy of *Outline 9–10.2* and go over the details, structure, and content of this project. As you do this, ask students to consider potential titles for their essays. (Remind them that *every piece of writing needs a title*; it should be clear and simple and tell the reader what the piece is about.) Also, instruct them to consider three subtopics that correspond to the structure of this essay (you'll help them with this) and to make notes onto their outlines. If they look closely at the *Outline*, they'll see that each subtopic is broken into three smaller topics, which we will call "examples." Here's what I mean.

As students write their essays, they are strongly encouraged to discuss each subtopic in terms of *three different examples*. This will help inform the reader, and (more important) will assist students with structure, organization, and development of ideas. By giving them this framework, we help our students avoid the high-school brand of writer's block, often expressed succinctly as follows: "I don't know what to write." Here is the assignment in detail:

### 1. Introduction

In your first sentence, tell your reader exactly (and clearly) what your essay is about. *For example, your first sentence might be as follows: For my entire life, I have wanted to be a writer.* State why this goal is worthwhile to pursue, and provide a brief overview of it. Your introduction should be one paragraph in length. Write this last.

### 2. First Subtopic: *Your Connection to the Goal*

First, give this subtopic a *heading* (a "title" at the left margin; see the example provided earlier). Describe your personal "history" with this goal. *Have you always wanted it? Why do you want it? Why (and how much) does it matter to you?* Tell your reader how you plan to pursue this goal. Use three different examples, and include a mixture of summary and commentary (first describe, then explain).

### 3. Second Subtopic: *More about the Goal*

Give this subtopic a *heading*. Describe the goal in greater detail so that the reader understands it more clearly. You can choose your own examples here, but you can also consider the following: *What do you know about this goal? What is its history? What prominent people are associated with it? Do you* know anyone who is associated with it? *What will it take to achieve this goal? Hard work? Talent? Education?* Use at least three specific examples to inform your reader about your goal (telling brief stories can be a very effective form of exposition). Again, include a mixture of summary and commentary.

## 4. Third Subtopic: *The Results of Reaching Your Goal*

Give this subtopic a *heading*. It's time to dream a little bit. *How will you know when you have achieved your goal? How will you feel, and what will you do when you attain your goal?* Use three different examples, and include a mixture of summary and commentary. (Note: in this subtopic, you will include an *illustration* related to the topic. In the third example, you will describe the illustration and discuss why you chose it and what it reveals about your goal. Here are two sites where students can choose copyright-free illustrations: *Photos for Class* provides "safe images that are available to be used . . . for educational purposes" ["Photos for Class"]. On *Pics4Learning*, "Teachers and students can use the copyright-friendly photos and illustrations" ["Pics4Learning"]).

## 5. Conclusion

Here, you will mention your goal once again and provide a brief summary of your essay. *What do you want the reader to remember about this essay?* End by encouraging others to pursue this worthwhile goal. This will be one paragraph; write it second-to-last.

## REMEMBER YOUR GOALS

This concludes our foray into the personal informative essay. This project is simple by nature, but it contains priceless foundational learning for fledgling writers. As you teach this project, keep in mind its most important aspects. As students compose this essay, they are learning how to organize knowledge and how to develop (and present) ideas by making friends with two sibling giants named *summary* and *commentary*.

As you teach the informative essay and transform your students into writers, keep things upbeat, optimistic, and fun. When students write personal essays on topics such as goals for the future, they are unwittingly composing the unwritten narratives of their lives, and this is a process that should be approached with joy. But tell them not to forget their goals for the future, because they're not done with them yet.

Ninth and Tenth Grade, Second Writing Project: *Outline 9–10.2*
The Informative Essay: "A Goal for the Future"

Name_____ Date_____
Title _____

For the title, state your ultimate goal in life. Example: I Want to Become a Writer and Author

1. Introduction. In your first sentence, tell the reader what your goal is. After that, confidently assert that this is a worthwhile goal. Do this in one paragraph. Write your introduction last.

2. First Subtopic: *Your Connection to the Goal* (include a *heading* for this section)
   a. Why do you want to attain this goal? What is your motivation?
   b. How will you pursue and achieve this goal?
   c. Describe why this is a worthwhile goal to pursue.

3. Second Subtopic: *More about the Goal.* Describe the goal in greater detail so that the reader understands it more clearly, using at least three specific examples (or provide brief anecdotes) to impart information on the topic (include a *heading* for this section).
   a. First Example (summary and commentary)
   b. Second Example (summary and commentary)
   c. Third Example (summary and commentary)

4. Third Subtopic: *The Results of Reaching the Goal* (include a *heading* for this section)
   a. How will you *know* that you have reached the goal?
   b. Reactions: How will you *feel* when you reach the goal, and what will you *do*?
   c. Include an *illustration* of the goal (include a copyright-free image, or draw a picture). Describe the illustration and why you included it.

5. Conclusion: Provide a brief summary of your essay. Describe why others might wish to pursue the same goal. This will be one paragraph. Write it second-to-last.

*This page is permitted to copy.*

*Chapter 3*

# Grades Nine and Ten: Third Writing Project

## *The Short Story: "You Attain Your Goal"*

Main Standard: 9–10.3:
Write narratives to develop real or imagined experiences or events using effective technique, well-chosen details, and well-structured event sequences.

*Author's Notes: In this project, the students are going to write a short story that grows out of the essays they wrote in the previous chapter.*

*Sub-Standard A:
Engage and orient the reader by setting out a problem, situation, or observation, establishing one or multiple point(s) of view, and introducing a narrator and/or characters; create a smooth progression of experiences or events.

*Author's Notes: In their short stories, students will have a clearly defined problem to overcome. They will write their stories in the third person.*

*Sub-Standard B:
Use narrative techniques, such as dialogue, pacing, description, reflection, and multiple plot lines, to develop experiences, events, and/or characters.

*Author's Notes: As students portray their characters, they will employ the rule "Show, don't tell," and they will use dialogue abundantly.*

Sub-Standard C:
Use a variety of techniques to sequence events so that they build on one another to create a coherent whole.

*Author's Notes: Students will sequence their stories by using the One-Story approach.*

\*Sub-Standard D:
Use precise words and phrases, telling details, and sensory language to convey a vivid picture of the experiences, events, setting, and/or characters.

*Author's Notes: Students will use imagery in their descriptions.*

Sub-Standard E:
Provide a conclusion that follows from and reflects on what is experienced, observed, or resolved over the course of the narrative.

*Author's Notes: In the conclusion of their stories, the characters will reflect on what they learned during their journeys.*

## WHAT'S THE STORY?

In this project, students are going to write their first short story. They'll find this exciting and mysterious, and they're also sure to wonder, *How will I do this? What will my story be about? What if I can't come up with any ideas?* And you'll assure them that they can definitely do it, so don't worry. In fact, they composed the basis for their short stories in the previous essay they wrote. (It's true; more on that later.) As students develop their plots, they will adhere to the One-Story structure of *Grail, Conflict, Resolution* (described in the introduction to this book). In a switch from the previous two projects, students will write their stories using a *third-person narrator*.

All stories are driven by plot and *especially* character, so students will have their characters speak to each other through the abundant use of dialogue. "Don't worry," you'll tell them. "You'll be able to do this. You've been using dialogue for your entire life." Students will also employ imagery in their descriptions, and they will utilize the rule "Show, don't tell." All of this will make for a fun, challenging, and creative project that will help our students to grow as writers and to explore a new and intriguing dimension of composition.

## WHAT ARE WE WRITING ABOUT?

We are going to make things easy on our students and give their stories a ring of great familiarity. In a sense, students have already started writing about this assignment. In the previous project, they wrote about a worthwhile goal for their lives. In these current stories, *each student will be the main character in the story he or she writes*. Additionally, the grail to be attained will be the goal described in the previous essay (this usually brings a sigh of relief).

As always, we will be using the five-part structure in our stories, and our three subtopics will be the elements of *Grail, Conflict,* and *Resolution.* Let's review these elements briefly; here is an example:

- *Grail:* I want to write a short story.
- *Conflict:* It seems very difficult, and I don't know how to do it.
- *Resolution:* Because I worked hard—and have an amazing teacher—I was able to write a terrific short story.

As you review the One-Story approach with your students, encourage them to start with a *situation*. They will place the situation in the introduction to their stories, and it will include the setting (time and place), the main character, and the main character's current situation (which likely involves a problem to solve). Here is an example of a situation (original to this book):

**The Infinite Forest**
Danny looked at his watch and saw that it was nearly seven o'clock. It was past dinner time, and he felt hungry. Through the trees, he could see the orange and yellow of the sun as it began to set for a night that would be cold and very dark. Danny stood without moving and listened to the sounds of the forest. A wind blowing high above the trees. A mourning dove, singing its lonely song of sorrow. A woodpecker somewhere very far away, hollow and hungry. An ancient river, frigid and merciless. The smell of fungus and damp earth and wet, rotting things.

Danny looked at the darkening skies and the trees and he saw nothing familiar. The forest held no signs and no comforts and no welcomes for him, and he suddenly knew that he was very lost. A sense of danger and a fear he had never felt before spread through his body and through his thoughts. His mouth tasted dry and metallic, and he felt very cold. His hands shook as he zipped his Windbreaker up to his neck. "Don't panic," he whispered to himself. "It'll be okay."

If you look at the brief example above (and all the clues it contains), you'll find the following elements, either stated or suggested:

- *Narrator*: This is a *third-person* narrator, which the students will be using. (If *Danny* were telling his story, it would be a first-person narrator.)

- *Character*: Danny. He comes from civilization, and he is quite vulnerable. The diminutive "Danny" (rather than "Daniel") suggests a young person. Other than that, we don't know much about him yet. Throughout the story, we will learn about him, just as he learns about himself.
- *Setting*: A forest, probably in present day (we have a wristwatch and a Windbreaker).
- *Situation* (and problem to solve): The main character is lost in a forest.
- *Grail*: He wants to survive. He wants to find his way out of the forest, back to civilization and safety.
- *Conflict*: It's getting cold and dark. He is lost. He has no survival equipment. Finding his way out will be difficult.
- *Consequences*: If he doesn't find his way out of the forest—and fairly soon—he will probably die.
- *Dialogue*: Two short sentences presented in quotation marks (because there's only one character, we might consider this *monologue*). They provide insight regarding the character's feelings. He is terrified and attempting to think clearly.
- *Resolution* (a wonderfully happy ending): After many trials and difficulties (described in the story), Danny will find his way out of the forest and get back to civilization and safety.

Teach (and encourage) your students to bring all the elements above into their writing. As you teach these components, also be sure to emphasize the following.

## THIRD-PERSON NARRATOR

There are several different types of narrators in the world of writing, but your students will write this story in the *third person*. Explain to them that the third person is not a character in the story. In most cases, this narrator presents the story to us impartially and objectively and uses the words *he*, *she*, and *it* (rather than *I* and *me*). There are several nuanced types of third-person narrator, but with our students, we'll focus on two basic ones:

- Third-person limited: This narrator is tethered to the main character and looks over the character's shoulder and describes the story from the character's perspective. This narrator also tells us what the character is thinking. The "Infinite Forest" excerpt uses a third-person limited narrator.
- Third-person omniscient: This narrator knows everything about the story and about all characters in the story, no matter where they're located. For

example, if the "Infinite Forest" were third-person omniscient (it's not), we might see a page break, followed by a sentence introducing a new section taking place in a different location. Here is an example:
- As Danny shivered in the forest, he had no way of knowing that his friend Michelle had already begun organizing a search party.

Tell your students that, in their stories, they can use third-person omniscient or third-person limited. They'll choose the best fit for their stories, and you'll help them with this decision.

## CHARACTERS AND DIALOGUE

Students will include at least two characters in their stories. One of these characters (the main character) will be strongly based on the student-writer. In a sense, this story will blend autobiography with fiction (and a bit of fanciful wish fulfillment). The other character may be a good friend to the main character (perhaps based on a friend of the writer). A third character (optional) may be a "villain," somehow enabling the conflict and seeking to frustrate the main character.

Tell your students that their goal is to create characters whom the reader can understand and recognize as discernibly human. As students develop their characters, they will describe them in terms of physical traits, personality quirks, and actions. It's always difficult for a writer to create a fully realized original character, so we'll make things simple for our students as they create their characters and ask them to focus on three main things:

- Describe the character's *appearance*. What does the character look like?
- Describe the character's *personality*. Is the character loud? Quiet? Shy? Athletic? Bookish? Aggressive? Kind? Hostile? Selfish? Generous? Lazy? Energetic? Etcetera.
- Describe what the character *says* and what the character *does*.

As students begin creating their characters, they should begin with the one based on themselves. That will be good practice, and they know that character pretty well.

When it comes to dialogue, tell students that their characters must speak to each other just as real people speak to each other (and they *do* have some experience in the art of conversation). Explain that the dialogue in their stories should help to define the characters and should also assist with exposition and push the plot along. As they compose their stories and begin to write dialogue, tell your students that a conversation is like a ball being tossed back and forth. The first character says something (thus tossing the ball to the other character), and the second character responds (tossing the ball back).

As students begin to generate characters' conversation, show them how to *format* dialogue. It includes specific punctuation (such as quotation marks), and it often contains tags describing the physical actions that accompany the characters' words. This is a fairly simple process, but it needs to be taught (and learned). See the example below:

> Danny picked up his phone and called Michelle. "Hey Michelle," he said. "I'm going walking today through the Infinite Forest. Want to come with me?" He smiled a little and waited for her answer.
>
> Michelle thought for a moment, and Danny heard a sigh of exasperation. "No," she said. "And you shouldn't go either. It's a really big forest, and it's supposed to get cold today."

Note how the example above contains *words* and *actions* (it also contains *foreshadowing*, but that's not a primary focus here). As we speak to others, we animate our words with physical gestures, and these constitute a high percentage of our communication. As your students write their dialogue, tell them to imagine how people *speak* and *act* when they talk to each other—and try to replicate that on paper. Share the above example with your students. Describe how the formatting assists with comprehension and how the dialogue reveals character and helps to push the story along. In this brief exchange, Danny is revealed as a bit impulsive and reckless, while Michelle is thoughtful and cautious.

## IMAGERY AND "SHOW, DON'T TELL"

Two very powerful writing techniques are *imagery* and a rule known as *"Show, Don't Tell."* Let's start with imagery. When you look at the word *imagery*, you'll undoubtedly see the word *image* embedded in it. Here, you may be tempted to think that imagery refers to describing things in terms of how they *look*. That's true, but it's only 20 percent of the story.

Imagery means describing things in terms of *all five senses*. How does something *look*, *sound*, *feel*, *taste*, *smell*? When we employ description in our writing, we should make an effort to use *imagery*—to describe things by using all of our senses. This is a highly effective writing technique, and it helps animate our writing in the mind of the reader.

As a general rule, however, it works very well to use *one or two* (and probably no more than *three*) senses in a single description. For example, look at the "Infinite Forest" excerpt above, and you'll find (individual) examples of imagery there that employ all five senses. These references make the writing more vibrant and muscular, and they help to place the reader silently (and nervously) by Danny's side.

And now we come to a rule known as "Show, Don't Tell." The concept here is rather simple, but it's difficult to learn it and use it in our writing. To put it rather simply, as writers, we should not simply *tell* our readers what we want them to perceive or understand; we should *show* it to them. This is a highly effective (even foundational) writing technique, and every writer should learn it and make it a habit. Consider the following three examples, all drawn from the "Infinite Forest." In each one, you will find a "showing" sentence, followed by a "telling" sentence:

- *Showing*: Through the trees, he could see the orange and yellow of the sun as it began to set for a night that was sure to be cold and very dark.
*Telling*: It was getting late in the day, and it was getting cold also.
- *Showing*: Danny looked at the darkening skies and the trees and saw nothing familiar.
*Telling*: It was getting late, and Danny was lost in a forest.
- *Showing*: His hands shook as he zipped his Windbreaker up to his neck.
*Telling*: Danny was cold.

In the three examples above, you can see the difference between "showing" something to our readers and merely "telling" it to them. "Telling" is information; "showing" is *art*. When we *tell* something to our readers, they can understand it and internalize it rather clinically. When we *show* them something, they can see it in their minds and explore it by using their imaginations.

## THE ASSIGNMENT IN DETAIL

After introducing the assignment and teaching your students the beauties of the One-Story approach, characterization, dialogue, imagery, and "show, don't tell," it's time to go over the assignment in detail. Hand out *Outline 9–10.3* and go over each part with your students. As you discuss the particulars of writing this short story, encourage your students to ask questions and to take notes onto the outline. Here are the five sections of this assignment:

### 1. Introduction

Here, students will introduce readers to the main character (again, the main character will be a stand-in for the student-writer). Students will provide the setting (time and place) of the story and describe the situation (which will likely include a character with a problem to solve).

## 2. First Subtopic: *The Grail*

Tell us what the main character wants or needs. Make this goal interesting and worthwhile, rather than comical and trivial (for example, "Danny wants potato chips with his lunch" is not sufficient, because it lacks meaning and narrative power). Describe why the goal is important to the main character. If the protagonist does *not* achieve the grail, there must be serious *consequences*. What are they?

## 3. Second Subtopic: *Conflict*

Someone or something is working to prevent the character from attaining the grail (and solving the problem). *Who or what is doing this? Why is this happening? What is the motivation?* Describe the conflict. Also, describe how the conflict makes it difficult for the protagonist to achieve the grail. *What are some things this character can do to overcome the conflict? How will the character learn, grow, and change as a result of being challenged like this?*

## 4. Third Subtopic: *Resolution*

The protagonist overcomes the conflict, attains the grail, and solves the central problem (instruct students to *give their stories a happy ending*). *How did this resolution happen?* Describe it in detail, because it gives us hope, teaches us about resilience, and teaches us about the character. Describe the character's reactions to attaining the goal, and describe the repercussions of this accomplishment. *How will this reverberate in the character's life? Will it positively affect the world? If so, how?*

## 5. Conclusion

Time to wrap things up. Don't leave any loose threads hanging, because we want the reader to feel the satisfaction of a proper ending. Here, the writer should reflect upon how the main character learned and grew and how attaining the grail was a difficult, but noble endeavor. The writer might also suggest that the lessons learned by the protagonist might work well for others—including the reader.

## THE DREAMS WE HOLD IN OUR HEARTS

And that concludes our first venture into writing a short story. Your students will enjoy writing this bit of fictional autobiography, so motivate them to approach this assignment with creativity, joy, and optimism. As students compose their stories, encourage them to use their imaginations freely and to write with confidence. The world of writing is the perfect place to explore our worlds and ourselves. It provides us a safe perch where we can peek at our future selves and play with the dreams that we hold in our hearts.

Ninth and Tenth Grade, Third Writing Project: *Outline 9–10.3*
The Short Story: "You Attain Your Goal"

Name_____ Date_____
Title _____

Give your story a title that is clear, interesting, and accurate to the story.

1. Introduction (write this last)
   a. Introduce readers to the main character(s).
   b. Provide the *setting* of the story (time and place).
   c. Describe the *situation* (what's happening).

2. First Subtopic: *Grail* (the goal pursued by the protagonist)
   a. What is the grail desired by the main character? Describe it.
   b. Why does the main character want this goal?
   c. If the protagonist does not achieve the goal, what are the *consequences*?

3. Second Subtopic: *Conflict* (the thing preventing the protagonist from attaining the grail)
   a. Describe the conflict.
   b. What is *causing* the conflict? Is another character involved in it?
   c. *Why* will the conflict be difficult to overcome?

4. Third Subtopic: *Resolution* (give your story a happy ending)
   a. *How* did the main character attain the grail?
   b. Describe this character's *reactions* to attaining the grail.
   c. How does this improve the character's life, others' lives, or the world?

5. Conclusion: *Reflection on the Events of the Story* (end on a positive note)
   a. What did the main character *learn* during this story?
   b. Are there any *lessons* here that readers can learn and benefit from?
   c. What is most meaningful about this story, to the characters—and the readers?

*This page is permitted to copy.*

*Chapter 4*

# Grades Nine and Ten: Fourth Writing Project

## *The Personal Reflective Essay: "Your Favorite Place" (First Draft)*

Main Standard: 9–10.4:
Produce clear and coherent writing in which the development, organization, and style are appropriate to task, purpose, and audience. (Grade-specific expectations for writing types are defined in standards 1–3 above.)

*Author's Notes: Students will write a personal reflective essay on their favorite place in the world. Alternate topics include writing about a favorite object, a favorite activity, or a favorite time in their lives. Students will write this in the first person. There are no sub-standards here.*

### PRODUCTION AND DISTRIBUTION OF WRITING

This standard is the first in a group of three standards called "Production and Distribution of Writing." For the first time in this writing program, we are going to bundle the three standards together and give students a three-part multimedia writing assignment composed of three different drafts of one grand, multifaceted assignment. Here is an overview of our next three projects:

- Chapter Four (this current chapter): The Personal Reflective Essay: "Your Favorite Place" (First Draft)
- Chapter Five: The Personal Reflective Essay: "Your Favorite Place" (Second Draft: Revising and Editing)

- Chapter Six: The Personal Reflective Essay: "Your Favorite Place" (Third Draft: *E-book*)

If you look at the standard's requirements, you'll see that they are rather minimalistic. They don't tell us *what* our students should write (that's up to *us*); they tell us *how* our students should write. In plain terms, this standard encourages students to write essays that possess the following foundational attributes:

- *Clarity*: The writing is clear and understandable.
- *Focus*: The essay discusses one central and clearly specified topic.
- *Development*: The main ideas are developed through description and analysis.
- *Organization*: Related ideas are presented in a logical and understandable sequence. (The element of *organization* is embedded in the five-part outline, so this will not be a major topic of discussion here.)

Beyond teaching those wonderful traits and methods of writing, this standard does not impose great strictures on us as teachers. Indeed, we can design any type of writing assignment that we desire. It's an exhilarating proposal, but also a daunting one. We have been given a marvelously blank slate, and (like our students) we are expected to create something beautiful and refulgent with meaning. What will it be? What sort of writing assignment will we choose and develop?

As it's still early in the year, let's give our students an assignment that will engage them as it teaches them the beauties and basics of writing. In this current project (the first draft of our three-part metaproject), students will write a *personal reflective essay*. This is a type of autobiographical essay about some significant aspect of the students' personal histories. Nonetheless, the student is not merely telling stories from past experience (which would be rather dull and meaningless); the student is mining and extracting meaning from the subject and passing it along to the reader.

And what will students be writing about? In this project, students will write about their *favorite place in the world*. In their discussions, they'll go far beyond discussing the place in a whimsical and nostalgic way. After choosing and describing the place, students will engage in *reflection* and *insight*, attempting to discover and reveal what the place really means to them and why it possesses such meaning in their lives. This is the most valuable component of these essays, but it is easier said than done.

## A THREE-PART HARMONY

This essay is rather straightforward in nature, so let's seize this opportunity to deliver several high-powered writing lessons. Before you begin teaching the content of this assignment, teach your students the three foundational elements mentioned above: *clarity, focus, development*. These are extremely important for young writers to understand and to learn, so teach them well. Let's start with clarity.

1. *Clarity*. This refers to the intelligibility of writing. *Is it clear and understandable? Does it make sense to the reader? Does it flow effortlessly?* Contrary to conceptions of writing that have taken root (culturally speaking), writing does not need to sound poetic and flowery, and it is not composed of fancy words that few use (or hear) on a daily basis. In fact, these things are often the hallmarks of *poor* writing or of something unnecessarily overwritten.

No, good writing is always clear and simple. *Clear and simple*. Why make the reader work harder than necessary? Tell your students that, as writers, they are working to convey ideas to the reader. Readers should understand their ideas and (if possible) enjoy the experience of reading their work. The elements of clarity and simplicity are wonderful assistants for fledgling writers, and they will appreciate this very much. Nonetheless, how, *exactly, can they implement these in their writing?*

Give them a rather unorthodox rule: tell them to *write the way they talk*. And *yes*, phrase it just like that: *write the way you talk*. As budding writers, they're all on a quest to develop a distinctive and individual writer's voice (they just don't know it yet). And here's the good news: they already have a unique voice. It comes out *when they speak*, because our speech patterns are as individual as our fingerprints. At this point, hands will go up, and students will say things like *this* (and you'll respond as indicated):

- But I don't speak good! (That's okay. You'll fix it through successive drafts.)
- But my grammar ain't so great! (Patience. That will improve over time.)
- But speaking isn't writing! (Yes it is.)

Tell them not to worry; those things will be addressed in the second draft (during the process of revising and editing). Explain to them also that learning to write takes a long time. It's not a flash of inspiration; it's a process of *growth*. Right now, we're interested in the larger aspects of developing their essays (and learning to write), which—at the moment—are *clarity, focus*, and *development*.

And now, let's discuss a pragmatic and understandable plan for your students. Tell them that in the early stages of writing, *ideas are more important than words*. This is extremely important, so emphasize it dramatically. They must begin by *writing and codifying their ideas* (in the way they speak) and *worry about wording later*. Think of it like this: when we build a house, we begin by preparing a solid foundation. We focus on *that* particular large task and make sure it's done right. Polishing floors and furniture comes later. It's the same with writing: *foundation first, polishing later*.

2. *Focus*. The *subject* of this essay is the student's *favorite place*. The *topic* of the essay is the particular place the student chooses (subject is *general type*; topic is *specific example*). And this leads us to a very important revelation that must not be overlooked: *topic is the most important part of an essay*. For students to produce a coherent piece of writing, they must know (and understand with *perfect clarity*) what they are writing about. You would be surprised at how often students don't know what they are writing about.

As you teach this essay, strive to help your students clearly understand what they are writing about. They should be able to state the topic of the essay in a single simple phrase or sentence. For example, if you ask students, "What's the topic of your essay?" their answers should sound like this:

- "I'm writing about Lake Winnipesaukee."
- "Stan's Book Bin. It's my favorite bookstore in the world."
- "My favorite place is next to my dog, no matter where we are."

See how narrow and focused those are? Those three students know exactly what they're writing about, so their essays are likely to be meaningful for the writer and the reader.

When students have chosen a specific and meaningful topic, they should write about that topic and nothing else. This will give the essay focus and unity (which are *extremely* important elements in an essay). This will impart a feeling of intentional design in the piece, and it will give the reader confidence in the writer. Above all, they must resist including unrelated material and (in particular) must not include flaccid fluff for the purpose of padding the essay and making it longer (a very common strategy among young writers).

Nonetheless, there is room for skillful interpretation here. The students' chain of association is likely to wander a bit, and they may generate writing unrelated to the main topic. As long as the discussion is *tangentially* related to the main topic, this material might be acceptable. Keep in mind, however, that everything the student writes must somehow *shed light on the main topic*.

This can be a bit difficult to learn and to truly understand, so offer this gentle guidance to your fledgling writers: *If you're not sure whether something is truly related to your topic, write it anyway. You can always delete it, edit it, or save it for another essay. And, if you're still not sure, ask me. I'll tell you whether or not it works for your essay.*

3. *Development.* The term *development* refers to development of ideas, which we discussed in chapter 2, when students wrote informative essays on a "Goal for the Future." As we taught that project, we introduced students to a simple (but highly effective) process of analysis that focused on *summary and commentary*. In this current chapter (and this project), we will once again encourage students to use the paradigm of summary and commentary as they explore and present their favorite places. However, as this essay is different, the *commentary* process will be different also.

After describing the place they chose (*summary*), students will provide *commentary* in the form of *reflection* and *insight*. These two elements are always necessary when writing reflective essays, and you can teach this format to students by offering them the acronym "DRI" (pronounced "dry"). DRI stands for *description, reflection, insight*, and these also happen to be the three subtopics of this essay.

Teaching the elements of reflection and insight can be a bit challenging, especially for fledgling writers. There are similarities between the two, and their differences consist not so much in *kind* but in nuance. You might introduce these concepts to your students as follows:

- *Reflection*: When engaging in *reflection*, writers consider what the topic means to them and to their lives in a deeply personal manner. The discussion here is the relationship existing between the *topic* and the *writer*. The discourse remains focused on the topic and how it has impacted (and continues to impact) the writer's life. *What exactly does it mean to the writer? Why does it hold this meaning?*
- *Insight*: When discussing *insight*, writers go *beyond the topic* and relate it to larger aspects of their lives (and of existence). The focus here is on what they have *learned* from the topic. They discuss the insights that they have gained over the years and how these lessons have impacted their lives and their ways of looking at the world. *What has the topic taught them about their worlds? About people? About their lives? About life in general?* Finally (and this is a *very* important element) *what can these insights teach the reader? How can these insights impact the reader's life, just as they impacted the writer's life?*

Understanding the difference between *reflection* and *insight* is difficult, so it may help to look at these through the prism of these two questions:

- Reflection: *What does this place really mean to me?*
- Insight: *What might this place mean for others?*

And now, let's take a close look at the requirements for this essay.

## THE ASSIGNMENT IN DETAIL

Give each student a copy of *Outline 9–10.4*, and go over each component in detail. Keep your explanations clear and simple, and encourage your students to take notes directly onto the outline. And don't forget to talk about the inner core of this assignment. This is a very personal essay, and you're hoping that students write it with *feeling* and *genuine emotion*. These things impart great meaning to one's writing, and they also help us to organize and interpret the narrative of our lives. Here are the five parts of the essay, presented in detail:

### 1. Introduction

Here, students will introduce the topic and provide an overview to the reader. They will name (or identify) the place clearly so that the reader understands the topic of the essay. They will describe the circumstances (how, when, and how often they visited the place or spent time at it). For example, an introduction might look like this:

> For five summers of my childhood (from my eighth year until my twelfth year), my parents and I drove up to Lake Winnipesaukee, in New Hampshire. It was our summer vacation. My aunt and uncle owned rental cottages on the big lake, and we stayed there for about a month during the cool mystery-magic of June. For the young me, it was like finding a land I had always wanted to live in, with the lake and the forest awaiting my arrival. And now, I want to tell you all about my time there, about some of the things I did, and how much it all meant to me.

### 2. First Subtopic: *Description*

Here, students will describe (in detail) the place they're writing about. Remind them to use *imagery*, incorporating the *senses* into their descriptions. The goal is to make readers feel like they know the place. As students compose this section, they should describe particular sights and scenes, activities, and the people (characters) they met there. They can also tell stories (anecdotes) of interesting things that happened there. Telling stories is a highly effective mode of exposition and is typically not taught to young students.

## 3. Second Subtopic: *Reflection*

This section grows out of the description in the previous subtopic. Here, students will *reflect* on the place, discussing how much it meant to them and *why* it meant so much. This can feel a bit abstract and difficult to explain, so you should illustrate this for your students by offering them examples, such as these:

- *This place is special to me, because . . .*
  - My father and I got to know each other.
  - I met my best friend there.
  - I fell in love there.

Note how these reflections venture beyond description yet are still anchored to the students' experience. As students engage in reflection, ask them to also consider how often they think of this place and why it means so much to them. To do this, they truly need to engage in private reflection, to identify the emotional connections they have with the place, and to translate those feelings into words. It is very challenging, but it's a tremendous learning experience.

## 4. Third Subtopic: *Insight*

In this section, students' discussions will venture beyond the place and move into more philosophical territory. Now, we are asking them to consider what they have *learned* from their experiences at—and their connections with—the place they have chosen. This too is challenging, so help them with their ruminations and offer them the following questions to assist their thinking:

- What did you learn there about the following: *life, people, growing up, friendship, happiness, sadness, family, love, nature, sports, work, responsibility*? Et cetera.
- If you never went to this place, how would you be different?
- How did this place make you a better person?
- What lessons did you learn there? How have they impacted your life?
- What lessons can the *reader* learn from your experiences at this place?

## 5. Conclusion

Students will conclude with a brief statement reinforcing the main points of the essay. They should also try to discern what the essay is *really* about. *What major themes surfaced during the writing of the piece?* They might also describe a future visit to the place. Your students have undoubtedly changed since their last visit—but what if the *place* changed also? *How would they feel? Would it tarnish their memories?* Finally, they can conclude by mentioning the most important thing they learned at the place—tacitly hoping that readers can learn it also.

## LEARN TO SEE MIRACLES

And this concludes the first draft of our three-draft project. In this personal reflective essay, we have taught our students foundational lessons of clarity, focus, and development of ideas. Perhaps more important, we have taken them on a journey that included forays into *reflection* and *insight*. These are two very different facets of analytical commentary, and they are quite challenging to learn and practice. Nonetheless, they are extremely valuable for students to learn how to evaluate the seemingly mundane experiences they have and to extract meaning and joy from the small, quiet miracles that occur around us—and *to* us—every day of our lives.

Ninth and Tenth Grade, Fourth Writing Project: *Outline 9–10.4*
The Personal Reflective Essay: "Your Favorite Place" (First Draft)

Name_____ Date_____
Title _____

Make sure your title mentions the place you're writing about.

1. Introduction: A brief overview of the topic (write this last)
   a. Introduce readers to the place you're writing about (brief overview).
   b. When did you go there? Why? How often? Et cetera.
   c. Briefly describe your first visit (and impressions) of the place.

2. First Subtopic: *Describe the Place*
   a. Give the reader a detailed description of this place.
   b. Introduce us to specific sights, activities, people, et cetera.
   c. Tell an illustrative story (such as a favorite memory) connected to the place.

3. Second Subtopic: *Reflection* (the prompts below are suggestions; they are not mandatory)
   a. How often do you think of this place?
   b. What is your favorite *aspect* of this place?
   c. Why does this place mean so much to you?

4. Third Subtopic: *Insight* (the prompts below are suggestions; they are not mandatory)
   a. What has this place taught you? What have you learned?
   b. How does this place enrich your life, even when you're not there?
   c. What can *the reader* learn from your insights?

5. Conclusion: A brief recap of the topic (includes some summary)
   a. What was this essay about? (a place). What was it *really* about? (themes).
   b. Describe a future visit to the place. How would you feel if it changed?
   c. What was the most important point of this piece? What did you learn—and what can your *readers* learn?

*This page is permitted to copy.*

*Chapter 5*

# Grades Nine and Ten: Fifth Writing Project

## *The Personal Reflective Essay:* "Your Favorite Place" (Second Draft: Revising and Editing)

Main Standard: 9–10.5:

Develop and strengthen writing as needed by planning, revising, editing, rewriting, or trying a new approach, focusing on addressing what is most significant for a specific purpose and audience. (Editing for conventions should demonstrate command of Language standards 1–3 up to and including grades 9–10 here [http://www.corestandards.org/ELA-Literacy/L/9-10/]).

*Author's Notes: In this project, we are going to improve the students' first draft by teaching the tandem processes of revising and editing. There are no sub-standards here.*

### A SECOND DRAFT

As you can see, this standard focuses on improving a completed draft of writing. The standard uses terms such as *revising, editing, rewriting,* and "trying a new approach." Clearly, the central focus of this standard involves taking a completed draft of writing and making it better. It also refers rather mysteriously to "Language standards" One through Three. If you consult these, you'll find that they refer to commonsense editing practices, such as grammar, punctuation, and spelling. They also encourage students to make stylistic choices to improve meaning and readability. (To read these standards in their entirety, see, "English Language Arts Standards, Language, Grade 9–10.")

As you teach the requirements of this standard, understand that it conveys learning via a pedagogical Trojan horse. It will appear to students that our goal is to improve their first draft of writing. This will certainly happen, but this improvement is a *by-product* of the learning occurring here; it is not the primary focus. The most important learning occurring here involves *teaching students how to revise and edit*. As students revise and edit their essays, they will learn that a piece of writing is not truly finished until it has been improved—and brought to its full potential—through rewriting the text and generating successive drafts.

As you begin this segment of teaching, explain the concepts of revision and editing to your students. If you ask them the differences between these two things, they probably won't know. Begin by telling them that *revision is "bigger" than editing*. Revision involves making *large* changes in the text that will alter (and improve) the *meaning* of the essay. *Editing* involves making smaller (proofreading) changes in the text, and it requires the writer to locate and correct mechanical and typographical errors in the essay. Because revision is bigger than editing, *revision comes before editing*. Revise first, edit later.

The following sections contain an overview of the processes of revision and editing. These are designed to give students a simple and basic introduction to this new and complex task. To assist students in their learning, *Outline 9–10.5* contains an outline of this process, rather than an outline of the project.

## REVISION AND LISTENING

When skilled writers compose, the text will begin to grow *organically*, making its own decisions. After a time, it will *speak to the writer* and make specific demands. This point is very important, and it bears emphasis and explication. As an experienced (or passionate) writer develops a text, *the text will begin speaking to the writer, describing where it wants to go and what it wants to express*. The quickening text takes on an autonomous life of its own and begins a silent dialogue with the author.

When this happens (and it will if the writer allows it), the writer becomes a *collaborator* with the organically growing text. The writer listens to the text and works with it, rather than directing it or hammering it into a preconceived shape. To improve an essay, a skilled writer must learn how to *listen to the text* and recognize when it is asking for something new, or stating that something isn't working (and needs to be altered or deleted). Because our students are still quite young, you will have to teach them this process. (Please note that this allowance of organic composition is the highest level of revision. It occurs *before* the revision proper occurs, and thus one may refer to it as *prevision*, a term original to this book).

When students revise, there are some specific things they'll need to do. Tell them to begin by *rereading the essay critically* (several times), looking for places where it can be improved. To put it simply, this involves adding more good stuff and getting rid of bad stuff. It requires the writer to expand certain sections while shortening (or eliminating) other sections. It often requires writers to alter the flow and organization of the piece by (for example) moving entire sentences, paragraphs, or sections from one location to another.

When beginning the revision process, students may wish to print out a hard copy of the draft and write comments on it in pencil (this is a very effective method, and it allows students a different and more tactile look at their work). Alternatively, they may wish to make comments directly onto the electronic draft. When doing this, most popular word processing programs have an *add comment* function that allows writers (and teachers) to make suggestions in the margin of an electronic document. This works well, but it needs to be learned and can be a bit cumbersome. The simplest and most intuitive method for editorial comments is to write comments directly into the text of an essay and to put these comments in a different color (*blue* is a calm and friendly choice for this).

## GREEN LIGHTS AND RED LIGHTS

As students reread their work critically, they should begin by looking for "green lights" and "red lights" in their writing. Green lights are places where something good is happening on the page. The writing is strong, the exposition is interesting, and the topic conveys valuable meaning. When students encounter green lights, they must retain them and (ideally) expand them further through additional description, reflection, and insight. Metaphorically speaking, it's a bit like this: *when you find a beautiful orange, squeeze as much juice from it as you can.* Recognizing, preserving, and expanding green lights is essential to bringing any piece of writing to its full potential.

Students must also learn how and when to *eliminate* material from their essays. As they reread their material, they must learn to recognize "red lights" in their writing. These are places where, for some reason, the writing is substandard or just isn't working. The exposition may be unclear or uninteresting, or it may contain long, plodding sections with excessive description and insufficient analysis. Perhaps a passage simply sounds like it doesn't belong in the essay. When this happens, students must reduce the length (and presence) of the passage or eliminate it from the essay entirely.

Very often, you'll find that the students' writing has wandered too far from the main topic (a very common mistake among new writers). If this happens, students should delete these unrelated passages. If they are retained in the final drafts, they will weaken and damage the focus and unity of the essay. This will dilute the meaning of the piece and will encourage the reader to lose faith in the writer. The topic of *focus* was covered in chapter 4, but you should discuss it with students once again. They have a completed draft of writing, so the discussion will now be *practical* rather than theoretical.

The process of deleting (or shortening) textual red lights will greatly improve one's writing, but it can be very difficult for writers (especially novice writers). If your students balk at eliminating their work, explain that *all* writers have a *delete button* (in their minds and on their keyboards). They use it with great frequency, and *it improves their writing*. Immeasurably. If your students are *still* reluctant to hit *delete*, have them create a folder titled "Storage Locker" and store the "temporarily excised" passage in there. It will lessen the sting of deletion.

Nonetheless, if an offending passage contains glimmers of green that may blossom into verdant beauty, encourage your students to shorten the passage while increasing the fecund flicker of meaning. In this manner, red lights can be converted into green lights. This can be difficult to learn—and to teach—so you might try this technique: cover the passage with your hand and ask the student to tell you *verbally* what she is trying to say and keep it to *one or two sentences*. When the student is finished speaking, ask her to write down what she just said, verbatim. It will probably be interesting, focused, muscular prose that will work well in the essay.

Revising is difficult to learn, but it can be distilled to a few simple principles. Increase the good stuff. Decrease the bad stuff. Don't include material if it's not related to (or doesn't somehow illuminate) the main topic. Finally, don't write *ten* sentences if the point can be made in *two* sentences. Don't make readers work harder than they have to.

## EDITING

As stated earlier, editing is "smaller" than revising, and thus it comes *after* revising. When your young writers have revised their drafts—when the drafts are focused and well organized, and all ideas are present and intelligible—it's time to edit. Editing (you'll tell your students) involves proofreading, correcting linguistic errors and weaknesses, getting rid of simple "mechanical" errors, and making sure the essay has a smooth and polished feel to it. This is a tall order for ninth and tenth graders. It requires a linguistic knowledge base that they likely don't yet possess (and won't acquire overnight), so you'll work with them on the basics and (as always) keep things simple.

First, tell your students that internet slang and texting abbreviations are not allowed in academic essays. You are not to use "ur" for *you are*; the number "4" for *for* is a wrong number, and to settle the question, "*to be* or not *2b?*," the answer is "not *2b*" (so don't use it). Besides that, keep things simple, focus on the obvious, and don't assume your students know the basics of editing or formal writing.

As you teach the fundamentals of editing, don't be afraid to discuss rudimentary items, such as starting sentences with a capital letter and ending them with a period. Tell your students to make sure their words are spelled correctly. Spell check is a great help with this, but it's not infallible (for example, students almost always spell the word *definitely* wrong, and it is *almost always* incorrectly "corrected" to *defiantly*). As for paragraph length, tell them to keep their paragraphs between one-third and one-half of a page. Along the way, teach your students the individual identities of two sets of cute triplets named *there, they're, their*, and *two, to, too*. Many *graduate* students still have trouble with these.

As for grammar, that's a long and difficult evolution, but (one hopes) it will improve with time, reading, writing, and the education process. Before students hand in their final drafts, instruct them to engage in some effective methods of editing that are not often taught. First, ask them to read the piece *out loud* to themselves and to friends and family members. They can also have others *read the essay to them* and flag errors that they hear. Very often, our ears can pick up grammatical errors and linguistic clumsiness that our eyes missed.

Students can also have someone else read the essay and look for errors (if professional writers can have assistants, then our students can also). Finally, after they hand in their completed drafts, *you*, the dedicated teacher, will indicate repeated errors in their essays and teach your students how to avoid them in the future. The processes of revising and editing are complicated and challenging, so keep things simple and teach your students where they *are*, rather than where they "should be." Always celebrate their small successes.

However, keep your teacherly dignity and don't celebrate too much, because our students aren't departing from their favorite places just yet. In the next chapter—the final one in this three-part cycle—we are going to do something very surprising and very special. We are going to convert our students' completed and polished drafts into beautiful, illustrated, actual *e-books*.

Ninth and Tenth Grade, Fifth Writing Project: *Outline 9–10.5*
The Personal Reflective Essay: "Your Favorite Place" (Second Draft)

Name_____ Date_____

Title _____

At this time, you may wish to revise your title.

## Revising and Editing: An Outline of the Basics

1. Revision: *Making large changes to the text. This may alter the meaning of the essay. Note: Revising is bigger than editing. Revise first. Edit later.*
   a. Reread the essay critically (several times), looking for places it can be improved.
   b. Write comments directly onto the hard copy or the electronic file.
   c. Look for *green lights*. When something is working, keep it and expand it.
   d. Look for *red lights*. When something is *not* working, delete it or shorten it.
   e. If a *red light* contains something good, increase the good part. Shorten the bad part.
   f. Preserve focus: When something is not sufficiently related to the main topic, delete it.
   g. Keep discussions brief and lean. Don't write more than the reader needs to read.
   h. Don't be afraid to hit the *delete* button. It will improve your writing.
   i. Create a "Storage Locker" file to save your deleted material (this is optional).

2. Editing: *Making smaller proofreading changes to the text. This is your chance to correct errors and to polish your final draft.*
   a. Avoid internet slang and texting abbreviations.
   b. Pay attention to basics, such as punctuation, spelling, and capitalization.
   c. Keep paragraphs between one-third and one-half of a page long.
   d. Learn to correctly spell (and use) *there, they're, their,* and *two, to, too.*
   e. Work on improving grammar. *Listen to your essay*. Read it out loud to yourself and to others. Have them read it to you. *Your ears will detect grammatical errors that your eyes miss.*

*This page is permitted to copy.*

*Chapter 6*

# Grades Nine and Ten: Sixth Writing Project

## *The Personal Reflective Essay: "Your Favorite Place" (Third Draft: E-book)*

Main Standard: 9–10.6:
Use technology, including the internet, to produce, publish, and update individual or shared writing products, taking advantage of technology's capacity to link to other information and to display information flexibly and dynamically.[1]

*Author's Notes: In this project, we will teach students how to convert their essays into e-books. Students will include up to three illustrations related to (and supporting) their essays. There are no sub-standards here.*

**TRANSFORMING YOUR WRITERS INTO AUTHORS**

The focal point of this standard is using technology (especially the internet) to get our students published. During this process, we will link to other information and present the material in an attractive and interesting format. How will we do this?

Using an online platform such as Google Docs, we could certainly have our students create documents in the format of e-books. We could begin this process by having our students design a cover (complete with title, author's name, and illustration). After that, we could show our students how to create a table of contents displaying chapters and corresponding page numbers. In this table of contents, the "Introduction" would be the introduction to the student's essay, and the "Conclusion" would be the conclusion of the essay.

Between these, the three subtopics from the essay would become the book's three chapters.

Each component of the e-book would include a supporting illustration from a site such as Photos for Class or Pics4Learning. The student would complete the book with an "About the Author" section (also listed in the table of contents), which would include a brief biography and a photo of the student. When students complete their e-books, you could have them share them to a classroom folder, then give each student access to the folder. This way, they are "published" to the folder, and the students can read each others' e-books.

You could also share students' work the old-fashioned way. Students could print out their work and create hard copies to populate a highly accessible classroom "library" that can be read by other students. All of this would certainly provide a rich learning experience, would yield a reasonably presentable product, and would be gloriously *free of charge*. Nonetheless, it lacks the dynamic presentation called for by the standard.

A more interactive and interesting option would be to use an internet-based program that allows users to create their own actual *e-books*. There are several of these programs available online, but the best choice for our fledgling writers is Book Creator (bookcreator.com). This program is intended for teachers and their students, and it suits our purposes perfectly. It is easy to learn, safe to use, and produces a beautiful end product. Let's take a closer look at it.

## BOOK CREATOR

Let's start with costs. Book Creator is not free, but it's not expensive either. Upon creating a free account, teachers receive a trial membership that includes forty free e-books (certainly enough for one class). After that, the school district (or the teacher) can purchase (for a surprisingly small price) a one-year subscription that allows students to create up to *one-thousand e-books*.

The interface of Book Creator is fairly simple and intuitive. It's easy to learn, fun to use, and generates a beautifully designed and professional-looking e-book (complete with animated pages turning). And how will you learn it? Simple. Book Creator has its own YouTube channel (Book Creator), and you can watch lots of their instructional videos. You can also watch videos posted by knowledgeable users of Book Creator. Some of these videos were created by teachers, and some were created by students (Book Creator, "Book Creator Tutorial for Students").

Both types work very well and show you Book Creator from both sides of the teacher's desk. You'll be surprised at how quickly you master this program, so don't be intimidated by the specter of learning new technology.

If you watch some of these videos and practice creating your own e-books, you'll be an expert in just a few days.

Book Creator is extremely versatile, and the combinations and variations possible are seemingly infinite. After you teach your students how to use Book Creator, you'll witness their creativity and excitement escalate. They'll start by choosing the *shape* of the book (portrait, landscape, square, etc.), and then they'll design the *cover*. They will include the title and their own name (lots of fonts, sizes, and colors to choose from), along with an eye-catching illustration.

When the cover is completed, students will add a table of contents to the next page. The table of contents will organize the information by chapters, and the chapter titles will relate to the subheadings that students have been using. For example, if the student is writing about Lake Winnipesaukee, the table of contents might look like this:

- Introduction: Hello, Lake! . . . . . . . . . . . . . . . . . . . . . . . . . . . . . . . . . . 3
- Chapter One: Lake Winnipesaukee. . . . . . . . . . . . . . . . . . . . . . . . . . . 4
- Chapter Two: Reflections in the Lake. . . . . . . . . . . . . . . . . . . . . . . . . 6
- Chapter Three: Insights Viewed through Lake Water. . . . . . . . . . . . . . 8
- Conclusion: Good-bye, Lake. . . . . . . . . . . . . . . . . . . . . . . . . . . . . . . 10
- About the Author. . . . . . . . . . . . . . . . . . . . . . . . . . . . . . . . . . . . . . . .11

If you look at the above table of contents, you'll note that it contains creative chapter titles. Encourage your students to do this; it's much more interesting than chapters titled, respectively, "Summary," "Reflection," "Insight." After the students complete their tables of contents, they will link each chapter title to its corresponding page number. This way, if you click on the chapter title, the book jumps directly to the chapter (you'll learn how to do this in Book Creator tutorials).

After that, students can add as many pages as they want (up to 999) and can customize each page in countless configurations. They can change the background, the color, the texture, and the font. They can add pictures, links, video, and audio. (For this project, students will add one picture to the cover and one picture to each chapter.) They can have the pages read aloud in a "robot" voice, or they can record their own voice and narrate their own books.

As the teacher, you will direct the entire process, keep an eye on your students' progress, and provide lots of instruction and encouragement. After teaching this program to the students, you will create a "library" for each of your classes and each of your assignments. Each "library" is essentially a classroom, and you will "invite" your students to join your library.

## DECISIONS, DECISIONS

Next, you will have a few important decisions to make. For example, you can choose "Students can enable collaboration," which allows multiple students to work together on a single e-book. (Although this Standard allows for "sharing," this project is personal and individual in nature, so you should *not* enable the collaboration feature for this particular assignment.) You can also enable students to read the other students' e-books. Here, you should *start* by selecting "no." During the composition process, you as the teacher (and "owner" of the library) will be able to read the students' developing e-books, but the other students will *not*.

However, when all books are completed, you will alter this setting and allow all students in the classroom ("library") to read their peers' books. This will be an engaging learning experience; it also fulfills the Standard's requirement to "publish" the students' work (albeit within the boundaries of the classroom).

You will also encounter a choice that states, "Students can publish their books online." *Do not select this for your students*, because there are privacy issues here. However, when all books are completed, you can select "Publish library online." This is not as comprehensive and ungoverned as it sounds, because you will also be able to choose limiters. The software will ask you "Who can read this library?" and will offer you several choices. At this point, you should select "Only people with the link and a password." In this manner, the students can provide these to friends and family and can have their work read by select individuals whom they know.

Book Creator emphasizes the safety of this choice, stating, "The URL for your book is private—it's not publicly searchable on Google. And you can choose whom you want to share it with. It's completely safe and means the book can be read on any device" (Kemp, "Publishing Your Book Online with Book Creator"). Books can also be "unpublished" at any time. Despite these safety precautions, do not allow students to include their full names, school, photographs of themselves, or any other identifying information. Ask them instead to sign the books with their first names, initials, or a nickname only.

## COFFEE OR TEA? DOGS OR CATS?

Now, let's take a moment to gather our thoughts and catch our breath. You have just received a good deal of information about a computer program, and you may be feeling a bit overwhelmed. This is to be expected, so please don't shut down, shut this book, and say, *I can't do this!* You *can* do it. You definitely *can*, and the rewards will be worth it. Start by watching some *YouTube* videos about Book Creator (watch the one I mentioned above. It's listed in the bibliography, and it's called "Book Creator Tutorial for Students." It's very helpful, and you'll love it).

After that, get a cup of coffee or tea and sit down with Book Creator and play with it. Don't worry over it—*play* with it. Playing is the best way to learn, so play with Book Creator; you will learn this program more quickly than you can imagine. And you'll really like it. Create some of your own silly e-books. Maybe you could write a short book about your dog or your cat, or about the best day you ever had. And, when you have learned the basics of Book Creator, *revisit the pages above*, and they will make much more sense to you. And then, when you know the program fairly well, teach it to your classes.

And now, let's take a close look at this project.

## IT'S TIME TO MAKE AN ILLUSTRATED E-BOOK

After your students understand the basics of using Book Creator (and practice on it), you'll explain this project to them in all its components. As you do this, be sure to model the creation of a simple e-book so that students can visualize the process. At this time, you should also give each student a copy of *Outline 9–10.6* and explain each component of this assignment, encouraging your students to take notes directly onto the outline.

As you introduce this project to students, emphasize that *most of it has already been completed*. Most of their effort now will focus on transferring the text of their *favorite place* projects onto the pages of their e-books. To do this, they will "copy and paste" sections of about two or three hundred words onto each page of the e-book. As they do this, they will exercise choice and creativity, and they will make their work look and behave like an actual e-book. And the end product is quite striking.

In addition to the text of their essays, students will also include a total of *seven* illustrations. Here are the elements that will include an illustration:

1. The Cover
2. The Introduction
3. The First Subtopic (Chapter One)
4. The Second Subtopic (Chapter Two)
5. The Third Subtopic (Chapter Three)
6. The Conclusion
7. About the Author (this will include a photo of the student)

When inserting illustrations, encourage students to place the illustrations at appropriate places *within the text*, rather than placing them at the end of each section (an uninspiring quick fix). This will give the books a more professional look, and the pictures will illustrate (with immediacy) the elements being discussed.

When illustrating their chapters, students will search for pictures that somehow capture the essence of each chapter (and subtopic). Book Creator makes this easy for students. To do this, students will click on the prominent "plus" sign (top right), then click on the word "Import." A search window will immediately open that allows for a modified and filtered search of *Pixabay* images (pixabay.com). Book creator declares the results appropriate for student use, stating, "Our Image Search is filtered to be safe, and copyright free (they are safe to use in your classroom)" (Kemp, "Add a Photo from the Image Search").

As students search for related images, inform them that they don't have to find images that capture their topics in *exact* terms. They can find images that relate to (or somehow *represent*) the topic. For example, let's say the student's essay is about an unforgettable summer spent on the shores of Lake Winnipesaukee. For Chapter One (the "description" chapter), it will be easy to find a picture of this beautiful lake. However, how will students illustrate *reflection* and *insight*?

For this more abstract component, the students will search for illustrations that somehow convey an idea discussed in the chapter. For example, *does the student talk about finding an arrowhead in the sand?* If so, the student might complement this discussion with a picture of an arrowhead. *Does the student discuss time spent in a canoe?* If so, the student might choose a picture of someone canoeing on a lake (even if it's *not* Lake Winnipesaukee). *Does the student reflect on things learned while staying at the lake?* Perhaps the student can find a photo of someone reading a book on the beach of a lake (and it can be *any* lake). As long as the images are somehow related to the text, this works beautifully.

After locating a suitable image, students will click on the image, then click "Add." Next, they will adjust its size and its location on the page. The process is simpler than it sounds, and the result is quite striking. These related illustrations will enliven the text and provide readers with a vibrant multimedia experience.

Students can also download their own original photos and bring these into their e-books (they will certainly do this for the "About the Author" section). After downloading a photo, the student will click on the "plus" sign and the word *Import*. Next, the student will click on the word *Files*, and select the photo he or she wants to include. This will give the e-book a very personal feel and will give each student a great sense of ownership and achievement.

After all, it's not every day that a young student becomes the author of a genuine e-book.

## WRITERS NEED READERS, RIGHT?

After your students complete their beautiful e-books, there is just one last thing to do, and it's rather celebratory in nature. When your classroom library is populated with your students' shiny new e-books, change the privacy setting on Book Creator and announce to your students that they are all published to the classroom library and *they can now read each other's e-books*. And then watch the flush of excitement spread throughout your classroom.

As the students read each others' e-books and learn about their lives and the wonderful places their classmates cherish, you can marvel at the marvelous things they (and you) have accomplished together. You have transformed your fledgling writers into authors of e-books, and it is a stunning achievement. As an educator, it's a rare moment to enjoy, and it's quite forgivable if—for just a moment—you look around your classroom and think a sweet and silent thought to yourself: *this is* my *favorite place.*

Ninth and Tenth Grade, Sixth Writing Project: *Outline 9–10.6*
The Personal Reflective Essay: "Your Favorite Place" (Third Draft: *E-book*)
Name_____ Date_____
Title _____

1. Cover
   a. Includes Title of Project; Student-Author's name; Illustration

2. Table of Contents
   a. Lists *all* components of this project, from "Introduction" to "About the Author"
   b. All titles linked to corresponding page numbers

3. Introduction
   a. Includes Creative Title; Full Text; Illustration

4. Chapter One (First Subtopic: *Description*)
   a. Includes Creative Title; Full Text; Illustration

5. Chapter Two (Second Subtopic: *Reflection*)
   a. Includes Creative Title; Full Text; Illustration

6. Chapter Three (Third Subtopic: *Insight*)
   a. Includes Creative Title; Full Text; Illustration

7. Conclusion
   a. Includes Creative Title; Full Text; Illustration

8. About the Author
   a. Includes Biography (one paragraph) and Illustration (Photograph of the Student)

*This page is permitted to copy.*

*Chapter 7*

# Grades Nine and Ten: Seventh Writing Project

## *The Literary Research Paper:* "Dreams and Loneliness in Steinbeck's Novella *Of Mice and Men*" (First Draft: Literary Analysis)

Main Standard: 9–10.7:

Conduct short as well as more sustained research projects to answer a question (including a self-generated question) or solve a problem; narrow or broaden the inquiry when appropriate; synthesize multiple sources on the subject, demonstrating understanding of the subject under investigation.

*Author's Notes: Students will perform a close reading of Steinbeck's novella* Of Mice and Men. *They will perform original literary analysis of the themes of* dreams *and* loneliness *within the novella. Alternate topics include writing about prominent themes in works such as* Fahrenheit 451 *(by Ray Bradbury);* Night *(by Elie Wiesel); and* I Know Why the Caged Bird Sings *(by Maya Angelou). Students will write this in the third-person. There are no sub-standards here.*

### RESEARCH TO BUILD AND PRESENT KNOWLEDGE

The next group of standards (Seven, Eight, and Nine) is called "Research to Build and Present Knowledge." In these three standards, the primary focus is performing and utilizing academic *research*. To teach the research process thoroughly and deeply, we are going to bundle these three standards together into a large and multifaceted three-part metaproject focused on composing a thorough and sophisticated research project. Here is an overview of the next three projects:

- Chapter 7 (this current chapter): The Literary Research Paper: "Dreams and Loneliness in Steinbeck's Novella *Of Mice and Men*" (First Draft: Literary Analysis)
- Chapter 8: The Literary Research Paper: "Dreams and Loneliness in Steinbeck's Novella *Of Mice and Men*" (Second Draft: Secondary Sources)
- Chapter 9: The Literary Research Paper: "Dreams and Loneliness in Steinbeck's Novella *Of Mice and Men*" (Third Draft: Creative Addendum)

As we take our students through these three related projects (that build on each other), we will proceed one step at a time and convey concepts clearly and simply. Our primary goal will be to introduce our students gently into the mystifying world of writing an academic research paper. This is an extremely important project, and, taught well, it will offer students the proper methods to compose a research project.

In doing this, it will boost our students' thinking and organizational skills and will help prepare them for the rigors of writing in college—and there is a tremendous need for this. In many cases, young students are *assigned* research projects, but they aren't truly taught how to *compose* them. In cases like this, they are given a task that they cannot complete. Consequently, the research paper becomes a confusing and stressful experience for the student, rather than an opportunity to learn. We are going to change all that.

## WHAT IS THIS PROJECT ABOUT?

In this project, we will teach our students the sequential steps of composing a research project. As we do this, we will move slowly and deliberately and present the steps in clarity and simplicity. This project will be based on John Steinbeck's wonderful novella *Of Mice and Men*, and that text will be the vehicle through which we teach the (related) processes of analysis and research. In this paper, students will analyze the two most prominent themes in the novella: *dreams* and *loneliness*. Along the way, they will learn a great deal about this text. More important, they will gain understanding of how to analyze literature and how to compose a research project.

As you teach this project, present it in such a manner that the students learn it not by rote but by a holistic understanding of its nature. Begin by giving your students an overview of the assignment, and do something highly unusual: convey to them the *philosophy* embedded in composing a research project of this nature. And what does that mean? It means a great deal, and it is spectacularly *not* a component of mainstream contemporary pedagogy.

If you read the standard above, you'll note that this research project is impelled by *answering a question*, which means that it is based (to an extent) on principles of inquiry-based learning. However, our fledgling writers will not create the question to answer (they are not yet ready for that type of open-ended inquiry). *We* (as teachers) will provide structure by creating the guiding question. It will be in the form of a declarative prompt, and here it is: *In John Steinbeck's novella* Of Mice and Men, *the two primary themes are* dreams *and* loneliness. *Write an essay in which you analyze the novella through the lenses of these two themes.*

When students understand the impetus of this project, we'll show them how to do it.

## THE PHILOSOPHY OF THIS PROJECT: *ORIGINAL WRITING FIRST, RESEARCH LATER*

We now arrive at the philosophy underlying this project—which is not often taught in the contemporary academy (especially to high school students). In this current project, *students will use the primary text as the exclusive source of "research."* They will interpret the novella through the lenses of the two themes and will generate their own original literary analyses. They will *not* look (yet) at other research sources (such as literary criticism), because this will shut down their original thinking. This point is very important, and it bears further explanation.

In this current project, students will write an essay in which they perform original literary analysis on Steinbeck's *Of Mice and Men*. The "research" they perform will be between the covers of the novella, and students will not include any outside (secondary) sources. This method can be termed "original writing first, research second." It is highly effective, and we will teach these principles with clarity and simplicity.

By composing an original analytical essay first, students will be required to perform their own literary analysis and will therefore avoid the dreaded practice known as *plagiarism*. Our fledgling writers will compose an original paper they can be proud of, rather than simply assembling the thoughts of others.

## LITERARY THEMES

Now, let's say that you have assigned your class to read *Of Mice and Men*. After introducing Steinbeck and discussing the novel's setting, situation, and characters, tell your students they are going to write a paper that analyzes the most prominent themes of the novella. At this point, teach students the concept of literary *themes*. All literature (if it is to be called "literature") portrays and examines important themes. And what are themes? They are ideas highly relevant to all of our lives and to the experience of being alive as a human being.

As you teach this, explain to students that stories function on two levels. There is the *visible* story—what is happening on the page—and there is the *invisible* meaning, which happens underneath the words. It is written in code, in invisible ink, and it resides in the margins, between the words and lines of the pages, and in the readers' intellect and imagination. It takes time to learn this new language, but you are there to help them.

When teaching this concept, give your class a list of themes they can understand—and that relate to their lives—and discuss them with your students. Here are ten themes that students will find engaging: *friendship, family, love, pets, growing up, school, bullying, sports, working, dealing with loss*. As you discuss these themes, stress to your students that by reading works of great literature, we learn about concepts that are deeply relevant to our lives. And why is this important? Because there is no owner's manual for understanding the experience of being alive on planet Earth. So, we turn to art and literature, and we live in those for a time, and these become our instruction booklets. We learn about life in *them*.

When the students have a sound basic understanding of the nature and purpose of literary themes, tell them they will examine *Of Mice and Men* through these two particular themes: *dreams* and *loneliness*. These siblings are the most prominent and important themes present in the text, and they run throughout its entirety. And what do they mean? *Dreams*, you'll explain to your students, are the main characters' *grail*. For George and Lennie, it means owning a place of their own.

Explain to your students that dreams are more intense and whimsical than "goals." Whereas goals may be pragmatic in nature, dreams live in the innermost sanctum of our hearts, and they whisper to us throughout all our lives. *I'm waiting for you*, they breathe in the silence between heartbeats; *I am here, waiting only for you*. Dreams are not our nightly slumberous apparitions; they are the things we want most deeply, in every pulsing molecule of our being.

When you explain *loneliness*, tell your students that there is a difference between being "alone" and living a life of frigid loneliness burning slowly in your bones. That sort of existential loneliness runs throughout all the characters in this novella—with the exception of the two main characters, George and Lennie. They are *not* lonely, because they have each other. Nonetheless, the story's tragic and unforgettable conclusion presages a life of stinging acid loneliness for George.

## AS YOU READ, TAKE NOTES

As you take students through this novel, tell them to read the novel through the lenses of *dreams* and *loneliness*. They are both present in the novel, and their appearance is not disguised by Steinbeck. He wanted us to understand what this book is really about. Tell your students to read with eyes open and pencil in hand, looking for instances in which these themes emerge. When students find quotes alluding to *dreams* or *loneliness*, they must flag them in the text with prominent annotations, because they'll need to find them later. Encourage your students to write these quotes down—preferably onto an electronic document—and to include the citations (author's last name and page numbers). These quotes will become the centerpiece of this project.

As students read (and fall in love with) this book, you'll need to provide guidance. Tell them to find at least three quotes that relate to the theme of *dreams* and another three quotes that relate to the theme of *loneliness*. Quotes regarding these themes are often quite long, but encourage your students to include the most relevant part of the quotes and to keep these no longer than about three lines (but they can go a bit longer, if necessary). When the students finish reading *Of Mice and Men*, each student should have assembled at least six quotes—three quotes on *dreams* and the other three quotes on *loneliness* (with page numbers attached to each quote). And the backbone of the paper will be complete.

## THE FIVE STEPS TO ANALYZING LITERARY QUOTES

When the students have their six quotes assembled on an electronic document, it's time to weave them into coherent literary analysis. Your students will not know how to do this, so you will have to teach them. This is difficult for fledgling writers, but you will instruct them with clarity, simplicity, and patience.

As students begin performing the beautiful act of literary analysis, tell them that it will be a bit like the "summary and commentary" analysis they performed in earlier chapters. However, the (literary) analysis students perform here is a bit different and will be composed of five steps. Every step here is crucial, and here they are:

1. Introduce the quote by describing the context and the situation. Whenever presenting and analyzing a quote, students must lead into it with *their own words and thoughts*.
2. Provide the quote, verbatim (and include quotation marks).
3. Include the *citation*. Because the quote comes from Steinbeck's novella, we technically don't need to include his last name. For teaching purposes, however, we will include his name and the page number where the quote occurs, as follows: (Steinbeck 15).
4. Explain the quote. Nothing fancy here; just paraphrase the quote and explain it to the reader. What does the quote mean, especially in terms of the story or character?
5. Analyze the quote. What is the "invisible" meaning embedded in it? This is where students will generate original analyses.

The analysis portion (step 5, above) is the most challenging part of this project, and it also contains the most important new learning occurring here. In this portion, students will interpret the quote and will relate the quote to the theme being discussed.

During this process, they will consider questions such as these: *What does the quote say about dreams or about loneliness? What is Steinbeck's message here? What does the quote teach us about the theme—in terms of the novella and in terms of life? What can readers learn from this quote? What can we learn about the story and the characters? Why do the characters feel this way? What does it teach us about people and human nature? What does it teach us about life in general?* Et cetera.

This entire five-step process can be successfully expressed in a single paragraph. Or, if the student's insight and ideas start to blossom, this might be presented in *two* paragraphs—one for description and the other for analysis. Ideally, the analytical portion should be longer than the quote itself, but this is new and it takes practice, so be patient with your students as they venture into this new and unfamiliar landscape. Work with them, give them guidance, and celebrate their small successes and the surprising insights they achieve (because there will definitely be some).

## TWO EXEMPLARS

Below you will find two exemplars of this process. Please share these with students and discuss them. The quote and passage below are about the theme of *dreams*:

> In chapter 3, George, Lennie, and Candy are alone in the bunk house. Lennie asks George to tell him (once again) about their dream to own a little place they can call their own. George tells Lennie that "we'd have a little house an' a room to ourself. Little fat iron stove, an' in the winter we'd keep a fire goin' in it. It ain't enough land so we'd have to work too hard. Maybe six, seven hours a day" (Steinbeck 63). In this quote, George describes his simple dream to Lennie. His highest goal in life is for them to own (together) a little farm with a cozy house where they can be comfortable and work for themselves, instead of for a boss whom they don't really know.
>
> This quote is important because it gives the reader a clear idea of the dream shared by George and Lennie. However, their dream is much more than owning a farm. The two friends want the emotional fulfillment that will come with owning (and living on) a place of their own. They will no longer fear being fired, and they won't have to sleep in a bunk house with other workers. They will have privacy and the pride that comes with a sense of true ownership. They will also be working for themselves and will sell (and eat) the fruits and vegetables that they grow. All of this will give them a deep sense of purpose and *spiritual satisfaction*, and this makes it a worthy dream to pursue.

This next quote and passage are about the theme of *loneliness*:

> Early in the novella, George and Lennie are spending the evening camping out in the open. When Lennie asks George to tell the familiar tale of their friendship, George states, "Guys like us, that work on ranches, are the loneliest guys in the world. They got no fambly. They don't belong no place" (Steinbeck 15). Lennie then excitedly interjects, *"But not us! An' why? Because.... because I got you to look after me, and you got me to look after you, and that's why"* (Steinbeck 15). In this dialogue, George describes the loneliness pervading their profession, while Lennie responds by asserting that it doesn't affect them, because they have each other.
>
> In this passage, Steinbeck introduces the novella's theme of loneliness and prepares us to enter a world inhabited by lonely characters. Nonetheless, George and Lennie are not lonely, because they have each other (a notion that brings Lennie great joy and emotional security). All it takes to avoid loneliness—the passage suggests—is to have the friendship and affection of another person. However, this is a bittersweet notion, because it also causes us to wonder what might happen if one of these friends disappeared from the other's life.

As you teach this concept, urge students to follow all five steps. Also, encourage them to read the quotes deeply and to understand what they're really saying. Remember, they must first understand the *visible* story before they can decode its invisible meaning.

## THE STRUCTURE OF THIS PROJECT

At this point, hand out *Outline 9–10.7* and go over it with your students. Encourage them to take notes on the outline and explain the following:

### 1. Introduction

Here, students will introduce the essay to readers. They will mention John Steinbeck's full name and the title *Of Mice and Men*. They will also mention the two themes they are discussing and will provide an overview of the essay. Students will write this last.

### 2. First Subtopic: *Dreams*

In this section, students will begin by introducing the theme of dreams to their readers. They will define the term "dreams," and they will state that dreams are a prominent theme in the text. After that, they will present the three quotes to the reader, along with their analyses. As they discuss each quote, they will utilize the five-part structure discussed above.

### 3. Second Subtopic: *Loneliness*

In this section, students will begin by introducing the theme of loneliness to their readers. They will state that loneliness is a prominent theme in the text and that nearly all of the characters are extremely lonely. After that, they will present the three quotes to the reader, along with their analyses. As they discuss each quote, they will utilize the five-part structure discussed above.

### 4. Third Subtopic: *Main Messages of This Pessimistic Novella*

Here, students will describe the main messages conveyed by the themes: *we will never achieve our dreams, and we will always be lonely.* After that, they will *evaluate the validity of these messages.* Yes, these melancholy messages are certainly true in the world of the novella. However, are they *necessarily* true in the real world? If not, students will write an original section in which they describe how and why these messages aren't always true in the real world. After all, there are people in the world who achieve their dreams, and there are people who are not chronically lonely. These are facts, not opinions. Nonetheless, we all remain susceptible to falling into the traps of frustrated dreams and frigid loneliness. How can we prevent these things from happening?

## 5. Conclusion

Students will end this essay by providing a summarizing review in which they reinforce their most salient points. Once again, they will mention the author and the title, along with the main messages of the novella. Last, they will discuss what the story teaches us about life and about human nature.

## JOINING THE CONVERSATION

When your students have completed these projects, congratulate them for doing something special. They have just performed original literary analysis on the most important themes contained within this brief masterpiece. But tell them also that these drafts, while complete as *essays*, are not yet truly finished. In the next project, we will expand their essays and buttress the students' findings and their analyses with the addition of (secondary source) literary criticism. As students engage in this next step, they will learn how to compose a genuine research paper, and they will join a conversation that has been going on for decades.

Ninth and Tenth Grade, Seventh Writing Project: *Outline 9–10.7*
The Literary Research Essay: "Dreams and Loneliness
in Steinbeck's Novella *Of Mice and Men*"
(First Draft: Literary Analysis)

Name_____ Date_____

Title _____

Make sure your title mentions the title, author, and themes you're writing about.

1. Introduction: A brief overview of the project. Be sure to include the title *Of Mice and Men*, the full name "John Steinbeck," and the themes *dreams* and *loneliness* (write this last).

2. First Subtopic: *Dreams*
   a. First quote and analysis (follow the five-step process)
   b. Second quote and analysis (follow the five-step process)
   c. Third quote and analysis (follow the five-step process)

3. Second Subtopic: *Loneliness*
   a. First quote and analysis (follow the five-step process)
   b. Second quote and analysis (follow the five-step process)
   c. Third quote and analysis (follow the five-step process)

4. Third Subtopic: *Main Messages of This Pessimistic Novella*
   a. We will never achieve our dreams.
   b. We will always be lonely.
   c. Evaluation and analysis: Are these messages true, in terms of real life? Why or why not? If not true, how might we overcome them?

5. Conclusion: A brief recap of the topic (includes some summary)
   a. Mention the title, author, and themes explored here.
   b. Describe the main messages of this novella.
   c. Describe what this novella teaches us about life and about human nature.

*This page is permitted to copy.*

*Chapter 8*

# Grades Nine and Ten: Eighth Writing Project

## The Literary Research Paper: "Dreams and Loneliness in Steinbeck's Novella *Of Mice and Men*" (Second Draft: Secondary Sources)

Main Standard: 9–10.8:

Gather relevant information from multiple authoritative print and digital sources, using advanced searches effectively; assess the usefulness of each source in answering the research question; integrate information into the text selectively to maintain the flow of ideas, avoiding plagiarism and following a standard format for citation.

*Author's Notes: In this project, students will locate, read, and annotate secondary sources on* Of Mice and Men. *After choosing relevant quotations to support the previous project, students will insert these into their essays and integrate them into the discussion taking place. Students will produce approximately two (or more) pages of new writing. There are no sub-standards here.*

### THE PRIMARY AND THE SECONDARY

In the previous chapter, our students wrote an original analysis of Steinbeck's marvelous novella *Of Mice and Men*. To do this, they studied the text through the lenses of two foundational themes running throughout the story: *dreams* and *loneliness*. As we taught this project to students, we discussed the *philosophy* of writing a literary research paper. It is essentially divided into two separate phases. In the first phase, the students write an original analysis of the primary text being studied (we did this in the previous chapter). When doing this, the student *will not consult any secondary sources*, because this will shut down the student's original thinking. (Note: The term "primary source" refers to an *original* artifact, such as a work of literature, while the term "secondary sources" refers to works written *about* the primary source.)

Now that the students' original draft is complete, we begin the second phase, in which we convert it from an essay into an actual research paper. To facilitate this transformation, our young writers will look at secondary sources and will locate quotes relevant to the themes being discussed. Next, they will insert these quotes in appropriate locations, integrate them into the discussion taking place, and make the analysis (and the paper) stronger and more convincing.

We can summarize this two-phase method as follows: *original analysis first; literary criticism second*. This is a highly effective approach that teaches literary interpretation *and* research, and it also makes plagiarism impossible. (Note: Although *paraphrasing* is a viable alternative to quoting, it is recommended that you encourage your fledgling writers to use *quotes* exclusively in this project. We will introduce paraphrasing in chapter 12.)

In this current project, we are going to take students through the entire process of locating and using research. Many different sources of research would work well for this project, but in this chapter, we are going to focus exclusively on *academic databases*. In a project like this, databases are the students' best choice for performing research. Besides being accessible and free of charge, they provide brief, reliable, highly focused articles and are a wonderful resource for students to learn and to use throughout all of their academic years.

We will also teach students how to create (and include) in-text citations and how to create a bibliography. All of this can be a difficult, cumbersome process for young writers, so we are going to proceed simply and take things one step at a time. In brief, there are five steps to performing and correctly using research, and we will teach all of these steps to students. Here they are:

1. Search for relevant sources.
2. Locate sources, and choose the best ones for the project.
3. Read the sources, look for relevant quotes, and annotate.
4. Integrate these quotes into the paper.
5. Create a bibliography.

## DATABASES

As you teach students how to search for high-quality resources, start by giving them a few basic rules. First, they cannot use search engines such as Google. While searches of this nature will likely return some good material, much of it is unreliable. Next, they cannot use Wikipedia as a source, because *anyone* with internet access can edit Wikipedia articles. Although Wikipedia articles tend to be accurate, they are not as *reliable* as articles provided by academic databases.

And what exactly are databases? To put it simply, they are reliable research sources that contain millions of scholarly articles. These databases are highly organized and categorized, and they provide information on all levels, from elementary school up through graduate school and professional scholars writing for publication. But how do we access academic databases?

Your school library probably has a subscription to a group of databases or to a single "digital library" called JSTOR, which is short for *Journal Storage* ("About JSTOR"). When teaching your students the art of research, you may wish to collaborate with your school librarian and arrange for your class to receive some instruction on using these resources. If your school library does not have databases, your local *public* library probably does. This is a fantastic resource and should not be overlooked. Everything there is free of charge, much of it is available online, and the ticket of admission is a current library card.

## OF SEARCHES AND BOOLEAN LIMITERS

Before students begin searching, give them this clear goal: they will get on the databases and find at least *two* articles that shed light on *Of Mice and Men* (especially the themes of *dreams* and *loneliness*). As students commence their searches, teach them about *Boolean limiters*, which are methods to help the search engine retrieve more accurate results.

Internet searches respond to several different limiters—such as *and, or, not* ("Boolean Operators and Nesting")—but the most effective limiter is the use of *quotation marks*. When students search for terms composed of multiple words (such as phrases, titles, and full names), they should *enclose the entire phrase in quotation marks*. This will cause the search engine to read them as a *specific term* (as if it's a single word), rather than as a group of individual words. For example, when performing searches for this project, students can use search terms that look like these (note that these searches are *not* case sensitive):

- "of mice and men" steinbeck
- "of mice and men" dreams steinbeck
- "of mice and men" loneliness "john steinbeck"

## OF STAPLES AND PENCILS

When students have located their two articles, have them print the articles out, staple each one together, and read the articles carefully and critically. Instruct them to read through the lenses of *dreams* and *loneliness* and to annotate in pencil (pencil marks create a gentle presence, and it's always helpful to erase mistakes). As students read their articles, they will search for quotes that somehow resonate with points made in their essays. When they find related quotes, students will flag the quote by circling it or underlining it. Their goal is to locate (and flag) three quotes related to the theme of dreams and another three quotes related to the theme of loneliness (for a total of six quotes).

When the students have located all six quotes, they will transpose them onto the electronic document containing the original project. They can do this by temporarily placing all six quotes beneath the essay, thereby creating a bank of quotes they will later integrate into their writing. When students transpose their quotes, *they must also include the citation.*

The citation students use will be similar to the one they used when citing the novella in the previous project. Once again, they will include the author's last name and the page number, as follows: (Kordich 35). However, if the database articles they find are not PDFs (which is likely), these articles will *not* have page numbers. When this happens, students will cite using *last name only*, as follows: (Kordich). Here are two examples of quotes and citations taken from a pair of articles recently found on two databases The first article relates to dreams; the second relates to loneliness (these do not have page numbers):

- "Reading closely their dreams could lead to an understanding about the role of dreams for the have-nots, or, perhaps, all people" (Kordich).
- "Pathos results from the novella's illumination of our human inability to transcend aloneness and loneliness" (Owens).

## INTEGRATING QUOTES INTO THEIR ESSAYS

In this section, we encounter the most important learning occurring in this chapter: *how to integrate research into the discourse taking place in the students' essays.*[1] First, *the student must decide where each quote belongs in the essay*. The purpose of these quotes (you'll explain to your class) is to reinforce (or echo) specific points they have made in their papers. When a student places a quote in an essay, the quote should relate to (and support) the points being made in proximity to the quote.

This will make their essays more authoritative and convincing; it will transform them into true research papers. Properly done, these secondary quotes will melt seamlessly into the text, and will help to make the paper feel organized, unified, and authoritative. To do this, we will once again follow the five-step method of using quotations (introduced in the previous chapter).

This process is a crucial bit of learning for our young writers, so we will review it with them, striving to produce deep understanding and long-term learning. After that, we will teach our students how to apply this technique to incorporating literary criticism into their original analyses. As you (re)teach this process, begin by reviewing the five steps. Here they are:

1. Introduce the quote.
2. Provide the quote.
3. Provide the in-text citation.
4. Explain the quote in their own words.
5. Analyze the quote, and discuss its relevance to the paper.

Let us now consider each step as it pertains to this project and to using secondary sources in general.

Introducing the quote means that the writer should put *his or her own words before the quote* so that the sentence does *not* start with quotation marks. For example, let's say that this is the quote and the citation: "Reading closely their dreams could lead to an understanding about the role of dreams for the have-nots, or, perhaps, all people" (Kordich). There are several ways to introduce this (or any) quote. Here are three methods, followed by examples relating to this project:

1. Provide a lead-in to the quote, in your own words:
   - It is important to understand the different dreams of the different characters, because "reading closely their dreams could lead to an understanding about the role of dreams for the have-nots, or, perhaps, all people" (Kordich).
2. Place the in-text citation (i.e., "Kordich states") *before* the quote:
   - Kordich states, "Reading closely their dreams could lead to an understanding about the role of dreams for the have-nots, or, perhaps, all people."
3. Truncate (omit) part of the quote:

- Understanding the dreams of the main characters "could lead to an understanding about the role of dreams for the have-nots, or, perhaps, all people" (Kordich).

If you look at the three examples above, you'll see that we have now performed three of the five steps: we have *introduced the quote*; *given the quote*; and *provided an in-text citation*.

The next step is to explain the quote clearly. The writer should not assume that the reader understands the quote, so the writer should explain the quote in simplified terms, *in his or her own words*. In this case, the explanation might sound like this: *When we understand the dreams of the main characters, we gain an understanding of the role that dreams play in the underprivileged—and possibly in all of humanity.*

And now comes the most challenging part of this process: generating an original comment that interprets the quote and relates it to the student's paper. After *explaining* the quote, students should provide an *analytical commentary* on the quote and (possibly) draw an original conclusion from the ideas there.

When teaching this, tell students that they must first *understand* the quote, and then *analyze* it. They must look deeply into it, and find thoughts and ideas that are not directly expressed in the quote. *What is the quote hinting at? What does it make you imagine? What ideas grow out of the quote? What does the quote suggest? What can we learn from the quote? How does the quote support points you make in the essay? How does the quote strengthen your essay?*

This sort of analytical commentary takes practice, so don't expect perfection or mastery from your students yet. The important part here is that they understand the concept and that they *attempt* to analyze the quotes they use. Working with the quote above, an analysis might sound like this: *In this quote, Kordich demonstrates a belief that by understanding the unfulfilled dreams of the main characters, we can gain an empathy into their lives and into the lives of all human beings. If we do this, we can develop an understanding of the importance of dreams, not just in the downtrodden but in every human being, everywhere.*

When we put all five elements together, they'll look like the passage below:

> It is important to understand the differing dreams of the different characters, because "reading closely their dreams could lead to an understanding about the role of dreams for the have-nots, or, perhaps, all people" (Kordich). When we understand the dreams of the main characters, we gain an understanding of the role that dreams play in the underprivileged—and possibly in all of humanity. In this quote, Kordich demonstrates a belief that by understanding the unfulfilled dreams of the main characters, we can gain an empathy into their lives and into

the lives of all human beings. If we do this, we can develop an understanding of the importance of dreams, not just in the downtrodden but in all of humanity.

If you look closely at the example above, you will note the presence of all five steps: (1) introduce the quote in your own words; (2) provide the quote; (3) provide the in-text citation; (4) explain the quote in your own words; (5) comment on the quote (analyze it and draw an original conclusion, if possible). And now, let us look at another exemplar passage in which we take Owens's quote about loneliness (provided earlier in this chapter) and apply the five steps to it:

> Owens believes that "pathos results from the novella's illumination of our human inability to transcend aloneness and loneliness." Reading this novella generates a great sadness in the reader, because it forces us to confront our own inescapable loneliness. However, this raises an implicit question: by confronting our existential loneliness, might we be able to deal with it in a manner that is healthier and more mature? Perhaps the enlightenment provided by Steinbeck can help us to consciously recognize the loneliness in all of humanity. And, if this leads us to a greater comprehension of the loneliness existing in ourselves and others, then perhaps we can take steps to alleviate the specter of loneliness in ourselves as well as other people.

If you look at the two examples above, you'll note that the *original writing* generated is a good bit longer than the quote. This is a positive occurrence, and it indicates that the writer is deeply involved with the material being discussed and has true ownership of the essay. As students begin learning this technique, encourage them to produce writing that is perhaps *two or three times longer* than the quote. Have them practice this method and apply their new skills to the six quotes they have located. It's a challenging prospect, but it's an excellent way for their voices to show up prominently in their essays. If they do this with all of their research, they will generate a paper in which they can take a sense of true ownership and feel a rightful sense of pride.

## THE BIBLIOGRAPHY

Because this is a research paper, the students will need to create a bibliography that lists their sources. Fortunately, the databases provide a luxury that makes this quite easy: they possess a function that creates the bibliographic entry for the user. When the students have chosen a database article they wish to use, tell them to locate a button labeled "Cite" or "Citation," and click on it. After choosing a citation style from the choices offered, the student will simply copy the bibliographic citation and paste it onto the bibliography.

So, let's say that we are making an MLA (Modern Language Association) bibliography for the two sources discussed here. Using the copy-and-paste function on the databases, it will look like this (note that these have been edited for brevity):

Works Cited

Kordich, Catherine J. "How to Write about *Of Mice and Men*." *Bloom's How to Write about John Steinbeck*, Chelsea House, 2017.

Owens, Louis. "Deadly Kids, Stinking Dogs, and Heroes: The Best Laid Plans in Steinbeck's *Of Mice and Men*." *Children's Literature Review*, edited by Jelena Krstovic, vol. 172, Gale, 2012.

**ANOTHER PERSPECTIVE**

When you complete teaching this to your class, give each student a copy of *Outline 9–10.8* and go over it with them. It's a different sort of outline, but it will be quite useful for our budding scholars. It includes the five sequential steps for *locating* research and the five sequential steps for *using* research. And, when your students have submitted their research papers on *Of Mice and Men*, congratulate them on completing a difficult and complex task. But tell them not to leave the farm and the world of the novella yet, because they have one more task to do. This one will be creative and will require them to write in the persona of a lonely man named George—who has recently lost a dream and a friend.

Ninth and Tenth Grade, Eighth Writing Project: *Outline 9–10.8*
The Literary Research Paper: "Dreams and Loneliness
in Steinbeck's Novella *Of Mice and Men*"
(Second Draft: Secondary Sources)

Name_____ Date_____

Title _____

**Table 8.1**

| STEP | PERFORMING RESEARCH AND LOCATING SOURCES | USING RESEARCH IN YOUR PROJECT |
|---|---|---|
| 1 | Search for relevant sources. Enclose multiple-word search terms in quotation marks. | Introduce the quote in your own words. You can give the author's name here or lead into it with an original phrase. |
| 2 | Locate relevant sources and choose the best ones for your project. | Provide the quote verbatim inside quotation marks. |
| 3 | Read the sources through the lens of your topic, look for relevant quotes, and annotate (in pencil). | Provide the in-text citation. For example: (Kordich 35) or (Owens). Include page numbers if available. |
| 4 | Integrate these quotes into the paper. (This process is described in the column to the right.) | Explain the quote in your own words. What exactly does it mean? Keep this clear and simple. |
| 5 | Create a bibliography. When using databases, click on "Cite" or "Citation," then copy and paste. | Write original commentary about the quote. Interpret and analyze the quote and discuss its relevance to your paper. How does it support your analyses? |

*This page is permitted to copy.*

*Chapter 9*

# Grades Nine and Ten: Ninth Writing Project

## The Literary Research Paper: "Dreams and Loneliness in Steinbeck's Novella *Of Mice and Men*" (Third Draft: Creative Coda)

Main Standard: 9–10.9:
Draw evidence from literary or informational texts to support analysis, reflection, and research.

*Author's notes: In this creative project, students will compose a diary entry written by George Milton. In this diary entry, George will reflect on the events of the novella and will allude to the themes of* dreams *and* loneliness. *Students will also make creative inferences about George's life after the events of the story. Students will write this in the first person (just as George would).*

*Sub-Standard A:
Apply *grades 9–10 Reading standards* to literature (e.g., "Analyze how an author draws on and transforms source material in a specific work [e.g., how Shakespeare treats a theme or topic from Ovid or the Bible or how a later author draws on a play by Shakespeare]").

*Author's Notes: This project aligns closely with Reading Standard 3, which encourages students to* "Analyze how complex characters (e.g., those with multiple or conflicting motivations) develop over the course of a text, interact with other characters, and advance the plot or develop the theme."

Sub-Standard B:
Apply *grades 9–10 Reading standards* to literary nonfiction (e.g., "Delineate and evaluate the argument and specific claims in a text, assessing whether the reasoning is valid and the evidence is relevant and sufficient; identify false statements and fallacious reasoning").

*Author's Notes: This sub-standard refers to "literary nonfiction," while* Of Mice and Men *is a fictional narrative. Sub-standard B will therefore not be a consideration in this project.*

## A DIFFERENT SORT OF PROJECT

Our students have been working very hard on their literary research projects, so it's time to give them a project that is creative and fun. Whereas the first two assignments were research-based, this current project will be a creative (and welcome) addition to the research paper that students have completed. In this project, students will compose a *diary entry* written by character George Milton.

If we look at the main standard, we note that it's rather brief, asking students to use textual evidence to support "analysis, reflection, and research." In the first two projects, students certainly performed their share of analysis and research. This current project will thus be primarily *reflective* in nature, and there will be two facets to this reflection.

First, their diary entries will portray *George* reflecting on the experiences he had with Lennie. Second, the *students* will reflect on the novella and their experience of reading it. As they write, they will also make imaginative inferences about the characters and situations in *Of Mice and Men*. This project will therefore be *creative, reflective, imaginative,* and *inferential*. It will be a potpourri of creative learning in which students can blend their prior knowledge of the text with fanciful glimpses into George's mind and the magical wonderings of "*What if.*"

## A DIARY ENTRY

Begin by telling students that this project will be a "coda" (a concluding section added) to their research papers and that this will be in the form of a *diary entry*. Here, transition to a discussion of the nature and purpose of diaries. As you introduce the concept of diaries, you might start by asking your students questions such as these: *What is a diary? What is the purpose of a diary? Does anyone here keep a diary? What might motivate a person to keep a diary?*

You can also present artifacts, showing your students an actual diary and photos of diaries and discussing with them the most famous diary ever written—the stunning masterpiece composed by Anne Frank, when she was a young teenager. Inform students that Anne Frank began her diary in 1942, just five years after Steinbeck published *Of Mice and Men*. Between the Dust Bowl, the Great Depression, and World War II, this time period was certainly a tumultuous (and often terrifying) period of history.

As you teach diaries to students, stress their unique qualities. They are a bit like blogs (a familiar reference point for students), but there is a crucial difference. Whereas blogs are public and intended for an indefinitely large audience, diaries are extremely private, deeply personal, and are very often confessional in nature. They are written for an audience of *one*—the writer—who jealously guards the diary and hides it or locks it to protect the contents.

And what does this privacy mean in terms of the things that are written there? It means that diaries are, by their nature, profoundly revealing and *true*. They reveal secrets locked deep within the writer's heart and things the writer would never reveal to anyone else. And why do people keep diaries? For the same reason Anne Frank kept hers: to express herself, to gain emotional release, to view her experiences and feelings on paper, and to help her navigate the contents of her mind and the complexities of the world. People keep diaries for all these reasons; they are among the most deeply personal and truthful forms of writing conceivable.

## THE TRADITIONAL FORMAT OF DIARIES

Tell your students about the *format* of diaries. Traditionally, they are written by hand. The diarist may write in them every day, or perhaps only when something interesting happens. Often, diary entries are structured a bit like letters to a friend. The diarist will always *date the entry* (with day, month, and year), which is very important for future reference. Some diary keepers address their entries "Dear Diary," while others may write to a person, real or imaginary, living or passed.

Anne Frank named her diary "Kitty" and treated Kitty as if she were a dear and intimate friend who was always present to listen to Anne's unburdenings. Accordingly, Anne began each entry by addressing it "Dear Kitty" and closed (and signed) it with the phrase "Yours, Anne." Our students will do something similar. They will address their diary entries "Dear Lennie," and they will close and sign their diary entries as follows: "Good-bye for now, Lennie. Your friend, George."

In terms of format, student diary entries will include the following four parts:

1. Date (sometime in the 1930s): For example, "February 26, 1936"
2. Greeting (or salutation): "Dear Lennie"
3. The diary entry
4. Closing and signature: "Good-bye for now, Lennie. Your friend, George"

## THE STRUCTURE AND PARAMETERS OF THIS PROJECT

To help students with this unique project, we are going to give them a good deal of structure (which is clearly reflected on *Outline 9–10.9*). Nonetheless, we are also going to offer students open-ended *choices*. These choices will boost engagement levels and animate students' inherent creativity. Each of the subtopics contains a prompt that requires students to use their imaginations and write something original. Tell your classes that they have great freedom in these segments, but the examples they choose must be related to the themes of each subtopic.

Students also have choices in the *presentation* of their projects. They can write by hand, if they choose, or they can write it electronically, using a script font. They can burn the edges of the paper (carefully), to give it an aged look. They can include purposeful mistakes, crossed-out words, misspellings, and poor punctuation. If they want, they can also incorporate the slang and the casual dialect of the novella, as long as it's "rated G."

Before they begin writing, briefly review the character and dialogue of George. Tell students that literary characters are just like real people. They are individual and unique, and they have their strengths, faults, and quirks. They do good things and bad things; they have a manner and speech patterns that are as unique and individual as fingerprints. All of this is revealed by what characters *say* and what they *do*.

And now, review some of George's actions and his dialogue. As you do this, ask students to consider the following: *How did he treat Lennie? What were some things George did? What were some of the things he talked about? Describe his personality.* (George tended to be rather outspoken and assertive. He was also fairly intelligent and was fiercely loyal to Lennie.) *What do all of these things show us about George's character and who he really is?*

After reviewing George's character, encourage students to continue (and develop) his persona in their diary entries. Urge them to *show* us George's character (instead of merely *telling* us) through George's actions and the things he says. Entreat them also to consider how George may have *changed and developed* after the events of the novella. *What did he learn? How did he change? How did he grow?*

## GEORGE AND HIS DIARY

Before students start writing, give them the *situation* of George and his diary. He is writing perhaps six months after the ending of the novella. This means that the events of the story—especially George's euthanasia of his best (and only) friend Lennie—are still quite fresh in his experience. He is deeply wounded, and the wounds are still raw in his mind and pulsing in his memory.

There is a good bit of psychology happening between George and his diary. Six months is not much time to recuperate after a terrible tragedy or a devastating loss, and George has just begun to process what has happened to his life and to his friend. And here, we can speculate about George's motivation for keeping a diary. It is helping him to heal. It allows him to feel less lonely, and it helps him to understand his ravaged feelings and the hole that has been torn in his life. He misses Lennie deeply, and writing diary entries to Lennie helps him feel connected to his old friend. In a sense, the diary has become a substitute for Lennie.

In the diary entries that students will write, George will reveal his deepest feelings about Lennie, their relationship, their experiences, and how he feels about losing his friend. In the diary entry, George's musings should be related (at least tangentially) to the themes of dreams and loneliness. The students can choose the *mood* of their pieces, making them melancholy (like the novella) or making them upbeat, with George enjoying a few friendships and formulating a new dream of something hopeful for the future. As you can see, there is a great deal of choice embedded into this assignment.

## THE COMPONENTS OF THIS PROJECT

As always, this project will be composed of five parts. The three subtopics will be organized chronologically, in a schema of *before*, *during*, and *after*. This organization works well for young students; it is logical, intuitive, and understandable. As students write their diary entries, instruct them to utilize the model of *summary and commentary* they have used previously. They will describe events and characters from the novella (this is the *summary* portion), and they will reflect upon and interpret the meaning behind and within them (this is the *commentary* portion).

Here is an overview of all five parts. As you'll see, each subtopic is broken down into three smaller sections following a pattern of *dreams*, *loneliness*, and *students' choice* (this structure will help students with organization and development of ideas). As you explain this project to students, distribute *Outline 9–10.9* as a visual reference and encourage students to take notes directly onto it.

### 1. Introduction

Students will commence the diary entry with a date (sometime during the 1930s) and the greeting, "Dear Lennie." They will also provide an overview of the diary entry, which means they will write the introduction *last*.

### 2. First Subtopic: *The Past*

*Dreams.* This section is essentially a review of the novella. In it, George will describe and comment upon certain events in the plot. He will discuss the dream that he and Lennie had. He will describe their modest dream and how it felt to have hope for the future. After that, George will comment on how it felt to lose that dream and that hope.

*Loneliness.* George will also allude to loneliness. He will discuss his relationship with Lennie and how it felt to have a close friend. He will also describe how it felt to lose Lennie, and he will evaluate his feelings on the enormous decision he made. *Is George happy with his decision to "protect" Lennie? Does he feel a sense of guilt? Does he feel both? Will he perhaps apologize to Lennie, or does he feel a sense of peace about his final act toward Lennie?*

*Students' choice.* The final component of this subtopic gives students *choice*. Here, students will choose an *event* or *character* from the novella and discuss it through a mixture of summary and commentary. This item may be related to the themes of dreams and loneliness, or it may be something else entirely. As long as it's meaningful and sheds light on George's state of mind, it will be appropriate for George's diary entry.

### 3. Second Subtopic: *The Present*

*Dreams.* In this section, students will use their imaginations and project where George might be six months after the apocalyptic conclusion of the novella. George will begin by telling Lennie about his current circumstances.

Where is he, and what is he doing right now? *Is he still in California, working on a farm? Is he walking down a dirt road or perhaps sitting in front of a campfire?* As students compose their responses, they will incorporate the theme of *dreams*. For example, *is George caught in a never-ending cycle of farm work, with no hope for the future? Or is he perhaps on a train, heading toward a new dream and a new start?*

*Loneliness.* In this discussion, George will allude to the topic of *loneliness* and write about his experiences with being lonely after the death of Lennie. For example, *in the past six months, was George able to make any friends? Has he given up on friendship? Is he hoping to someday get married? Does George now accept loneliness as an inescapable part of life? Does the diary—and the memory of Lennie—keep George company and help him to feel less lonely?*

*Students' choice.* Students will close this section with a topic and discussion of their choice. Here, they will use their imaginations and their knowledge of the text (and George) to project and infer something about George's life after the novella. Here are some possibilities to consider: *At night, when George sleeps, does he dream about Lennie? Is George depressed? Is George heading back to his hometown to see family members? If asked, what might George tell others about Lennie? How might he explain the things that happened?*

### 4. Third Subtopic: *The Future*

*Dreams.* In this section, students will write about George's concerns for the future. He is living in a dangerous world, and there is no surety to be had here. Nonetheless, he is still rather young (probably in his thirties) and is considering the rest of his life and the possibility of finding happiness and perhaps security. *What is George's attitude toward dreams in general? Does he have any dreams left, old or new? Has he decided that people never achieve their dreams? Or does he perhaps formulate a modest plan for his old age?*

*Loneliness.* George will also wonder if he'll be lonely for the rest of his life. *Has he accepted loneliness as a part of human existence? Or does he ponder ways to escape loneliness?* For example, George may consider the possibility of getting married. Perhaps his new dream is to meet a nice woman and to buy a little house and settle down with a day job. *What kind of job would George like? Does he want to have kids?* If George could manage such a feat, he would attain a beautiful dream of autonomy and would banish forever the specter of loneliness from his life.

*Students' choice.* Students will conclude this subtopic by making another choice. Here, George will discuss something that worries him. *Does it have* to do with money? Is he unemployed? Is he out of food? Did he get in trouble for some reason? Is there a problem with his health?* Students have great freedom here to choose an interesting problem for George to solve. They should also choose an interesting potential solution—because that's something that George would do.

## 5. Conclusion

Students should conclude their diary entries with George discussing his plans for tomorrow and for the near future. He can also send a very personal message to Lennie. What might George want to say to Lennie after all that's happened? *Will he apologize to Lennie? Will he tell Lennie that he misses him? Will he ask Lennie to "watch over" him in this dangerous world?* Finally, George will close and sign the diary entry by writing *"Good-bye for now, Lennie. Your friend, George."*

## GOOD-BYE FOR NOW

And that concludes our triptych of writing projects on Steinbeck's marvelous novella *Of Mice and Men*. When students complete their diary entries, staple them to the research paper and congratulate them on completing several tasks impressive for young students.

First, they read and internalized one of the great short works of American literature. Next, they performed original literary analysis on its two main themes (which are central to the human condition). After that, they converted their interpretive essays into research papers. Last, they wrote original, creative addenda in the form of a diary entry. These would be striking achievements even on the college level.

The next project is our last project of the year. In it, our students will look back on the year, reflecting on all the wonderful things they wrote and all the wonderful things they learned. They will also take a tentative glance into next year, trying to predict all the things they're going to find in the assignments—and in themselves, as well.

Ninth and Tenth Grade, Ninth Writing Project: *Outline 9–10.9*
The Literary Research Paper: "Dreams and Loneliness
in Steinbeck's Novella *Of Mice and Men*"
(Third Draft: Creative Coda)

Name_____ Date_____
Title _____

Give your diary entry a creative title.

1. Introduction (write this last)
    a. Give it a date during the 1930s, for example: *February 26, 1936.*
    b. Start it with *"Dear Lennie."*
    c. Provide an overview of this diary entry.

2. First Subtopic: *The Past* (refer to memories and events from the novella)
    a. *Dreams:* What were they? How did it feel to lose them?
    b. *Loneliness:* How did it feel to have a friend? How did it feel to *lose* a friend?
    c. *Your Choice:* Choose an event or character from the novella and write about it.

3. Second Subtopic: *The Present*
    a. *Dreams:* What is George doing right now? Does he feel any hope for the future?
    b. *Loneliness:* Is George lonely? Or does he have any friends?
    c. *Your Choice:* Use your imagination to discuss a topic about George's current life.

4. Third Subtopic: *The Future*
    a. *Dreams:* Does George believe he'll attain his dream?
    b. *Loneliness:* Will George be lonely for the rest of his life?
    c. *Your Choice:* Discuss something in the future that worries George.

5. Conclusion
    a. Where is George going next? What will he be doing?
    b. George sends a message to Lennie: *Thank you? I'm sorry? Good-bye?* Et cetera.
    c. Closing and signature: *"Good-bye for now, Lennie. Your friend, George."*

*This page is permitted to copy.*

*Chapter 10*

# Grades Nine and Ten: Tenth Writing Project

## *The Reflective Essay: "Looking Back on a Year of Writing"*

Main Standard: 9–10.10

Write routinely over extended time frames (time for reflection and revision) and shorter time frames (a single sitting or a day or two) for a range of discipline-specific tasks, purposes, and audiences.

*Author's Notes: This is the final project of the year, and will be reflective in nature. In it, students will compose three brief individual essays in which they reflect on the writing they did this year, on the growth they experienced, and on the upcoming year of writing. Students will write in the first-person. There are no sub-standards here.*

### RANGE OF WRITING

And now, we arrive at the final writing project of the year, which grows from the sole member in a "group" of standards called "Range of Writing." As you can see, that title calls for students to compose multiple projects of differing natures. The standard itself calls for students to compose projects in which they engage in the process of "reflection." Being the final project of the year, this is a bittersweet moment, but it also represents a wonderful opportunity for students to review the writing they produced and to evaluate the growth they experienced.

All of this is a perfect way to wrap up a year of writing. In those two elements—*range* and *reflection*—we have the systole and diastole of this final assignment. In this project, students will reflect on the year through a lens of positivity and optimism and will compose three brief, engaging projects. To do this, they will look at the nine writing assignments they have completed, and they will reflect on their progress and development as writers and human beings, along with another rapidly approaching year of writing. These three assignments are expressed in the three subtopics of this assignment, and they are a multidimensional trio.

(Note: If your students are completing their sophomore year, they will have completed *two* years of writing. Theoretically, we could have them look back over the past two years [nineteen assignments in total], but this is not recommended. That's a great deal of ground to cover, and students would find that an overwhelming, distasteful experience. So, we'll focus their reflections on *one* year of writing.)

To heighten engagement levels, this trio of projects contains a great deal of variety. Although presented through the choreography of a five-part essay, students will have great autonomy in choosing the things they write about. We will supply structure by asking students open-ended questions intended to spark reflective thinking, and the students will have great freedom in choosing the answers they provide. The dance of this antiphonal exchange is designed to activate prior knowledge and to reinforce the lessons they learned during the year.

We will also offer our students variety in the *type* of essays they will write. Each of the subtopics will be written in a different textual *format*; here are the subtopics and the formats that students will use:

a. First Subtopic: *What Was Your Favorite Writing Assignment?*
   - Students will write this in the format of a *journal entry*.
b. Second Subtopic: *What Did You Learn, and How Did You Grow?*
   - Students will write this in the format of an *interview*.
c. Third Subtopic: *Notes to Your Next-Year Self.*
   - Students will write this in the format of an *email to their future selves*.

## THE THREE NEW WRITING FORMATS

Begin this project by describing the three writing formats to students. The prospect of learning (and writing in) three new formats may alarm your budding writers, but tell them to *keep calm and write*—this will be a joyful and creative end-of-the-year project that allows them to showcase their new learning. All three formats are rather simple, and they function as engaging, creative ways to present the writing that students will do. Let's now consider the three formats in detail.

## THE FIRST SUBTOPIC: *JOURNAL ENTRY*

In the first subtopic, students will write *journal entries* in which they discuss the previous year of writing. Begin this project by teaching students how to write a *journal entry*. Journals (you'll tell your class) are a bit like diaries (a subject very fresh in their minds). But how do journals and diaries differ? The distinctions are nuanced and fuzzy around the edges, like a blurred Venn diagram, and they are subject to some interpretation. Nonetheless, you will *define your terms* (remember that from chapter 1?), and tell your students how the term "journal entry" is being used in this assignment.

Journals tend to be less event-based than diaries and are based more in *feelings* and *emotions*. They are not written *to* anyone; there is no "Dear Diary" or dear anyone else. They are private, but perhaps not as deeply private as a diary. They are the writer's thoughts and moods at the moment, scribbled down in truth and shining in the vivid fluorescence of reality as perceived by the author's mind.

Journals tend to be a bit more casual and less structured than diaries; they are more creative, and they do much to project the writer's current concerns and states of mind and capture them on paper. For example, an incident may inspire the writer to compose a *poem* or *short story*. This would make for a spectacular journal entry but might seem out of place in a diary entry.

Tell students they will write their journal entries in the form of an *internal monologue* (sometimes called an *interior monologue* and quite similar to *stream of consciousness*). And what does "internal monologue" mean? It refers to the stream of thoughts pulsing in their minds, because we all tend to think in words and language. Our thoughts are expressed in language, even in the privacy of our silent, beating minds. So the term "internal monologue" essentially means *the sentences taking place in my mind as I think and process information.*

To help students understand this, give them a three-minute free-write in which you ask them to write their thoughts and make them visible on paper. Encourage them to write whatever is occurring in their minds, even if it seems trivial and silly (as long as it's *rated G*). This is a very freeing experience for a writer. It is excellent practice and makes for a marvelous gateway into the process of writing a freely expressed journal entry.

Also, tell your students that journal entries written in the kaleidoscope of flashing emotion tend to have a casual feel in which the rules of formal writing are suspended in favor of raw expression. So, encourage them to write their journal entries with a casual creativity rather than a formal scholasticism—as long as they're presenting the truth in their own unique writer's voices.

## THE SECOND SUBTOPIC: *INTERVIEW*

This subtopic is rather unusual and assigns each student a starring role in the narrative. Here, *the student will be interviewed by another person*. During this interview, the student will answer three questions about the *learning* and *growth* that took place over the year (these questions are located on *Outline 9–10.10*). But who will conduct the interview?

Each student will choose the interviewer. They can choose someone real or fictional, living or passed. However, because we want this project to be upbeat in tone, the interviewer must be someone whom the student likes and respects. It can be a family member, superhero, athlete, celebrity, friend, et cetera. In the student's narrative, the interviewer will sit down with the student and ask three questions, and the student will respond truthfully. The only new element here is the format, which will be *structured like the dialogue in a play*. Nonetheless, it's quite simple; to teach it, show students this example (the first question in the second subtopic):

> WILLIAM SHAKESPEARE: So, Timmy, what was challenging about the writing thou didst this year? How didst thou overcome these challenges?
>
> TIMMY: Well, Mr. Shakespeare, I found it very difficult to find time to write. I'm very busy with school and sports, and when I get home, I'm very tired. And sometimes I find it difficult to think up ideas to write. But then I started to come up with ideas during the day, and when I was at soccer practice. And then, when I got home, I would sit down and write for exactly one hour each night, after dinner. And then, in the morning, I would read over what I wrote and edit it a little bit. I did this every night, and I started to get pretty good at writing. Even though I'm really busy, it wasn't so much of a problem anymore.

See that? If you look at the structure and the details, you'll see that it's very simple to format. Put the interviewer's name in caps and state the question (verbatim, from *Outline 9–10.10*). Then, provide the student's name (or simply "ME") in caps, and the student's response, with one paragraph for each question. As students begin composing their answers, tell them to write their responses in a "conversational" manner, because an interview consists of two people chatting with each other. And how should students do this? Simple: tell them to *write the way they talk*. This is a very powerful writing technique, and it's usually where we do our best writing.

## THIRD SUBTOPIC: *EMAIL*

Your students are in high school, so they're probably very familiar with sending and receiving emails. However, the recipient and subject of this email are rather unusual: they are writing it to *themselves* in the next grade, and the subject is the *future*.

In terms of formatting, this email will contain the parts of a properly written email. It will contain a greeting (perhaps, "Hello, Michelle in the Eleventh Grade!"), a message (three paragraphs answering the three questions on *Outline 9–10.10*), a closing (perhaps, "Your younger self"), and a signature (perhaps, "Michelle in the Tenth Grade"). Also, tell students that, because this is an email, they are encouraged to use the casual, informal writer's voice they use when emailing a friend.

To compose this part of the project, students will actually write an email to themselves, print it out, and attach it to the assignment. They'll find this interesting and fun because it lends a trippy multilayered realism to this project. They are sending an email to their future selves, and who will be receiving it? Their future selves. And how cool is that?

So, those are the three formats in which students will present their writing. There is a good deal of variety, choice, and engagement here, and these projects are designed to be fun and casual. And now, let's take a close look at the things they'll be writing.

## OKAY, THOSE ARE THE FORMATS. ... WHAT ARE WE WRITING ABOUT?

When you finish teaching students the three different *formats* they'll be using, it's time to teach them the *content* that will be filling those formats. Begin by describing the underpinnings and process of this yearly reflection. This sort of long-term reflection will begin with *rereading the nine pieces they wrote this year*. After that, they will reflect on the writing they performed, the growth they achieved, and their feelings about writing in the next grade level.

As students perform their reflections, they will utilize the "summary and commentary" model of analysis they used during the year. In brief, here is the two-step process: after describing the subject being discussed, they will reflect on (and interpret) what it meant to their writing and to their lives. As students formulate their responses, encourage them to keep their descriptions and conclusions *optimistic* and *positive* in nature. This will help your students to write more meaningfully (and more happily), and it will foster a buoyant relationship between the writer and writing and between the reader and the writer.

At this time, hand out *Outline 9–10.10* and go over all five parts. As always, encourage your students to take notes directly onto the Outline. They know the *shapes* of the magic lamps; it's time to describe the genies they'll place inside.

### 1. Introduction

Students will begin their reflections by providing readers with an overview of this project and with some overarching statements regarding the year of writing they have just completed. Remind them to keep all of their discussions *positive* in nature. Write this last.

### 2. First Subtopic: Journal Entry: *What Was Your Favorite Writing Assignment?*

In this section, students will reflect on the writing they produced. It will begin with students rereading their (nine) projects and choosing a favorite. As they begin writing, remind them that they're writing in the format of a *journal entry* and should compose an internal monologue in an aura of casual spontaneity. Nonetheless, remind them also that guidance and structure are provided in the three questions on the outline. Tell them to write one paragraph for each question.

They'll begin by discussing their favorite writing project, answering questions such as the following: *What was the assignment? What did they write about? Why did they choose this topic?* Next, they'll describe *why* this is their favorite assignment. *What, specifically, do they like about the piece of writing? What is their favorite part? When they reread the piece, what did they find surprising, gratifying, or interesting?* Finally, they'll engage in some speculative thinking. If they were to expand the piece of writing by adding a new section, *what would they write about? Why would they add this topic? How would it improve the writing?*

### 3. Second Subtopic: Interview: *What Did You Learn, and How Did You Grow?*

In this section, students will reflect not on their writing but on *themselves* and their development as writers and human beings. Remind students that they're writing this section in the format of an *interview*, so it should have a casual, conversational feel to it, like a transcript of two people chatting (formatted like a play). The structure of this section is rather simple. Students will answer three questions posed to them by an interviewer of their choice, and they will write one paragraph for each question.

In the first question, students will describe the challenges they encountered this year as they learned to write. *What, specifically, did they find difficult? What was the most challenging writing project they composed? What made it so challenging? How did they overcome these challenges, solve problems, and complete their writing assignments? How did it feel to solve problems and to emerge more knowledgeable on the other side?*

Next, students will identify the *three favorite writing techniques* they learned and used this year. This is challenging, so you can offer them this list to choose from:

- The Five-Part Outline (as an organizational tool)
- The rule "Show, Don't Tell" (to make writing more vivid)
- Imagery: Using the senses (often two, or perhaps three) in your descriptions
- Summary and Commentary (a two-part model of description and analysis)
- The One-Story Approach to writing fiction (Grail; Conflict; Resolution)
- The "Green Light" and "Red Light" approach (for revising and editing)

After students choose their favorite techniques, tell them to frame their responses by naming the technique and then describing it (this is the *summary and commentary* paradigm, and it will be an excellent review for the students). After that, they will discuss how (and where) they used each technique. *In what assignments did you use it? How did you use it? Why do you like this technique? How did it improve your writing?*

Students will conclude this section with a brief rumination on how they grew this year as writers, as students, and as human beings. *Did their attitudes toward writing change? Did they get a sense of satisfaction after completing a writing project? Did they become more confident as writers? Did they improve as students? Did they become more organized? Did their study habits improve? Did they mature and grow, in general?*

### 4. Third Subtopic: Email: *Notes to Your Next-Year Self*

In this subtopic, students will discuss their feelings about the upcoming school year. In the format of an *email to their future selves* (i.e., "Dear Timmy in the Eleventh Grade"), students will answer the three questions on the outline, writing a paragraph for each question and utilizing an informal writer's voice.

They'll begin by describing their goals (as writers and students) for the next grade level. As students develop their answers, encourage them to articulate clear goals and to describe a logical strategy for reaching each goal. *What do you want to accomplish, in terms of writing? Where do you need to improve as a writer and a student? What are your writerly and scholastic strengths, and what are your weaknesses? How will you continue to improve your writing skills? How can you become more successful as a student?*

Next, students will give some advice to their future selves. How can they succeed next year as writers, students, and human beings? They will begin by considering the challenges they expect to face next year. *What difficulties do you foresee? How might you convert these into opportunities for learning, growth, and success? What are some strategies that will help you develop as a writer? How will you adjust to the demands of a higher grade level and the difficulties of a new and challenging writing curriculum?*

Finally, students will write a brief anecdote that describes and defines who they are *today*. An "anecdote" (as used here) is a short story that focuses on a specific (and meaningful) incident that happened to the student. The anecdotes that students write must be true (nonfiction), and they must be *optimistic in nature*, revealing positive characteristics about the students.

As students compose their anecdotes, they will use the summary and commentary paradigm, explaining the anecdote and then describing what it reveals about them. *Have they done something difficult or overcome adversity? Do they have a particular talent? Have they performed an act of kindness? Have they worked hard to improve some aspect of their lives? Have they recently had a noteworthy accomplishment? Do they have a particular dream they want to achieve?* And so on. (This section may be longer than a paragraph.)

## 5. Conclusion

Here, students will wrap up this project (and the year) and place a figurative bow on the year of writing they have just completed. To begin, they will describe *their favorite moment* of the past year, perhaps putting it in the form of a *story* (telling stories is a wonderful—and largely overlooked—mode of exposition in academic writing). Next, they will offer an overall statement about the writing they performed, the wonderful things they learned, and the growth they achieved—and they will present it all in positive terms.

Last, they will say good-bye to a terrific year of writing and learning. A glorious summer has arrived, beckoning to our students in the golden light of late afternoon. Nonetheless—and our students will never admit to it—they'll miss the writing they did in your classroom—and they'll miss you too.

## PORTFOLIOS

And this concludes a year of writing, growth, and learning. When you hand these reflections back to students—along with your kind comments and suggestions for improvement—tell your students to put them all in a folder, to label it "Writing Portfolio," and to include the grade (ninth or tenth) that they just completed. Tell them also to put their ten projects in chronological order—and not to lose them! These assignments (you'll tell them) are like *time capsules* (a theme we'll revisit later in this book). They tell a story of hard work and of learning and growing during a period in their lives that is formative, important, and priceless.

And now, let's turn to a new year of writing.

Ninth and Tenth Grade, Tenth Writing Project: *Outline 9–10.10*
The Reflective Essay: "Looking Back on a Year of Writing"

Name_____ Date_____
Title _____

1. Introduction: Provide an overview of what this essay is about. Keep your ruminations and observations positive and provide some statements about the year of writing. Write this last.

2. First Subtopic: Journal Entry: *What Was Your Favorite Writing Assignment?*
   a. Which assignment was it? What did you write about?
   b. Why is this your favorite assignment? What did you like best about it?
   c. If you had to *add* something to this assignment, what would it be?

3. Second Subtopic: Interview: *What Did You Learn, and How Did You Grow?*
   a. What was challenging about the writing you did this year? How did you overcome these challenges?
   b. What are your three favorite writing techniques that you learned and used?
   c. How did you *grow*—as a writer, as a student, and as a person?

4. Third Subtopic: Email: *Notes to Your Next-Year Self*
   a. What are your goals for next year, as a writer and a student?
   b. Give some advice to your next-year self. How can your future self succeed as a writer and continue to grow and develop—as a writer, student, and person?
   c. Write a brief anecdote that describes and defines who you are today.

5. Conclusion
   a. What was your favorite *moment* in this past year of writing? Tell a story!
   b. Formulate a positive, optimistic statement about this year of writing.
   c. Say good-bye to this year of writing.

*This page is permitted to copy.*

*Chapter 11*

# Grades Eleven and Twelve: First Writing Project

## *The Argumentative Essay:* "Are Cell Phones Good for High School Students?" (Part One)

Main Standard 11–12.1:
Write arguments to support claims in an analysis of substantive topics or texts, using valid reasoning and relevant and sufficient evidence.

*Author's Notes: In this argumentative essay, students will evaluate and discuss cell phones in the lives of high school students. Alternate topics include social media, video games, ways to deal with cyberbullying, and evaluating the link between technology and loneliness. Students will write in the third person.*

*Sub-Standard A:
Introduce precise, knowledgeable claim(s), establish the significance of the claim(s), distinguish the claim(s) from alternate or opposing claims, and create an organization that logically sequences claim(s), counterclaims, reasons, and evidence.

*Author's Notes: Students will begin their essays with a clear thesis statement. They will include at least one counterargument and will organize their essays by using the five-part outline.*

*Sub-Standard B:
Develop claim(s) and counterclaims fairly and thoroughly, supplying the most relevant evidence for each while pointing out the strengths and

limitations of both in a manner that anticipates the audience's knowledge level, concerns, values, and possible biases.

*Author's Notes: Students will include evidence for their major claims and their counterarguments. This evidence will be based on the students' experience and will be presented in a logical and convincing manner.*

Sub-Standard C:
Use words, phrases, and clauses as well as varied syntax to link the major sections of the text, create cohesion, and clarify the relationships between claim(s) and reasons, between reasons and evidence, and between claim(s) and counterclaims.

*Author's Notes: Students will use transitional words, phrases, and sentences, such as* however, nevertheless, next, additionally, afterward, because of this, as a result, on the other hand, the next day, *et cetera.*

Sub-Standard D:
Establish and maintain a formal style and objective tone while attending to the norms and conventions of the discipline in which they are writing.

Author's Notes: Students will write this project in the third person. They will use a formal "academic" voice, proofreading carefully, and refraining from using the slang and abbreviations often used when sending emails and text messages.

Sub-Standard E:
Provide a concluding statement or section that follows from and supports the argument presented.

Author's Notes: Students will provide a brief conclusion to this project (probably one paragraph long). The conclusion will include elements of summary and a final assertion that the writer's point of view is the correct one.

## TEXT TYPES AND PURPOSES

We begin this new year of writing with a group of three standards called "Text Types and Purposes." These standards encourage students to compose three different types of writing projects: *the argumentative essay, the informative essay*, and a *narrative essay* that can be fiction or nonfiction (essentially an exercise in *storytelling*). In these three projects, our students will compose three discrete pieces united by the subject of technology, and the main focus of the examination will be *cell phones*.

In chapter 1, we introduced our students to the argumentative essay through a project in which they evaluated the merits of "Television and Streaming Video" and its impact on their lives. This current project builds on that theme and the learning that occurred there, and it continues its examination of the students' relationship with technology in its various forms.

In this current writing assignment, students will write argumentative essays in which they evaluate the effects that cell phones have on the lives of high school students. This topic is carefully chosen for the demographic we're teaching, because cell phones (and technology in general) pose an enormous presence in the lives of most teens (and will thus heighten engagement levels in students). On a more serious note, the shadow cast by electronic devices is vast, troubling, and worthy of evaluation.

According to a 2019 study (undertaken by educational organization Common Sense), approximately 90 percent of teenagers aged sixteen to eighteen own cell phones (Rideout and Robb, 7). Perhaps more surprising (and somewhat disturbing), the study also determined that teens spend about *seven-and-a-half hours each day* looking at an electronic screen—"not including for school or homework" (Rideout and Robb, 22). In this project, we encourage students to evaluate their relationship with cell phones and to think about the effect these devices are having on their lives.

## TIME FOR A REVIEW

The requirements of this standard are quite similar to last year's standard and slightly increase the demands on students. As we teach this project, we will review the process of composing an argumentative essay, focusing on its components and format, the correct use of evidence, and a logical organization. Students will write this essay in the third person, using a formal academic voice, and will continue their use of transitional words to give the essay a feeling of coherence.

As you begin this project, conduct a review of the structure of an academic argument in order to activate students' prior knowledge (before beginning, the reader may wish to review chapter 1). Begin by reminding students of the purpose of the persuasive essay, which is to present the writer's perspective to the reader in a manner that is formal, fair, and logical for the purpose of convincing the reader that the writer's point of view is the correct one (or is at least worthy of consideration). Now, let's review the four major parts of the academic argument.

# A FOUR-PART HARMONY

The four parts of the academic argument comprise *thesis*, *definition of terms*, *evidence*, and *counterarguments*. Students will include all of them in their essays, and here they are in terms of this assignment:

## 1. Thesis

Remind your students that the thesis will likely be one sentence and will be the *first sentence in the essay*. The thesis will grow out of the essential question for this assignment, which is this: "Are Cell Phones Good for High School Students?" By nature, this is an "A or B" question, which means that it will produce two types of thesis statements. Here they are, rendered in simplicity:

- "Cell phones are good for high school students."
- "Cell phones are not good for high school students."

## 2. Definition of Terms

In this section, students will define terms (perhaps three) as used in the essay. Here, they can briefly define cell phones as portrayed in the project, including details such as types of cell phones, major brands, and technological capabilities (for example, it has internet access, texting capacity, video games, educational apps, etc.). They can also define (and explain) the particular *aspects* of cell phones they'll be discussing in their essays. Doing so will help the reader better understand the arguments students will make.

## 3. Evidence

Students will use evidence to "prove" their arguments. This essay will *not* be based in research but on the students' direct experience, knowledge, and observations of high school students using their cell phones. Students can also, if they want, "interview" friends or other high school students and include these findings as evidence.

## 4. Consideration of Counterarguments

In this section, students will describe at least one valid opposing point of view. After that, they will argue that this point of view is not compelling, is somehow deficient, or does not outweigh their main arguments. When doing this, students can *partially agree* with the counterargument (a very effective technique), and they can then expose its inherent weaknesses. Describing and discrediting counterarguments strengthens the main argument and increases the writer's authority on the subject.

## QUALIFYING ARGUMENTS

After reviewing the purpose and four major components of the academic argument, it's time to introduce this project to your students. Emphasize that they are about to write an essay in which they will evaluate cell phones as a positive *or* negative element in the lives of high school students. They'll find this exciting, and they'll say "It's both," and they'll be correct, of course. There are two valid sides to this argument. However, this project will challenge them to choose a side and argue their position clearly and convincingly.

As they formulate their arguments, you will once again explain "qualifying" arguments to your students. They encountered this concept in chapter 1, where it was presented to them in optional terms. In this current essay, students are required to include *qualifications* in their arguments. This means that their arguments will not depict the issue in black-and-white terms, but in shades of nuance and degree. For example, let's say that a student is arguing that cell phones are a *negative* force in the lives of high school students. This hypothetical student might write a qualifying argument that sounds something like this:

> I'm not saying that high school students can't have cell phones at all. I'm saying that access to cell phones must be regulated, and there should be some rules to use them. For example, students should *not* be able to use cell phones in school. Also, when students are home, they should not use cell phones past nine o'clock at night. And one more thing: students should not play video games on their cell phones for more than one hour each day. There are better things to do than play games on a cell phone.

That is a well-constructed qualifying argument that supports the student's thesis. The student is *not* suggesting that cell phones should be completely off limits to high school students (which would be unreasonable). The student is applying sensible qualifications (or *conditions*) to regulate cell phone use. Now, let's take a look at a hypothetical student who is arguing the opposing view, that cell phones are a *positive* force in the lives of high school students. A qualifying argument by this student might sound like this:

I know that students using cell phones in school can sometimes be a problem. But we should not force students to leave their cell phones at home. Cell phones are a safety device. What if parents or guardians need to contact a student about an emergency? What if students need to contact parents (or someone else) about an emergency at school? In cases like this, cell phones can literally save lives.

This argument is also highly effective. The student does not advocate for unlimited use of cell phones (an inherently problematic point of view) but argues legitimate reasons for students to have in-school access to cell phones. Indeed, both arguments are highly effective. Note how both writers consider the issue from all sides, yet stick to the main thesis, and offer qualifying arguments that support the thesis in reasonable terms. Even though the students argue opposing sides, they both make very compelling sense and would be hard to dispute. Show these arguments to students and encourage them to use similar logic and qualifying arguments as they formulate their own positions on the issues they argue.

## YOU MUST CHOOSE WISELY

When the students understand the underpinnings of this assignment, it's time for them to pick a side. Begin by having a class discussion on the topic of cell phones, prompting students to recognize and discuss the good points and bad points of these devices.

When your class understands the inherent duality of cell phones, ask them to take out a pen and a sheet of paper and write their names on the paper. Next, have them draw a "t-chart" on the paper, labeling the left column "Good Points of cell phones," and the right column "Bad Points of cell phones." Next, give them a three-minute free-write in which they list at least three positive aspects of cell phones and at least three negative aspects about them.

When the three minutes are up, ask them to decide which is stronger—the good points of cell phones or the bad points? When they have chosen one side over the other, have them circle the topic and hand it in. And then, congratulate your students. They have just chosen the thesis they will argue in a very meaningful essay.

## THE PROJECT IN DETAIL

When it's time to explain the finer points of this project, distribute *Outline 11–12.1* and go over it with your students. As you do this, encourage them to take notes on the outline and to ask lots of questions. Here are the five parts of this assignment described in some detail:

## 1. Introduction

The first sentence of this essay will be the thesis statement, expressed clearly and simply. After that, students will write a few sentences (perhaps four or five) describing what this essay is about. This will be one paragraph long, and (as always) students will write this *last*.

## 2. First Subtopic: *Definition of Terms*

As stated earlier, students will define and describe the (perhaps three) terms and elements *as they are being used* in this essay. This will help the reader understand the argument taking place.

## 3. Second Subtopic: *The Main Arguments*

This is the most important part of this assignment. It is where students present their main arguments in favor of the central thesis. Encourage your writers to showcase *three supporting examples*, which (if they blossom) may be presented in three different paragraphs. Each example should include a mixture of *summary and commentary*. In the *summary* portion, students will explain the item being discussed. *Is it excessive texting? Potential for cyberbullying? Valuable educational apps? The safety provided by cell phones?* In the *commentary* portion, students will argue how this example reinforces the central thesis of the essay. Remind students to include conditions and qualifying arguments.

## 4. Third Subtopic: *Counterarguments*

Here, students will include at least one carefully chosen counterargument. Again, they will use a mixture of summary and commentary. Students will begin by describing a counterargument and validating its meaning (at least partially). After that, they will use qualifying arguments to expose deficiencies in the counterargument and to show why the central thesis presents a more compelling position. Counterarguments are challenging for students to learn, so teach this concept clearly and encourage students to keep this section simple and sensible.

## 5. Conclusion

Review the major points of the argument and wrap things up in simple terms. Students will restate the thesis, provide an overall statement of their findings, and affirm that the central thesis is the correct position on the issue. This should be one paragraph long and may be composed of perhaps four or five sentences.

## A MAP FOR AN UNKNOWN LANDSCAPE

This concludes our students' second excursion into the world of the persuasive essay. Constructing a logical and sensible academic argument is a terrific learning experience for our students, and they'll be using it over and over as they proceed through their educations and through their lives.

However, there is other valuable growth occurring here also. Students are learning to examine important issues through consideration of all sides and in terms of nuance and degree. Perhaps more important, they are also considering their personal relationships with cell phones. The cell phone is a recent apparition in students' lives—and on the landscape of human history—and we're not really sure about its long-term effects. Nonetheless, asking questions is a great place to start. Perhaps we can find some answers on our upcoming journey through the world of *research*.

Eleventh and Twelfth Grade, First Writing Project: *Outline 11–12.1*
The Argumentative Essay: "Are Cell Phones
Good for High School Students?"

Name_____ Date_____
Title _____

Tell the reader what this essay is about, and include your position on the issue.

1. Introduction. Your first sentence is your thesis statement. After that, write three or four sentences providing an overview of this project. Write your introduction last.

2. First Subtopic: *Definition of Terms.* Give perhaps three terms. What types of cell phones will you be discussing? Which *aspects* will you be discussing? Explain these clearly to your reader.
   a. Define and explain your first term
   b. Define and explain your second term
   c. Define and explain your third term

3. Second Subtopic: *The Main Arguments.* Provide at least three examples that support your thesis. For each, include a mixture of summary and commentary. Be sure to include conditions and qualifying arguments.
   a. First Example (summary and commentary)
   b. Second Example (summary and commentary)
   c. Third Example (summary and commentary)

4. Third Subtopic: *Counterarguments.* Think of at least one valid argument (up to three) against your position. Describe why your position is stronger than the counterargument. Again, remember to include qualifying arguments.
   a. First Counterargument (necessary)
   b. Second Counterargument (recommended, but not necessary)
   c. Third Counterargument (helpful, but not necessary)

5. Conclusion: Restate your thesis statement and summarize your essay. Close by affirming that your position is the correct one. Write the Conclusion second-to-last.

*This page is permitted to copy.*

*Chapter 12*

# Grades Eleven and Twelve: Second Writing Project

## The Informative Research Essay: "Cell Phone Addiction" (Part Two)

Main Standard 11–12.2:
Write informative/explanatory texts to examine and convey complex ideas, concepts, and information clearly and accurately through the effective selection, organization, and analysis of content.

*Author's Notes: In this project, students will write an informative research essay in which they discuss the topic of cell phone addiction. Alternate topics include the history of cell phones, social media addiction, and cyberbullying. Students will write this in the third person.*

\*Sub-Standard A:
Introduce a topic; organize complex ideas, concepts, and information so that each new element builds on that which precedes it to create a unified whole; include formatting (e.g., headings), graphics (e.g., figures, tables), and multimedia when useful to aiding comprehension.

*Author's Notes: Students will organize this essay by using the format provided on* Outline 11–12.2. *For each subtopic, they will include a heading and one photo or illustration.*

\*Sub-Standard B:
Develop the topic thoroughly by selecting the most significant and relevant facts, extended definitions, concrete details, quotations, or other information and examples appropriate to the audience's knowledge of the topic.

*Author's Notes: Students will utilize research for this project, extracting quotations and paraphrases from the sources they find.*

Sub-Standard C:
Use appropriate and varied transitions and syntax to link the major sections of the text, create cohesion, and clarify the relationships among complex ideas and concepts.

*Author's Notes: Once again, students will use transitional words, phrases, and sentences, such as* however, nevertheless, next, additionally, afterward, because of this, as a result, on the other hand, the next day, *et cetera.*

Sub-Standard D:
Use precise language, domain-specific vocabulary, and techniques such as metaphor, simile, and analogy to manage the complexity of the topic.

*Author's Notes: When discussing aspects of the topic that are not common knowledge, students will provide appropriate definitions and explanations.*

Sub-Standard E:
Establish and maintain a formal style and objective tone while attending to the norms and conventions of the discipline in which they are writing.

*Author's Notes: Students will compose this project in the third person. They will employ a formal "academic" voice, refraining from using the slang and abbreviations often used when sending email and text messages.*

Sub-Standard F:
Provide a concluding statement or section that follows from and supports the information or explanation presented (e.g., articulating implications or the significance of the topic).

*Author's Notes: Students will provide a brief conclusion to this project (probably one paragraph long). The conclusion will include elements of summary, a call to take this problem seriously, and an affirmation that cell phone addiction can be overcome.*

## A RESEARCH PAPER RELEVANT TO STUDENTS' LIVES

This standard calls for students to write an essay on a complex real-world issue. Beyond that stipulation, it allows us a great deal of freedom and choice, so we are going to seize this opportunity and teach students how to write a research paper. This is a challenging (but very important) task for developing writers, so we're going to harness engagement levels and have students write a paper on the theme of *cell phone addiction*. This paper will be primarily research-based, but students will also interact with the research and generate their own original insights. For each subtopic, students will include an explanatory (and creatively worded) heading and an illustration that is eye-catching and related to the topic being discussed.

This is a challenging assignment, so we'll take our students through each step. Along the way, we will focus on two primary goals. First, we will teach students about the *task*. Students can't write a paper if they don't understand what they're doing. Second, we are going to take them through every step of this process, presenting each phase in clarity and simplicity. Let's take a look at the task and how you'll explain it to students

## PART I: UNDERSTANDING THE TASK

### 1. What Is the Topic?

The topic of cell phone addiction is relevant to a disturbingly high percentage of our students. And what is cell phone addiction? In brief, it involves excessive and obsessive cell phone use despite physical, emotional, and social damage to the user. And it is *very* common, especially among high school students.

According to a recent survey by the Pew Research Center, "Fully 95% of teens have access to a smartphone, and 45% say they are online 'almost constantly'" (Anderson and Jiang). This has become an enormous (and often unrecognized) problem in the lives of many high school students. Writing a paper on this topic will benefit our students in two ways: first, it will engage them as they learn to write. Second, it will teach them about this serious problem, providing an effective dose of self-awareness.

As you introduce this project to your students, begin by discussing the topic of cell phone addiction. During this introduction, do a three-minute free-write in which you ask students to evaluate their own cell phone use. *How much time do you spend on your cell phone each day? What do you normally do with your phone? Could you live without your phone for a day? For a week?* Et cetera. After discussing students' results, explain that they are going to write an informative research essay on the topic of cell phone addiction.

## 2. What Kind of Paper Are We Writing?

This is an *informative research* paper, which means that students will *not* be taking a side on the issue (as they did in the previous chapter). The purpose of an informative essay is not to persuade but to *teach readers about a significant issue*. It is an important genre of writing, and it needs to be taught well and understood deeply. When your fledgling writers understand the *type* of paper they're composing—along with its *purpose*—it's time to explain its structure. Show them this simple outline, and discuss each part:

1. Introduction (introduce the topic to readers)
2. First Subtopic: Overview of cell phone addiction
3. Second Subtopic: Symptoms and problems
4. Third Subtopic: Ways to treat this addiction
5. Conclusion (summarize the main points)

As you can see, the subtopics are clear, simple, and intuitive. They offer a logical progression of exposition, proceeding from overview, to detailed discussion, to treatment options. It's a simple and sensible organization. When students understand the *structure* of this project, it's time to begin the *research* component. Research is necessary for this topic (you'll explain to them), because they are not experts in this field—nor are they expected to be.

## PART II: HOW TO WRITE A RESEARCH PAPER

Now that students understand the task, we will teach them *how to do it*. This is a complex process, and it is not often taught well. Composing a research paper takes time and understanding; it consists of a cycle of steps which proceed sequentially and logically. We will now take our students through the entire cycle, presenting each step in clarity and simplicity. It begins with research.

### 1. Research; Bibliography; In-Text Citations

Rather than using the databases (as we did in chapter 8), we are going to introduce students to the process of utilizing research gathered from the open internet. However, we are going to simplify things and skip (for now) the process of *locating and evaluating* internet research. In an effort to make this process *understandable* for students, we will present them with three *prescreened* sources gathered from the open internet. Here they are, in bibliographic format (note that each entry contains the URL for locating the resource). Feel free to share this information with students, perhaps posting the links to your online classroom:

## Works Cited

Hurley, Katie. "Teenage Cell Phone Addiction: Are You Worried about Your Child?" *Psycom.net: Mental Health Treatment Resource Since 1996*. 16 November 2020. Accessed 12 July 2021. www.psycom.net/cell-phone-internet-addiction.

"Limit Your Device Not Your Life: Discover Change That Lasts." *reSTART*. 2019. Accessed 18 July 2021. https://www.netaddictionrecovery.com/.

TEDx Talks. "Quit Social Media." YouTube Video, 13:50, 19 September 2016. Accessed 15 July 2021. https://www.youtube.com/watch?v=3E7hkPZ-HTk&t=6s.

When the bibliography is complete, teach your students a useful tip for making their in-text citations. If you look at the sources above, you'll see that they start with an author's last name, or a title. Here is the rule: to make in-text citations, *always use the first part of the bibliographic entry*—either the author's last name, or the title of the piece (whichever is present). If sources have page numbers (unusual for websites, unless they are PDFs), students should include those also. The three sources above do *not* have page numbers, so the in-text citations are as follows:

- (Hurley)
- ("Limit Your Device Not Your Life")
- (TEDx Talks)

## 2. How to Use Research

And now we come to the heartbeat of this project and the most valuable learning occurring here: *how to use the research we gathered*. Now that students have their sources, they will read the websites and watch the video, looking for relevant quotes to use in their papers. But what, exactly, are they looking for? The answers are found on *Outline 11–12.2*.

Give your students the outline and explain each component. As you can see, each subtopic consists of *three examples* to discuss (for a total of nine examples). For each example, *students will find a quote that provides the information requested*. And where will students find this information? They will find it in the three sources we gave them.

To find the information they need, students will read their sources through the lens of each example, looking for a quote that pertains to it. Because there are nine examples, students will find nine quotes for this research paper. When students find quotes, they will place them on an electronic document (along with the in-text citations). These nine quotes will form a "bank" of quotes, and they will become the backbone of this project.

This is a simple process; nonetheless, we must teach it to our students. It begins with reading the websites (to do this, students can read the websites online, or print them out and annotate in pencil). But how will students cite the video? Simple. They will "read" the video by watching it and will *listen for quotes* that illustrate an example.[1] When students locate a relevant quote, they will *transcribe it verbatim* onto the electronic document. Quotes from videos are a valid source of research, and students will treat them the same as textual quotes—presenting them in quotation marks and including in-text citations.

## 3. The Proper Use of Quotes

When the students have created their bank of nine quotes, it's time to convert them into a research paper. At this point, pause for a teachable moment and explain to students the philosophy of a properly developed research paper.

A research project should not be a mere assemblage of others' thoughts; the student must stand proudly within the text as a writer and critical thinker. In a paper of this nature, how much "ink" should belong to the student? About 50–75 percent is a good suggested range. This way, the student will feel a sense of ownership for the project and can rightfully feel a sense of pride. But how do students convert a bank of nine quotes into a proper research paper? They proceed methodically, one quote at a time.

Tell students that for each quote they will perform a five-step process. We taught this in chapters 7 and 8; nonetheless, we'll review it briefly here:

1. Introduce the quote. Here, students will put *their own words* before the quote.
2. Provide the quote, verbatim, in quotation marks. Explain here that students can also *paraphrase* quotes (this is new learning for students). Paraphrasing (you'll tell them) means they can phrase the quotes *in their own words*, perhaps simplifying or shortening it. When doing this, *quotation marks are not necessary*, but in-text citations *are*. Emphasize this very important point: *paraphrases must always be cited*, because they are not original to the writer. If they're not cited, it's *plagiarism*.
3. Provide the in-text citation. This will include source information, such as author's last name or title of article and page numbers (if available). Examples: (Smith); (Jones 35).
4. Explain the quote in their own words, focusing on its relation to the paper. (This may not be necessary if students paraphrase the quote in clear terms).

5. Comment on the quote and discuss its relevance to the thesis or the topic of the paper (this is the most challenging part of this five-step process). Here students will generate original insights and conclusions drawn from the quote. *What is present within the quote? What does the quote suggest? What can we learn from it? How does the quote support the writer's thesis? To what aspect of the quote would you like to draw your readers' attention?* Et cetera.

When teaching this process, you should model it for students. For example, let's say we're searching for information that illustrates the third example on the outline, which is "Describe some statistics." In reading Hurley's article, we find this relevant quote:

> Results of a 2016 Common Sense Media Report found that 50 percent of teens "feel addicted" to mobile devices, while 59 percent of parents surveyed believe that kids are addicted to their devices.

If we apply all five steps to that quote, we can make it the nucleus of a very effective paragraph. As you read the following paragraph, note the inclusion (and location) of all five elements. Note also that the quote has been truncated because the earlier portion was deemed to be unnecessary for the point being made:

> Teens and their parents recognize this problem, because "50 percent of teens 'feel addicted' to mobile devices, while 59 percent of parents surveyed believe that kids are addicted to their devices" (Hurley). In this quote, we see that half of teens admit they are addicted to their phones, while more than half of parents worry that their kids are addicted. This is definitely a problem, and it is obviously affecting families, and not in a good way. Teens and their parents recognize the presence of cell phone addiction, and it is driving families apart. When teenagers spend more time on their cell phones, they are spending less time with their families. This is bad for family relationships.

Feel free to share this example with students, indicating where each of the five steps is located in the paragraph. This process for using research is straightforward and is highly effective. The only challenging step is the last one, because it requires interpretation and inferential thinking. Nonetheless, this can be learned, and fluency will come with practice. Tell your students that their interpretations can be brief, but they must somehow reflect the quote and shed light on the paper's main topic. Interpretation is an evolving skill.

## 4. Polish, Revise, Edit

As students transform their quotes into polished and scholarly paragraphs, remind them to include other elements that will give their research papers a very academic feel. Encourage them to include transitions, so that paragraphs and elements flow smoothly from one to another. Instruct them to apply an explanatory (and *interesting*) heading to each of their subtopics, and remind them to include a related illustration with each of their subtopics. As mentioned in chapter 2, two good places to locate copyright-free images are Photos for Class and Pics4Learning. Finally, remind your students to revise and edit carefully before submitting their projects.

## THE PROJECT IN DETAIL

After teaching the philosophy and skills of composing a research paper, explain each component of this project, and ask your students to take notes directly onto *Outline 11–12.2*.

### 1. Introduction

Here, students will introduce the topic to their readers and will mention how serious this problem is. As always, they will write the introduction *last*.

### 2. First Subtopic: *Overview of Cell Phone Addiction* (include a *heading* and *illustration*)

In this section, students will use research (three quotes) to describe how high school students use cell phones with tremendous frequency. They will also provide an overview of cell phone addiction. *What does it look like? What are the telltale signs of cell phone addiction? How do we know when a teen is addicted?* They will provide some alarming statistics of this problem.

### 3. Second Subtopic: Symptoms and Problems (include a heading and illustration)

Here, students will use research (three quotes) to describe cell phone addiction in detail and will explain how teens obsessively use cell phones. *What apps do they use? How prevalent is texting among teenagers? What social media do they use? What types of video games? How much time do teens spend on their cell phones?* Next, they will describe the *physical* problems that can result from cell phone addiction, such as texting while driving, sleep deprivation, and sedentary lifestyle. Finally, they will discuss the dire *emotional* damage that can occur as a result of cell phone addiction.

## 4. Third Subtopic: *Ways to Treat This Addiction* (include a *heading* and *illustration*)

In this final subtopic, students will use research (three quotes) to offer a hopeful overview of the ways to treat and overcome cell phone addiction. For example, they may suggest healthful approaches, such as family-wide monitoring of cell phone use and limiting the amount of time spent on a cell phone. They may encourage replacing cell phone use with healthy "unplugged" pursuits, such as sports and other outdoor activities. They will conclude this section with a brief discussion of rehab programs and some of the methods used in those environments.

## 5. Conclusion

Students will conclude this paper with a brief summary of its salient points. They will once again mention the seriousness of this problem and will conclude with an optimistic statement that there is hope for those afflicted by cell phone addiction.

## DISPELLING THE MYSTERY

The research paper is a very important element in our students' educations and in their lives. As they move through their academic careers, they will encounter this form of writing over and over, and they need to handle it well—which means they need to *understand* it. Unfortunately, the research paper is not often taught as it should be taught—with clarity and simplicity—and, for most students, it remains an abject mystery. Students regard it with a mixture of dread and confusion; it produces great anxiety because *they don't know how to do it*.

In the methods described in this chapter, we dispel the eternal mysteries of the research paper. We break it down into clearly defined steps that orbit a subject deeply connected to students' lives. All of this is designed to generate understanding and engagement in students' minds and to remove the aura of mystery surrounding the research paper. Perhaps more important, this paper encourages students to consider their own relationships with cell phones and to evaluate the shadow these devices are casting over their lives.

Eleventh and Twelfth Grade, Second Writing Project: *Outline 11–12.2*
The Informative Research Essay: "Cell Phone Addiction"

Name_____ Date_____
Title _____

Mention the subject of the essay, along with a descriptive comment.

1. Introduction: Introduce the topic to your reader. Include a comment about how serious this problem is. Write your introduction last.

2. First Subtopic: *Overview of Cell Phone Addiction* (include a *heading* and *illustration*)
   a. What do teens use cell phones for?
   b. What does cell phone addiction in high school students look like?
   c. Describe some statistics.

3. Second Subtopic: *Symptoms and Problems* (include a *heading* and *illustration*)
   a. First Example: Obsessive and nearly constant use (texting, social media, video games, etc.)
   b. Second Example: Physical problems (driving while texting, lack of sleep, sedentary lifestyle, etc.)
   c. Third Example: Emotional problems (anxiety, depression, schoolwork suffering, social withdrawal, family problems, etc.)

4. Third Subtopic: *Ways to Treat This Addiction* (include a *heading* and *illustration*)
   a. First Example: Monitor and regulate *amount* and *type* of cell phone use.
   b. Second Example: Replace cell phone use with healthy "unplugged" activities.
   c. Third Example: Describe rehab programs.

5. Conclusion: Provide a brief summary of your essay, a call to take this problem seriously, and an affirmation that cell phone addiction can be overcome. Write this second to last.

*This page is permitted to copy.*

*Chapter 13*

# Grades Eleven and Twelve: Third Writing Project

## *The Reflective Short Story: "A Day without My Cell Phone" (Part Three)*

Main Standard 11–12.3:
Write narratives to develop real or imagined experiences or events using effective technique, well-chosen details, and well-structured event sequences.

*Author's Notes: Students will write a short story in which they spend an entire day without their cell phones. Alternate topics include writing short stories about traveling backward in time to a world before technology or attending a summer camp (or some other social experience) in which no cell phones are allowed. Students will write this in the first person.*

*Sub-Standard A:
Engage and orient the reader by setting out a problem, situation, or observation and its significance, establishing one or multiple point(s) of view, and introducing a narrator and/or characters; create a smooth progression of experiences or events.

*Author's Notes: In their stories, students will use the One-Story approach. They will include at least two characters. The main character will be the narrator, who is a stand-in for the student.*

*Sub-Standard B:
Use narrative techniques, such as dialogue, pacing, description, reflection, and multiple plot lines, to develop experiences, events, and/or characters.

*Author's Notes: Students will include dialogue and reflection; they will also employ the rule "Show, Don't Tell."*

Sub-Standard C:
Use a variety of techniques to sequence events so that they build on one another to create a coherent whole and build toward a particular tone and outcome (e.g., a sense of mystery, suspense, growth, or resolution).

*Author's Notes: The structure and organization of this short story will be embodied in* Outline 11–12.3.

Sub-Standard D:
Use precise words and phrases, telling details, and sensory language to convey a vivid picture of the experiences, events, setting, and/or characters.

*Author's Notes: Students will use imagery in their descriptions.*

Sub-Standard E:
Provide a conclusion that follows from and reflects on what is experienced, observed, or resolved over the course of the narrative.

*Author's Notes: In their conclusions, students will reflect on the experience of living without cell phones for a day. They will also reflect on the role of cell phones in their lives.*

## A SHORT STORY ABOUT CELL PHONES

This is the final project in our triumvirate of texts on cell phones. In the previous chapter (a research paper on cell phone addiction), you held a three-minute free-write in which you asked students if they could live without their cell phones for a day. Now, we are going to answer that question more fully in the form of a short story.

In this short story, students will compose a narrative in which they portray themselves existing for a day without a cell phone (or any other form of technology). These stories will be written in the first person, and each student will play the starring role in her or his short story. These stories will be told by a first-person narrator (*I, me, mine*), and the narrator will be a realistic depiction of the student. They love this sort of thing.

As you introduce this project to students, make sure they understand that it will be a fanciful projection, a grand wondering in which they use their imaginations to explore a "what if" scenario of an actual day without their cell phones (surely an ominous specter in their lives). Our students have been working very hard, and this project is intended to be a whimsical interlude, a fun exploration of an imaginary path they may have to tread someday. You never know. It is also an opportunity for students to review and practice their writing skills and to reinforce and activate earlier valuable learning that lies fallow in the fields of their fertile minds.

As always, we'll give our students guidance and structure during their journeys. When students understand the basics of the project, along with its tone (it is intended to be entertaining rather than grim), give them a *four-minute free-write* to spur their thinking on the subject. Ask students to take out a piece of paper and a pen and make a "t-chart." Above the horizontal line on the left, tell them to write "My Feelings." Above the horizontal line on the right, have them write "My Actions." Then, give them this prompt:

> I want you all to think about your connection to your cell phone and the role it plays in your life. And now, I want you to imagine that you have to spend an entire day without your cell phone. On this particular day, there is no school, and there is no technology at all. You have nothing scheduled. No practice. No homework. The whole day is a blank canvas for you to fill and enjoy. How will you feel? What will you do?
>
> In the left column of your chart, I want you to take two minutes and write your feelings about this situation. How would you feel spending an entire day without your cell phone? In the right column, I want you to take another two minutes and write down your *actions* during this time. What would you do? Got it? The time begins—now!

And watch them write.

When the four minutes are up, have a spirited discussion about how this situation would make them feel and what they would do. *Would some students find it liberating? Would some feel lost without their cell phone?* Have them add notes to their charts during the discussion, and tell them to keep these charts. They just performed a highly effective prewriting exercise called *brainstorming*, and they'll use these notes later.

## REVIEW AND ACTIVATE PRIOR KNOWLEDGE

Before beginning the actual writing of this project, review some of the writers' techniques you taught your students last year (repetition creates deep learning). Here are three highly effective techniques that students will include in their writing. We covered these earlier in the book, but a little review is good for the soul—and it's good for learning also.

## 1. Show, Don't Tell

This is a very powerful technique that creates visual images in the minds of readers. It helps them to picture the action and the characters in their minds, as if they're watching a movie. Here is an example of showing versus telling:

- *Telling:* The sun was very bright that day.
- *Showing:* Hake looked into the sun and blinked; his eyes went blind for a moment in the searing yellow light.

## 2. Imagery

Imagery is highly effective for creating memorable descriptions. Here, the writer will describe something in terms of our five senses. However, the writer should strive to include one or two senses in a single description (and usually not more than three). Here is an example of imagery in an extended description (original to this book):

- *Imagery:* Swan closed her eyes for a moment and felt happy. She felt the boards of the boat beneath her feet, solid and reassuring. She felt the ocean moving around the boat; it seemed somehow joyful, inviting her soul to a slow dance on the shining ripples of the sea. She listened and heard something very faint and faraway—the laughter of a seagull, maybe—and Swan was alive to her breathing and the smell of salt in the air. Faint scent of fish somewhere, all lean and silver muscle, swimming and silent and beautiful.

That description is vivid—but a bit unusual. It doesn't offer any visual descriptions, and this is because the main character's eyes are closed. Nonetheless, it makes effective use of three remaining senses—*feeling, hearing*, and *smelling*.

## 3. Dialogue

When students write their stories, they must employ *dialogue*. Their characters must speak to each other like real human beings having a back-and-forth conversation. These conversations should be fairly brief (it *is* a short story), and they should feel realistic and natural. They should also show us what's important to the speaker—a facet of character development—and they should provide soft exposition by moving the plot along.

As you review the process of writing dialogue, remind your students of all these things. Some of them will find it difficult to write dialogue, so give them some tips. Here is the most effective tip for fledgling writers: *write the way people talk*. When your students are writing their dialogue, encourage them to "hear" their characters speaking and then write down what the characters say to each other.

When your students are writing the narrator's dialogue, remind them that they are the narrator, so the narrator's voice should sound exactly like the student's. A conversation is like tossing a ball back and forth. One character says something (and tosses the ball), the other responds (tossing the ball back). Also, remind students to format their dialogue correctly, to include physical mannerisms (when the text calls for it), and to state who is speaking. Here is an example of dialogue (original to this book):

> When Skye opened the door, she looked at Jester in surprise. "Hi Jess," she said.
> "Hi. Sorry I couldn't call you," Jester said. "My phone's in the shop."
> "Well, that's weird," Skye said. "I left mine at school yesterday." The two looked at each other, waiting for one of them to speak.
> "So . . . it's weird being without a phone, isn't it?" Jester coughed a little. "What should we do?"
> Skye thought for a moment. "Hey," she smiled, "wanna go to the lake? Swimming? We can bring lunch."
> Jester's eyes widened, and he smiled at the thought. "Great idea!" he said. "When do you wanna go?"
> "*Right now!*" Skye said, and they both laughed. "And when we're on the beach, and we talk, we'll pretend we're texting each other," she said, and they both laughed again.

## THE ONE-STORY APPROACH

As students compose their stories, they will once again employ the One-Story approach. They used this in chapter 3 of last year, but we'll review it once again and relate it to this current project. In the One-Story structure, there is a problem to solve, and there are three parts to this problem-solving sequence: *grail*, *conflict*, and *resolution*. Here they are:

1. *Grail*: The main character wants something. This is the goal or "grail" of the story.

In this story, there are two grails—one is "visible"; the other is "invisible." The *visible* grail is the cell phone. *The student wants his or her cell phone back.* The *invisible* grail is what the story is *really* about, and it gives the story narrative power. Here it is: *the student must learn how to live without a cell phone*. In pursuit of this grail, the student must not merely tick away the hours of suffering until reunited with the beloved cell phone. The student must find meaning, satisfaction, and joy in a world existing beyond the phone's tiny screen. This is the *true* grail of the story, and it is infinitely more meaningful than a character finding a missing cell phone.

2. *Conflict*: Something is making it difficult for the main character to obtain the grail.

In this story, there are two conflicts present—one for each grail. To regain the cell phone (the *visible* grail), the student must make a physical journey of several miles (at least five). To obtain the *invisible* grail, the student must learn how to exist meaningfully for one day without the cell phone. Along the way, the character will find meaning, happiness, and growth. This will be difficult for students because they have developed a dependent bond to the cell phone and will likely feel lost without it. As you teach this, be sure to explain the deep literary structure to your students: *the physical journey is a metaphor for the emotional journey taking place.*

3. *Resolution*: the character obtains the grail (usually a happy ending) or does not obtain the grail (usually an unhappy ending). If the character does not attain the grail, there will be harmful consequences (these can be openly described or suggested by the action and characters).

By the end of the story, the student will regain the cell phone. More important, the student will have experienced a wonderful day and a great deal of emotional growth. As the narrator reflects on the events of the day, the writer will describe the narrator's emotions and the things that she or he learned from this experience.

## RULES OF THE GAME

After you take your students through the prewriting phase, teach them in detail about the story they're going to write. Here are the rules for this project:

1. Setting: your story takes place in the present day, in the real, recognizable world. There can be no magic, dragons, teleportation, and so on. This is a realistic story and will include *no impossible elements*.
2. Your cell phone must be at least five miles away from where you are.
3. You cannot use any electronic devices at all—no computer, television, recorded music—nothing that requires gas, electricity, or batteries. You're on your own!
4. You cannot take any kind of motorized transportation (no cars, planes, motorcycles, etc.). You must walk, ride a bicycle, skateboard, rollerblade, canoe, kayak, swim, et cetera.
5. There must be at least one other character in this story besides you.

6. This story must be upbeat and optimistic in tone (and you should have fun writing it!).

## THE ARCHITECTURE OF THIS STORY

Here is a detailed outline of this story:

### 1. Introduction

Here, you will provide the *setting* of this story (the time and the place) along with the *situation* (very important). You wake up one morning to discover that your cell phone is missing. Of course, you are very upset about this. *Where is your cell phone, and why is it there? Is it out for repairs or some sort of upgrade? Did you drop it somewhere? Did you leave it in a store? Did one of your friends take your phone as a prank? Did someone call your house and say,* "I found your cell phone; please come and get it"? *Or is it something else entirely?*

After you remember (or learn) where your cell phone is, you make a plan to go and get it. It is at least five miles away from you, and it will be a long and difficult journey (remember, you can use *no motorized conveyances* at all). You are not looking forward to this journey—but wonderful things are about to happen. You get dressed and head outside. *Where are you going?*

### 2. First Subtopic: *An Unplugged and Unexpected Occurrence*

You begin your journey, alone. *Are you walking? Riding a bicycle? Riding a skateboard?* In this first segment, you will describe something unexpected that happens to you. This will be a brief anecdote, like a short story within this short story. *What will you do? What will happen? Will you see something amazing? Will you meet someone interesting who tells you a great story? Will you fix something or solve a problem? Will you help another person? Will you rescue an animal?* Describe it, and then comment on it. *Why is it significant?* And then continue on your journey.

### 3. Second Subtopic: *You Do Something Unplugged with a Friend*

Along your way, you encounter a friend (possibly based on one of your real-life friends). *Is this meeting accidental or do you knock on your friend's door?* You tell your friend about your predicament, and (surprisingly) your friend is also without a cell phone. *Are these occurrences related?* The two of you talk and decide to do something interesting and fun. *What will it be?*

*Will you play some sort of game or sport? Will you meet other friends? Will you go to a park? Will you go for a run or do some other form of exercise? Will you go see a play, game, or concert?* Describe the activity and comment on the meaning you found there. You part with your friend, and you continue your journey, alone.

### 4. Third Subtopic: *You Do Something in a Natural Setting*

In this final episode, your journey brings you into contact with some spectacular form of *nature*—and something very interesting happens there. This is the final leg of your journey and to reach your destination, you must pass through some sort of natural setting. *Will you walk through a forest? Paddle a canoe across a lake? Swim out to an island? Climb a mountain? Descend into a canyon? Walk along an ocean beach and then swim out to a large yacht? Venture into a forbidding cave?* Describe your adventures in nature, and describe your rapturous reunion with your beloved cell phone.

### 5. Conclusion

You are happily reunited with your cell phone, and it's time to go home. *Will you call someone for a ride? Or will you return home the way you came—because it was so much fun?* In either case, you will use the journey home to reflect on your experiences. In your reflections, discuss the following: *What was your favorite part of the day? What was most surprising about your day unplugged? And—very important—what did you learn? How has this experience changed you? How have your feelings toward your cell phone—and the world—changed? As a result of today, how will you live your life differently?*

## A HAPPY ENDING TO OUR STORY

In this project, we ask students to imagine a life (briefly) without a cell phone. This is intended to be engaging and fun, but it contains valuable learning also. In addition to the writing lessons it offers, this project implicitly exhorts students to examine and question the relationship they have with their cell phones—and this is an important real-world aim. Through writing this story, students will remember that a world exists beyond the screens of their cell phones.

Properly taught and presented, this project will kindle self-awareness in students. In its highest actualization, it will encourage students to put down their cell phones and experience the real world and all it has to offer—and this will be a dynamic and liberating experience. When this day occurs, students will be rewarded with spectacular and unforeseen adventures in the real world—gloriously unplugged—and this is a happy ending to any story.

Eleventh and Twelfth Grade, Third Writing Project: *Outline 11–12.3*
The Reflective Short Story: "A Day without My Cell Phone"

Name_____ Date_____

Title _____

1. Introduction (write this last)
   a. Provide the setting (time and place).
   b. Provide the situation.
   c. Start your journey.

2. First Subtopic: *An Unplugged and Unexpected Occurrence*
   a. What is your mode of transportation?
   b. Describe what happens (tell a story).
   c. Comment on it. *Why is it significant or meaningful?* Continue your journey.

3. Second Subtopic: *You Do Something with a Friend*
   a. Whom do you meet, and how do you meet this person?
   b. What do you do with this person?
   c. Comment on this activity. *Why is it meaningful?* Continue your journey.

4. Third Subtopic: *You Do Something in a Natural Setting*
   a. Describe the natural setting.
   b. What happens there?
   c. Comment on it. *What did it mean to you?* Complete your journey.

5. Conclusion
   a. You get your phone back (describe this reunion).
   b. Retrospective summary of the events of the day. *What happened?*
   c. Reflect on the experiences of the day. *How have they changed you? What did you learn?*

*This page is permitted to copy.*

*Chapter 14*

# Grades Eleven and Twelve: Fourth Writing Project

## *The Personal Research Essay: "My Ideal Career" (Part One)*

Main Standard 11–12.4:
Produce clear and coherent writing in which the development, organization, and style are appropriate to task, purpose, and audience. (Grade-specific expectations for writing types are defined in standards 1–3 above.)

*Author's Notes: Students will choose an "ideal career" and write a personal research essay on it. Alternate topics include* careers they would *not* like to attempt *and* specific colleges and programs of study that interest them. *Students will write it in the first person; there are no sub-standards here.*

### PRODUCTION AND DISTRIBUTION OF WRITING

This next group of three standards is called "Production and Distribution of Writing." As you can see, it involves students generating high-quality writing and somehow sharing this with others. We are going to accomplish these goals by bundling these three standards together (thematically) and having students compose three discrete projects on an "ideal" career they would like to explore. Here are the next three projects:

- Chapter 14: The Personal Research Essay: "My Ideal Career" (this current project)
- Chapter 15: The Creative Essay: "My Ideal Career: Workplace Log Entries"

- Chapter 16: The Oral Presentation: "My Ideal Career"

Junior and senior years of high school are the perfect time for projects of this nature. The students are beginning to think about their futures; they are starting to wonder about the colleges they might attend and potential careers to explore. Properly presented and taught, these next three projects will be pragmatic and constructive for students, engaging them and helping prepare them for adulthood. These projects also accord beautifully with the Common Core's "Anchor Standards for Writing," which call for teachers to develop "college and career readiness" in students.

This project is rather unusual. It combines the informative research paper with the personal essay—a feat not often attempted in the contemporary academy. Nonetheless, this is a powerful combination that will unite different techniques and will engage students as it teaches and reinforces research and writing skills. In this paper, students will perform research on a topic closely linked to their interests. Here is a brief outline of this project:

1. Introduction
2. First Subtopic: *Describe Your Ideal Career*
3. Second Subtopic: *Describe the Training and Education Your Career Requires*
4. Third Subtopic: *Describe Why You Want This Particular Career*
5. Conclusion

## A STEP TOWARD YOUR FUTURE

Begin this project by discussing it with your students and providing an overview (which will include the outline above). To get them thinking, have them brainstorm potential topics in a three-minute free-write. During this exercise, students will list at least three careers, along with reasons why they find them interesting.

When the three minutes are up, have a spirited discussion about these potential careers. If students say, "I'm not going to college" or "I don't know what I want to do," motivate them to write from their imaginations. This essay has autobiographical aspects, but it also contains fanciful aspects of wish fulfillment. In other words, *every student will complete this project*.

Be sure to emphasize the fun and creative aspects of this project, but tell students that they are not to make a joke out of it. They mustn't write anything too outlandish or that couldn't actually happen in real life. Nonetheless, encourage them to dream big and to imagine careers that may seem impossible now but that could actually happen in the future. Unlikely dreams often lead to extraordinary success.

## MORE FREEDOM, MORE CHOICE

Our students are growing toward independence, so we are going to give them more freedom to explore and make choices. In this project, students will choose their own individual topics and then (for the first time) perform research on the open internet. This is an enormous open-ended task. What will they do?

We can't merely tell students, "Go on the internet and find some info about your career," because the results would be disastrous. There is very good learning to galvanize here, so we will give students freedom within a framework of structure and guidance. Begin by telling students that there are different *types* of resources available to them. In this project, we will offer students the following four (the first three are mandatory; the fourth is optional):

## FOUR TYPES OF RESOURCES

1. *Websites*. Each student must find at least one reliable website on her or his chosen career (this will provide information for the first subtopic, in which students will describe the career). For example, a student might find a website devoted entirely to a single profession, such as *nursing*. This website should be fairly current (ideally, no more than five years old), readable, and well-organized. It should also provide a comprehensive overview of nursing, from initial education to certification and onward through the different types of nurses (and nursing) in the field. This source is mandatory.
2. *College, University, and Vocational Training Websites*. This type of website will provide information for the second subtopic, which focuses on the training and education necessary for the career. Legitimate operating institutions overwhelmingly tend to provide excellent (and well-maintained) websites that will provide students with information that is current, comprehensive, and of high quality. This source is mandatory.
3. *Videos*. Each student will include one video in his or her paper. And how will they do this? These are upper-level students, so they can certainly search on YouTube. Why overlook the obvious? Once there, they will search for a high-quality video relating to his or her career. This video

must be well-produced, relatively recent (ideally within five years), and provide informative material about the career. This source is mandatory.
4. *Interview*. Here, students can interview someone who works in the field or who retired from the profession. This person might be well-known to the student, such as a parent, guardian, relative, or acquaintance. The student can also conduct an interview through email or over the phone. For example, the student might email (or call) an institution and *very politely* request an interview with someone who works in the profession. In any case (in-person, email, or phone), the student will ask *three questions* about the profession (and no more than three). Here are three good questions to ask:
   - What is (or was) your favorite part of your job?
   - Why is this an important profession?
   - Would you encourage someone to do this job? Why or why not?

Interviews are a terrific form of primary source research. When conducting interviews, the student will provide an in-text citation for each quote and will include the interview in the bibliography (this will be discussed later in this chapter). This source is *optional*.

## LOCATING AND EVALUATING INTERNET RESOURCES

Performing research on the open internet is more difficult than it sounds. The internet is enormous, and it contains a great deal of good information as well as bad information. This means that students must learn how to perform skillful searches and then evaluate their findings in terms of reliability. This is extremely difficult for young students. It must be taught clearly and well, and it takes practice.

As we teach this project, we are going to teach our students the basics of locating and evaluating internet research. As students begin their searches, encourage them to use a well-known search engine (such as Google) and remind them to use their *Boolean limiters*. We taught our students how to do this in chapter 8—a long time ago—so let's do a quick review now.

Boolean limiters provide an easy way to get results that are fewer and more relevant. There are a variety of Boolean limiters to use ("Boolean Operators and Nesting"), but the most effective one is the use of *quotation marks*. By enclosing multiword search terms in quotation marks, the search engine will (essentially) read the search terms as a single word and deliver fewer—and much more accurate—results. Here are some examples:

- "child psychologist"

- "small business owner"
- nurse

Note that the first two search terms are presented in lowercase letters, because search engines are not case-sensitive. Note that the last search term *omits quotation marks*, because it consists of a single word: *nurse*.

When students locate potentially relevant results (such as websites and videos), they'll need to *evaluate* them. This process is challenging for young students, so you might introduce this through a simplified process, called the BOWA method (original to this book). BOWA stands for *Biased, Old, Who, Accurate*. These four steps involve students asking (and answering) questions about the sources they locate. Here are the steps and some questions to ask:

- *Biased*: Is the information extremely biased toward a point of view? Is it propagandistic in nature? Does it involve some sort of political agenda? If so, these are bad signs. If the material seems *objective* in nature—presenting the material fairly—this is a good sign.
- *Old*: How old is the source? When was it created? As stated earlier, students should (in general) try to use sources no older than five years. In the academic world, newer sources are usually more preferable.
- *Who*: Who made the source? What person or institution wrote or compiled the information? For example, was it a university, museum, or other notable institution? Was it created by a professor or some other type of expert? If so, these are all good signs. If it was created by a person or institution with no legitimate credentials in the field, don't use it.
- *Accurate*: How accurate is the material? Are there any visible errors? Does the source have a low-quality (or "homemade") look (and feel) to it? Is it poorly written? Is it poorly organized? Does it omit important information? If so, these are bad signs.

As students search for resources, give them assistance and evaluate their sources for final approval. When students have found their three (or four) resources, have them immediately create a bibliography and in-text citations. For the websites and videos, we will use the following formats:

- Author. "Title of Webpage." *Website*. Date of publication. Date of access. URL.
- Author. "Title of Video." *Video Platform*. Length of video, date of publication. Date of access. URL.

When citing an interview, here is the bibliographic format we will use (the in-text citation will be the last name of the person being interviewed):

- Last name, first name. Type of interview (personal interview; phone interview; email interview). Place of interview. Date of interview.

And now, let's look at an example.

## TIME TO KINDLE LEARNING

Let's say that a student wants to become a firefighter in the New York City Fire Department (FDNY). After doing research, the student has assembled four reliable resources: a website about the FDNY; an interview with a retired New York City firefighter; a video about FDNY physical fitness, and a website about the FDNY Fire Academy. The bibliography looks like this (and *yes*, you should share this with students):

### Works Cited

"Firefighter: Get Hired." *JoinFDNY*. Accessed 15 August 2021. https://www.joinfdny.com/careers/firefighter/.

Horan, John. Telephone interview by the author. New York. 15 August 2021.

Join FDNY. "FDNY Fire Academy: An Overview of the FDNY Fire Academy's Physical Fitness Standards." *YouTube* Video, 6:19, 29 January 2015. Accessed 16 August 2021. https://www.youtube.com/watch?v=NxgAy6Fp_Ao.

"Studying at the Fire Academy." *JoinFDNY*. 15 February 2017. Accessed 15 August 2021. https://www.joinfdny.com/fdny-fire-academy/.

When students have gathered their resources, it's time to begin interacting with the research. Our students have done this before, but they're young, and it's a complex process and bears reviewing. Repetition is a valuable learning technique; it creates changes in the brain and deep, long-term learning (the author discussing Coyle in "Mindset in Your Library," 21).

At this time, give each student a copy of *Outline 11–12.4* and go over each component (this way, students will know what they're looking for). As students read their research and view their videos, tell them to look (and listen) for three relevant quotes in each resource. To do this, they will examine their resources with the three subtopics in mind.

When students find a useful quote, they will place it verbatim onto an electronic document, enclosing all quotes in quotation marks and including in-text citations. Their goal (you'll tell them) is to create a "bank" of (approximately) nine to twelve quotes (all drawn from their resources), presented in an order that corresponds with the *Outline*. When students have done this—when they have located and transcribed all their quotes—they have just created the backbone of the paper, and this is a significant achievement. Now they will develop each quote, adding their own unique and original voices to the project.

## HOW TO USE QUOTATIONS

At this point, our students will develop their quotes into an organized and readable paper. Their own voices (you'll remind them) should constitute about 50–75 percent of the words in the paper. To do this, we will once again use the five-step method students last used in chapter 12. Review this process with your students, because they're young, and it's challenging. Once again, here are the steps:

1. Introduce the quote. Here, you will put *your own words* before the quote.
2. Provide the quote, verbatim, in quotation marks. You can also *paraphrase* quotes in your own words. Remember: *paraphrases must be cited.*
3. Provide the in-text citation.
4. Explain the quote in your own words, focusing on its relation to your paper. (This may not be necessary if you paraphrase the quote.)
5. Comment on the quote. *What does it reveal about the profession being discussed? How do you feel about the information being revealed? How (and why) does this information increase your enthusiasm for the profession? How does it impact your thoughts toward the profession?*

And now, let's start putting the pieces together. Let's say that our budding firefighter interviewed someone who retired from the FDNY. How would the student include this research in the paper? By following the five steps above and by importing the verbal exchange in the form of *dialogue* (just as they did in the previous project). Here is an example of the five-step process being used for a quote gathered from an *interview*:

> I was able to speak on the phone with John Horan, a retired lieutenant in the New York City Fire Department. I began the interview by asking him, "What was your favorite part of being a firefighter?" He said, "I really liked helping other people. It felt great putting out fires and saving people from burning buildings. I also really liked the camaraderie among the firefighters. We were like a family. This was important, because your life depends on the people you work with" (Horan, John).[1]
>
> I could see that Lieutenant Horan loved two things about the job: saving people from deadly fires and all the great friends he made on the job. I really liked hearing this, because it's my dream to have a career where I can help other people. Also, I love making new friends. I have lots of friends now, and maybe

some of them can become firefighters too. It would be great to work with my friends, putting out fires and saving lives.

When you share this excerpt with students, indicate the presence (and placement) of all five steps to properly incorporating research in an academic paper. This process takes practice, but it's a very precious bit of learning that is almost never taught in the contemporary classroom. It is the alchemical bit of magic that will help their writing to leap off the page and blaze with life.

And now, let's take a closer look at each component of this project.

## THE PROJECT IN DETAIL

### 1. Introduction

Students will state the profession they will be discussing and describe it in one or two sentences. They will also emphasize their desire to pursue this career. As always, they will write the introduction *last*.

### 2. First Subtopic: *Describe Your Ideal Career*

Students will describe the profession for the reader. After providing an overview of the career, students will consider the following: *What are the typical duties of a person in this field? What can they expect to do on an "average" day? Why is this career important? What are the best parts of working in this field? What are some challenging aspects of working in this field? To do well in this career, what qualities should a person possess?*

### 3. Second Subtopic: *Describe the training and education your career requires*

In this section, students will describe how a person gains entry into this profession. In doing this, they will consider the following: *Does the career require a college (or graduate) degree? If so, describe the program of study. Is the career vocational or civil service? Is there an entrance exam? Describe the training or education required to begin working in this field. Does this career require a license or final exams to pass? If so, describe them.* Et cetera.

### 4. Third Subtopic: *Describe Why You Want This Particular Career*

Here, students will describe what led them to want this particular career. *Why do they want to do this? What are their favorite aspects of this job? How much would it mean to them to work in this field?* To illustrate this section, they can relate a story or a brief anecdote. This section is rather personal in nature, so it may not require the addition of research.

## 5. Conclusion

In this section (likely one paragraph), students will mention the career once again and emphasize their desire to work in this field. They might conclude with a statement on the happiness this career will bring them, or how they look forward to helping other people, or the satisfaction they'll experience from somehow improving the world.

## COLLEGE AND CAREER READY

In this project, we assisted students as they performed research to learn more about careers they would like to explore. A paper of this nature and on this subject works beautifully for our upper-level students, conveying a number of important lessons. The freedom and choice embedded in this project will help students prepare for the *laissez-faire* challenges of college-level writing, along with the increased freedom they'll find as they transition into the independence of college and career.

These projects also represent an excellent illustration of the power of writing to convey pragmatic life-lessons that can help us to navigate an unwritten future and all the marvelous possibilities it contains. However, the students' venture into the workplace isn't over, so they can't punch out just yet. They're about to discover that the world of work often has room for creativity.

Eleventh and Twelfth Grade, Fourth Writing Project: *Outline 11–12.4*
The Personal Research Essay: "My Ideal Career"

Name_____ Date_____
Title _____

Be sure to mention your career in this title.

1. Introduction
   a. Name the profession you're discussing.
   b. Describe the profession in one or two sentences.
   c. Emphasize your desire to pursue this career.

2. First Subtopic: *Describe Your Ideal Career*
   a. Provide an overview of the profession.
   b. Provide details of the profession (typical day, good points and bad points, etc.).
   c. Describe the qualities a potential employee should possess for this career.

3. Second Subtopic: *Describe the Training and Education Your Career Requires*
   a. Describe the education and training necessary for this career.
   b. Discuss entry exams or other requirements necessary for employment.
   c. Discuss final exams or licensing requirements, et cetera.

4. Third Subtopic: *Describe Why You Want This Particular Career*
   a. Describe what led you to this career (perhaps tell a story).
   b. Tell the reader why you want to do this.
   c. If you attain this career, how much would it mean to you?

5. Conclusion
   a. Restate the career.
   b. Emphasize your enthusiasm for this field.
   c. End with a bright, enthusiastic statement.

*This page is permitted to copy.*

*Chapter 15*

# Grades Eleven and Twelve: Fifth Writing Project

## *The Creative Essay:* "My Ideal Career: Workplace Log Entries" (Part Two)

Main Standard 11–12.5:

Develop and strengthen writing as needed by planning, revising, editing, rewriting, or trying a new approach, focusing on addressing what is most significant for a specific purpose and audience. (Editing for conventions should demonstrate command of Language standards 1–3 up to and including grades 11–12 here [http://www.corestandards.org/ELA-Literacy/L/11-12/]).

*Author's Notes: Students will compose fictional workplace log entries in which they describe daily activities and a significant problem that occurs. Alternate topics include writing a* diary *entry titled* "A Day in the Life at My Intended College, Studying My Intended Major." *Students will write this in the first person; there are no sub-standards here.*

### THINK AND IMAGINE

This is the second project in our group of three projects about the students' "ideal career." It will piggyback on the previous assignment, and it will allow students to utilize their new knowledge of an "ideal" career. However, this project will be *creative* in nature. Does this conform to the standard above? Yes, it does. It will be unique and engaging, and therefore it falls under the standard's open-ended suggestion for students to try "a new approach." It will also give students experience writing a new and different type of composition.

As you introduce this project to students, tell them that they are about to compose a piece of *realistic fiction*. Using their new knowledge of the profession, they will imagine that they are now working in the job of their dreams (the same one discussed in the previous essay). This paper will essentially be a "day in the life" narrative in which they chronicle their workplace activities over the course of one day. It will commence with "punching in" at work and will conclude with "punching out." Let's assume an eight-hour workday.

Tell your students that many workplaces keep "logs" of daily activities and significant events that occur in the workplace. A "log" (you can tell your students) is like a diary of daily occurrences in a workplace. In these logs, employees record incidents such as broken equipment, industrial accidents, unusual events, power outages, floods, storm damage, missing items, and injuries on the job (etc.). When something significant happens in a workplace, an employee will open the book, provide the date and time of the event, and then describe it clearly. This becomes an official record for the institution.

Today, many workplace logs are electronic and stored online. However (we'll explain to our classes), our budding writers will imagine they are writing workplace log entries in old-school log books. They are large and leather and battered, and they are absolutely beautiful. Sometimes the old ways are really hard to beat. Here is a brief outline of this project:

1. Introduction: *Arrive at Work (Punch In. Include Date and Time)*
2. First Subtopic: *Your Usual Daily Activities*
3. Second Subtopic: *A Problem Arises (it is central to your profession)*
4. Third Subtopic: *You Solve the Problem*
5. Conclusion: *Depart Work (Punch Out. Include Time)*

## LET'S GET STARTED

When students understand the basic flow and scope of this project, elaborate on it more fully. As you describe it, incorporate storytelling techniques, and say something like this:

> We are in a good place! You have all chosen an ideal career to explore. You've done research on it, thought about it, and written about it. Now, we are going to use your new knowledge and write a realistic fictional narrative *about your career. It's sort of like writing a short story, but in a different format. And let me emphasize that you have great freedom here to write the sort of narrative that you want to write. So have fun! Be creative!*
>
> Now, let's say that you have been hired in your ideal career, and you've been there for about six months. Your new workplace has a daily "log" that you

must fill out, sort of like a diary. Every day, you are required to write several log entries describing the things you do and anything interesting or significant that happens in the workplace. This is very true, and many workplaces use daily logs.

So today, you arrive at work, and it starts off just like any other day. You punch in, do your normal log entries and your usual tasks, and then—uh-oh—something serious happens. You are confronted with a large problem that you must solve, and it is centrally related to your profession. (For example, if you are a firefighter, you must put out an enormous fire.) Other employees can help you, but the ultimate responsibility is yours.

Here is your mission: you must understand the problem, consider possible solutions, implement the best solution, and finally solve the problem. When you are done, you will write a long and fascinating entry in the daily log book. Got it? You're going to love this writing assignment!

## FREE-WRITE

After describing the assignment, give your students a three-minute free-write. During this time, they will brainstorm on paper and activate their new knowledge about their chosen careers. They will do three exercises for one minute each, and here they are:

- *First Minute*: Write down three "typical" daily tasks for your ideal career.
- *Second Minute*: Write down three large problems you might be required to solve.
- *Third Minute*: Write down three potential solutions to those problems.

When the three minutes are up, ask students to share this information with the other students, and ask students to provide feedback to the speaker. As the discussion warms up, have your students take notes as new ideas develop and circulate around the classroom.

## WRITING TECHNIQUES

As students compose this project, they will again use (and practice) their fiction-writing techniques. Once again, we will encourage our students to employ the rule "Show, Don't Tell" and to use imagery. This time, however, we will encourage them to combine the two in their descriptions. Let's review both and then combine them in a single descriptive paragraph.

## 1. Show, Don't Tell

Students will employ this rule in their descriptions, because it is *the single most effective* way to create visual images in readers' minds. It is challenging to learn and more difficult than it sounds, but it will greatly improve the power of our students' writing. Here is a brief example:

- *Telling*: Juan could run really fast.
- *Showing*: Juan was the fastest firefighter we ever had. I once saw him race a German Shepherd just for fun, and I swear he crossed the finish line first.

## 2. Imagery

As students write their log entries, they will use *imagery* in their descriptions. When doing this, they will describe things in terms of the *senses*. Remember, two senses per description usually work well, and three is usually overdoing it). When writing extended descriptions, the writer can use as many senses as the description calls for:

- *Imagery*: That night, after the big fire, we all had dinner together in the firehouse. It was nice sitting with everyone. The kitchen was warm and clean, and I could smell steak and potatoes cooking. Scent of coffee brewing and something sweet baking in the oven. *Coffee cake*, I thought. The voices were hushed and tired, and a song played on the radio. It was something low and sweet from the 1940s, and everything just seemed perfect.

Hand out that description to students and ask them to flag the senses it uses and where it uses them. It is an *extended* description, and you will find references to all five senses. Here they are:

- *Touch*: The kitchen *feels* warm
- *Sight*: The kitchen is *clean* (a visual perception)
- *Smell*: The scents of good food cooking
- *Taste*: Suggested by all the culinary descriptions
- *Hearing*: The voices and the song on the radio

And now, let's take a look at the two techniques (*showing* and *imagery*) working together in a single passage. It's an effective pairing, so let's encourage our students to use it. The example below combines the techniques *show, don't tell* with *imagery*. When these elements work together, they create powerful descriptions designed to linger in readers' minds.

- The fire lit up the night sky like an insane carnival flashing orange and yellow and red. I could hear loud crackling sounds like splitting timbers, and the heat it emanated felt like I was standing near the surface of the sun. The smell of acrid smoke was terrible. It made me cough and vomit. As I picked up my hose, I saw with horror that the fire had spread to the buildings next to it on each side and that the siding on them was melting and their windows were starting to crack.

The description above (original to this book) is vivid and combines the two techniques quite successfully. It *shows* (rather than *tells*) the enormity of the fire. It also employs *imagery* to create a vivid sensory impression of the ferocity of the fire. Hand the passage out to students and ask them to flag all the sensory descriptions (there are clear references to *seeing, hearing, feeling,* and *smelling*).

After discussing the imagery in the passage, you can ask your students to flag points where the passage employs the technique of *showing* descriptions to the reader, rather than *telling* them. Here are three:

1. The fire "lit up the night sky."
   - This *shows* us that the fire is huge.
2. The smoke causes the firefighter to "cough and vomit."
   - This shows us that the smoke is terrible and is repugnant to human lungs.
   - It also shows us (and this is quite subtle) the courage and dedication of the firefighter, who picked up the hose rather than move to safety.
3. The fire "spread to the buildings next to it," and "the siding on them was melting and their windows were starting to crack."
   - This shows us that the fire is *big* and is getting bigger.
   - It also shows us that the fire is incredibly *hot* and is extremely dangerous.

## 3. Dialogue

As our students compose their log entries, they have great freedom to let the narrative grow organically and to see where the story takes them. (Very often, we do our best writing when we allow the story to unfold naturally and follow it to wherever it leads). Tell your students that they can, if they want, create and include other characters. If they do this, they should give these characters names and describe their appearances and personalities. These characters may be silent in the narrative, but they should perform a function or somehow assist the student.

The student can also (if the narrative demands it) reproduce conversations between the student and another character. If they do this, they'll format the dialogue exactly as we taught them to. They'll tell us who's speaking, assign physical movements to the speaker, and make the dialogue sound natural and human. Here is our fearless firefighter, checking on a friend who has been injured:

> I walked over to my friend Juan. He was sitting on the ground, rubbing his ankle.
> "Hey, Juan," I said, "are you hurt?"
> Juan looked up at me and winced. "A little," he said. "I twisted my ankle coming down the stairs. Might be fractured."
> "Okay," I said. I checked his jacket and pants for scorch marks. "Any burns?"
> "No," he shook his head. "I got lucky. Just the ankle."
> "Don't worry," I told him. "I'll get you some help. You'll be up and running in no time." And I winked at him.

### WHAT'S THE PROBLEM?

In previous chapters, our students have composed their fictional narratives by using the One-Story approach (*grail, conflict, resolution*). In this current project, we are going to alter that method—*slightly*—and add to our students' repertoire of literary knowledge. When teachers explain story structure to students, they often describe stories as a situation in which "a problem needs to be solved" (hereafter referred to as the "Problem-and-Solution" method).

When teaching works of literature, these educators will ask students to identify the problem that needs to be solved, along with its eventual solution. It's a simple method and an effective gateway into understanding story structure. Let's look at an example.

In chapters 7, 8, and 9 of this book, we composed three projects on Steinbeck's marvelous novella *Of Mice and Men*. Now, let us consider a question central to the construction of that story: *what was the problem to solve?* The question is actually more complex than it appears, because there were several problems to solve. Here are three of them:

- George and Lennie needed a steady job.
- Lennie needed to stay out of trouble (the story's central problem).
- When Lennie got in trouble, George needed to "protect" his friend.

As we teach this current project, we will direct students to use the Problem-and-Solution method. In their log entries, they will describe a challenging problem (connected to the profession) and how they eventually solve it. Please note that this does *not* contradict or displace the One-Story method; indeed, it is a simplified variation of it. Consider the following:

- **Problem-and-Solution Method**:
  - *Problem*: A large and dangerous fire is burning.
  - *Solution*: A firefighter puts the fire out.
- **One-Story Approach**:
  - *Grail*: A large fire must be extinguished.
  - *Conflict*: The fire is enormous, very dangerous, and growing larger.
  - *Resolution*: The firefighter courageously fights the fire, eventually putting it out.

Structurally, the two have much in common. However, whereas the Problem-and-Solution method focuses on *plot*, the One-Story approach focuses on *characters*. And now, here's what we're going to do.

### FOR EXAMPLE

When students write their entries, they will format them like genuine workplace log entries. They will include the day and date, the time of the occurrence, a detailed description of the events being discussed, and a signature at the end of the day. Here is an example of a brief log entry; students will format it as follows:

### OFFICIAL LOG BOOK: FDNY ENGINE 82, THE BRONX, NY

Thursday, August 19, 2021, 6:52 a.m.

I just arrived at firehouse Engine 82 in the Bronx. Looks like a quiet morning so far. Juan Carlos is the house-watch, and I checked in with him. Lt. Horan is the officer on duty. He assigned me to clean the kitchen after the morning meal (although he's my father, he treats me just like anyone else). The kitchen looks pretty good right now. I hope it's not too messy after breakfast. Besides cleaning the kitchen, I have some other things to do. I have to check the ladders and hoses and make sure they're ready if we have a fire. If I have time, I also want to polish the fire truck. It looks great when it's . . . wait, there's the alarm. I have a feeling this will be a big fire. I have to go.

## THE PROJECT IN DETAIL

When all the teaching and prewriting activities are complete, hand a copy of *Outline 11–12.5* to each student and go over each component in detail. Instruct them to take notes onto their Outlines. Here is the project in detail:

**1. Introduction: Arrive at work (punch in, or sign in. Include day, date, and time)**

Here, students will name the job and describe the setting. *Where are you located?* Also, describe your workplace. *What does it look like? Who else is present? What sort of work-related equipment is in this place?* Help the reader to picture the work environment. Describe your goals for the day.

**2. First Subtopic: *Your Usual Daily Activities***

You read yesterday's log entries. *Did anything interesting happen yesterday?* Look at today's schedule. *What's on the schedule? Will it affect you?* And now, you do a work-related task of your choice. *What will you do?* Describe it. You're surprised to see that it's already lunch time. Enter the *start* and *end* times of your lunch.

**3. Second Subtopic: *A Problem Arises* (one that is central to your profession)**

A very large problem arises. It is directly related to your profession. Describe the problem in detail. *How does it start? How serious is it? How do you feel about the problem? Are you nervous? Excited? What are the consequences of not solving the problem?* Set the stage for what follows.

**4. Third Subtopic: *You Solve the Problem***

You want to solve the problem, so you begin by thinking of some possible solutions. Describe some of these, and then choose the best one. *Which do you choose? Why? How do you solve the problem?* Describe this process in detail. *What happens after you solve the problem? What are the results?*

## 5. Conclusion: Depart Work (punch out, include time, sign the log book)

Reflect on today's events and the problem you solved. *How are you feeling right now?* (probably pretty good). *What did you learn from the problem you solved? What kind of experience did you gain? What can others learn from your experience? How did these events make you appreciate (and value) your job even more?* Punch out (or sign out) and include the time. Sign your name to the log book—because another day is done.

## A JOB WELL DONE

This project contained a great deal of valuable learning for our students. It allowed them to practice (and learn) a great variety of writing skills and to utilize their new knowledge of ideal careers in a format that was creative, unique, and fun. In an ironic pairing, this project required them to use their imaginations as they approached the very real world of work.

And what about *you*—the dedicated teacher reading this book? What will you write in *your* daily log book? What problems did *you* solve today, in the small and infinite world of your classroom? As you teach this assignment—and all the other assignments in this book—remember to rejoice in the job you are doing and in the small miracles that your students achieve every day.

Make no mistake, you are solving problems and offering solutions every time you walk into your classroom, and you are improving the world one student at a time. And what does this mean? The answer is simple. It means that you—*you, intrepid teacher*—really do have the ideal job. Let's all keep this in mind as we move through our days, and let us hope that someday our students can say the same thing.

Eleventh and Twelfth Grade, Fifth Writing Project: *Outline 11–12.5*
The Creative Essay: "My Ideal Career: Workplace Log Entries"

Name_____ Date_____
Title _____

Be sure to include "Log Book" and mention the specific workplace.

1. Introduction: Arrive at Work (Punch in, include date and time. *Don't ever be late!*)
   a. Name the job and describe the setting. Where is it located?
   b. Describe the conditions and people present. Help the reader to envision it.
   c. Describe your goals for the day.

2. First Subtopic: *Your Usual Daily Activities*
   a. You read yesterday's log entries and today's schedule. What's happening?
   b. You do a task of your choice. Describe it.
   c. You have lunch (include the start and end times).

3. Second Subtopic: *A Problem Arises* (It is central to your profession)
   a. How does the problem start?
   b. Describe the problem and its seriousness.
   c. What are the consequences of *not* solving the problem?

4. Third Subtopic: *You Solve the Problem*
   a. What are some possible ways to solve this problem?
   b. Which do you choose? How do you solve the problem?
   c. What happens *after* you solve the problem?

5. Conclusion: Depart Work (punch out, include time, sign the log book)
   a. Reflect on today's events. How are you feeling right now?
   b. What did you learn from the problem you solved? What can others learn?
   c. How did this experience increase your appreciation for your job?

*This page is permitted to copy.*

*Chapter 16*

# Grades Eleven and Twelve: Sixth Writing Project

## *The Informative Oral Presentation: "My Ideal Career" (Part Three)*

Main Standard 11–12.6:
Use technology, including the internet, to produce, publish, and update individual or shared writing products in response to ongoing feedback, including new arguments or information.

*Author's Notes: Students will prepare (and deliver) oral presentations on their ideal career. Alternate topics include giving a presentation on their "Intended College and Major." Students will write in the third person. This presentation will be at least five minutes long. There are no sub-standards here.*

### LET'S TALK

And so we arrive at our third and final project on the students' ideal career. This project is going to be different from the others, because it will begin as a series of electronic slides and culminate in an oral presentation given in your classroom. It's an unusual writing assignment, but it accords beautifully with this standard, fulfilling its requirement to create writing by using technology and to "update" writing projects. But what about *publishing* their work? By speaking in the classroom, our students will "publish" their ideas into their peers' pulsing minds.

In this project, we continue the pragmatic nature of this triad of assignments and teach our students a very important real-world skill: *public speaking*. This will be very helpful to our students, and they will almost certainly use it in the not-too-distant future. Remember, they're getting ready to enter the worlds of college and the workplace, and the experience of public speaking will help them to grow as students and as people. This is very difficult for most students, but with our support, they will confront their fears in safety and emerge stronger and more confident on the other side—and have lots of fun doing it.

## WHAT ARE WE DOING?

First, let's talk about the software program we'll be using. There are a number of excellent presentation platforms available (such as PowerPoint and Prezi), but we'll be using Google Slides. It's free, is simple to use, and exists within the widely adopted (and increasingly utilized) Google Classroom.

To start this project, introduce it to your students and motivate them, like this:

> *We are going to do one more project on your ideal career, and it's going to be lots of fun. Think about what you have accomplished: you have written a research essay on your career, and you have written creative log entries on it. You are an expert on your topic! And now, you are going to share your knowledge with your classmates. We are going to do oral presentations! (insert dramatic pause here). Stop groaning, you're going to love this.*
>
> *We will write these presentations on Google Slides. You'll create five amazing slides, and you will talk to the class for about five minutes. This means you'll speak for about one minute for each slide, and your information will be drawn from the two writing projects you did. At the end of your presentation, you will say, "Thank you for listening. Are there any questions?" And then you'll answer a few questions. Speaking of which . . . who has a question?*

## WHAT'S ON THE PROGRAM?

Your students' familiarity with Google Slides will vary, so you will teach it to all of them, especially as it relates to this project. Introduce it clearly, and keep it simple. You might start by showing them a seven-minute video produced by Super Schoolhouse (the URL is in the References). This video is intended for younger students, but it is remarkably clear and is a terrific resource for learning Google Slides (even for adults).

After that, walk your students through the creation of a template for this slide presentation (demonstrate this on a large screen, if possible). As you do this, create a five-slide presentation that will include a title slide and four information slides. Show students how to choose a theme, how to format each slide, and how to apply a fancy transition from one slide to another. You will also teach your students how to connect with an audience.

Here is the goal. The presentation will be well organized and visually attractive, but *it must not compete with the speaker*. Your students will *not* load the slides with text. The students will *not* stand up there and read to the audience. The presentation will function like an *outline* to organize the students' thoughts, and *the students will relate to their audience*. Nonetheless, the presentation will follow the structure of all our writing projects. The first slide is the introduction, slides two, three, and four are the subtopics, and the fifth slide is the conclusion. Here is a brief outline of this project:

1. Introduction (First Slide): *My Ideal Career*
2. First Subtopic (Second Slide): *Three important aspects of this job*
3. Second Subtopic (Third Slide): *Training needed for this career*
4. Third Subtopic (Fourth Slide): *A day in the life of this career*
5. Conclusion (Fifth Slide): *This is a fantastic career*

Explain this underlying philosophy to students: *the presentation is just an outline*. Students will use it to organize their thoughts, and they will speak to the class in *natural conversational language*. The slide presentation will illustrate (and require) the leap from *idea* to *speech*.

## HOW TO DESIGN AND FORMAT SLIDES

The *title slide* will include three elements: the title of the presentation (this will include the career being discussed), the student's name, and an eye-catching photo relating to the career. Each *information slide* will also have three elements: a title (indicating the slide's topic), three examples of the topic (presented as *bullet points*), and a photo related to the slide's topic. These slides are intentionally minimalistic. They are designed to organize the speaker's thoughts and to help the audience follow and understand the presentation.

Here is an information sheet containing the sequential steps to creating a presentation using Google Slides. Please hand this out to students:

## TEN STEPS TO CREATING A TERRIFIC PRESENTATION

1. Open a new browser window and go to *slides.google.com*.
2. Open a "blank" slide presentation. You now have a blank *title slide*.

3. Choose an attractive *theme* (on right side). You now have an *interesting* title slide.
4. Where the title slide says "Click to add title," write the title of your presentation (be sure to mention the career you are discussing). Where it says "Click to add subtitle," write your name. Add an informational photo.
5. Find the *plus sign* (on the top left). Next to the *plus sign* is a small *down arrow*. Click on the down arrow and find the *layout* labeled "Title and two columns" (a good choice for this project). Click on it, and a new slide will appear. Do this a total of four times. You now have a total of *five slides* (one title slide and four information slides).
6. Each information slide has a central topic. Write this topic where it says "Click to add title." Do this on all four information slides.
7. Your information slides all have two columns (or boxes). In one column (right or left), write down *three examples* of the slide's topic (present these in a *bulleted list*). You will discuss each example separately.
8. In the remaining (empty) column, paste a photo (or illustration) related to the slide's topic.
9. When your presentation is complete, be sure to edit for meaning and aesthetic appeal. Alter elements such as wording, placement of photographs, and font (style, size, color).
10. Click on "Transition" (top, center). Then, select an interesting transition effect (on the right) as you cycle from one slide to another. Next, click on "Apply to all slides" (under the transition menu). This is a terrific finishing touch, and it will make your presentation look very professional.

## HOW TO USE YOUR NEW SLIDES

When students present a slide to the class, they will spend about *one minute* talking about it. They won't stare at the slide, or read from it. The slide is a guide for the speaker and a visual aid for the audience. When the speaker transitions to a new slide, the speaker will glance at the slide and introduce the topic to the class. Next, the speaker will glance at each individual bullet point and then turn to the class and talk about them in *natural, conversational language*.

Finally, the student will speak about the photo (or illustration) contained on the slide. Photos and illustrations are terrific visual aids and will help the audience to understand and envision the subject being discussed. During this segment, the speaker will draw the students' attention to the photo and discuss it with a mixture of summary and commentary. First, students will describe the photo. *What is it a picture of?* Next, students will discuss the photo in relation to the slide's main topic. *What can we learn from this photo? How does it shed light on the career being discussed?*

## TIME FOR AN EXAMPLE

In figure 16.1, you will find an exemplar slide, created especially for this book. This would be the *second slide* for a presentation on a career as a New York City firefighter. It contains information for the *first subtopic* of this project, which is *Three Important Aspects of this Job.* Below the slide (in italics), you will find an example of how a student-presenter might narrate it. Remember, *students will not write their entire narration*. They will write bullet points on their slides (essentially creating an outline), and they will use that information as a springboard into natural, conversational language.

> *I think everyone knows that firefighters put out fires. But did you know that they also do lots of other great things? For example, they respond to medical emergencies, such as heart attacks and serious injuries. Firefighters also help with bad car accidents. If someone is trapped in a car that has been crushed, they have this tool called the "jaws of life." It can force a car door open, and it can also cut the roof off a car. Firefighters will also respond to calls for different kinds of catastrophes. They can provide help with things like explosions, floods, and collapsed buildings.*

### Firefighters Do More Than Put Out Fires. They Also Handle:

- Medical Emergencies
- Automobile Accidents
- Disasters (such as explosions, floods, and collapsed buildings)

**Figure 16.1. Slide Example**[1]

> *If you look at this picture, you'll see a fire engine called a "pumper." It is the main fire engine used to put out fires. It contains ladders and lots of hoses. These hoses can be connected to form very long hoses. Firefighters take these long hoses into burning buildings and put the fires out. The pumper also contains a big tank of water. This is helpful for smaller emergencies, such as car fires. But no matter what firefighters do, their main goals are always helping people and saving lives.*

The slide is effectively formatted, designed, and written. The slide's topic is clearly expressed and adheres to the requirements of the first subtopic. The slide contains three examples (presented as bullet points) that explain the slide's topic very well. It contains a photograph taken by Hennelly for *The Chief* that is attractive, interesting, and related to the slide's topic.

The student's narration is also very successful. It is clear and concise and illustrates the three examples in a manner that is natural and conversational. The student's discussion of the photo also works very well and follows the summary-and-commentary paradigm. It begins the *summary* portion with a simple and literal description of the photo. It then transitions to the *commentary* portion, where it describes the "hidden" aspects of the photo, relating them to the slide's main topic. And if you read the slide out loud—and time yourself—you'll note that it takes about *one minute*, which is just right for this presentation.

Please give your students a copy of the slide, along with its narration. It will be a helpful guide for them as they compose this project. If they can absorb and practice the principles depicted here, they are on their way to becoming effective public speakers.

## THE PROJECT IN DETAIL

Now, let's take a close look at each component of this project. Hand each student a copy of *Outline 11–12.6* and encourage them to take notes directly onto it. Remind students that for each slide they will speak for about *one minute* (thus ensuring a five-minute presentation) in a natural and conversational manner. They will also discuss the *photo* embedded on each slide, relating it to the topic being discussed. Please share the following information with your students:

**1. Introduction (First Slide):** *My Ideal Career*
**(include informational photo)**

On this slide, students will write a title that includes the career they are discussing, and they will provide their full name. While this slide is presented, they will introduce themselves (we all know their names, but this is good practice) and state the career they are discussing. They will describe the career briefly, and state how they got interested in it.

**2. First Subtopic (Second Slide):** *Three Important Aspects of This Job* **(include informational photo)**

When students advance to the second slide, they will discuss three significant aspects of this career. These can be *tasks* central to the profession, *equipment* used by workers in the field, special *vehicles* unique to the job, et cetera. The purpose of this slide is to give audience members a sound understanding of the basics of this profession.

**3. Second Subtopic (Third Slide):** *Training Needed for This Career* **(include informational photo)**

In this slide, students will discuss the training and education necessary for this career. As they develop this slide, they can consider the following questions for discussion: *Does this profession require a college degree? Does it require a graduate degree? Is a written examination necessary to "get on" the job? Does it require vocational training? Is some sort of "academy" required? Do employees need to complete an internship of some sort? Is a license or certificate required to work in this field?*

**4. Third Subtopic (Fourth Slide):** *A Day in the Life at This Career* **(include informational photo)**

Here, students will essentially take their classmates through "a day in the life" working in this career. They will describe the profession's everyday tasks, along with some of its more exotic elements. They will also describe some characteristics of this job. *Is it dangerous? Fun? Exciting? Interesting? Lucrative? Challenging? What is the starting salary? What is the potential salary?* Et cetera.

## 5. Conclusion (Fifth Slide): *This Is a Fantastic Career* (include interesting photo)

Students will begin with an optimistic description of their three favorite things about this career. Next, they will tell the class in very human terms why this career interests them (possibly relating a brief anecdote). Finally, they will conclude their presentations by saying, "Thank you for listening. Are there any questions?" This is very important; it conveys a clear signal that the talk is finished. The speaker will call on the students with raised hands and answer their questions. After all, the speakers are newly minted experts in this field.

## START WRITING

When the students understand the structure and flow of this project, it's time to start writing the *content* that will populate the slides. As students do this, they will be guided by *Outline 11–12.6*, and they will draw their information from their previous two writing projects.

The *Outline* is quite detailed and directive, and it exemplifies lessons on structure and organization. However (you'll tell students), the *Outline* is a guide, not a commander. As students compose this project, encourage them to exercise *choice* and *creativity*, treating the *Outline* as a map to be interpreted, not an authority to be obeyed. If you revisit the exemplar slide above and its sample narration, you'll note that they embraced the *spirit* of the *Outline* rather than the "letter" of the *Outline*.

When students are ready to start composing the content of their slides, instruct them to begin by *writing onto a Google Doc*. They will write this in the form of an outline, and it will closely follow the structure, organization, and content suggested by *Outline 11–12.6*. When complete, these outlines will contain (on one or two pages) the complete text of the students' slide presentations. This will enable students to view their budding presentations in their entirety, helping to ensure unity and prevent unnecessary repetition. Encourage students to keep each item brief. Each line represents an idea to be discussed, not a text to be read.

When students complete writing the content of their presentations, they will carefully paste each item onto their Google Slides. When this is complete, instruct students to read through the presentation several times, editing to improve meaning, accuracy, and visual appeal. When students are finished editing, they will be the authors of a terrific presentation and the owners of a sprightly sense of pride.

## A JOB WELL DONE

As you guide your students through this project, be cognizant and empathetic about their feelings toward public speaking, because some of them will have a tough time with this. While teaching the academic aspects of writing and creation, also teach your students how to *prepare* for public speaking. The most important mode of preparation is *practice*.

Tell them to rehearse their entire presentations *at least five times*, from start to finish, with no interruptions—and to *time* themselves. They can practice in front of a computer and (one hopes) in front of a mirror as well. Even better, they can practice in front of other (sympathetic) people who can alert them to unconscious verbal tics and awkward habits. This is extremely important, and their confidence will increase in proportion to how much they practice.

And this concludes our trio of projects on interesting careers. We've taken our students on quite a journey. We moved from a research paper to a creative assignment to an oral presentation. Along the way, we delivered valuable real-world lessons on interesting careers and public speaking. These projects contain a great deal of valuable learning for our students. They also embody the power of writing to leap off the page, into the real world and into the lives and minds of others—which is how all good writing should work.

Eleventh and Twelfth Grade, Sixth Writing Project: *Outline 11–12.6*
The Informative Oral Presentation: "My Ideal Career" (Part Three)
Name_____ Date_____
Title _____

Mention the career and say something optimistic about it.

1. Introduction (First Slide): *My Ideal Career* (include informational photo)
   a. Introduce yourself (your name will be on the slide).
   b. State the career and describe it briefly. Discuss the photo (summary and commentary).
   c. How did you get interested in this career? (Talk to the class extemporaneously.)

2. First Subtopic (Second Slide): *Three Important Aspects of This Job* (include informational photo)
   a. Describe some of the main tasks of this career.
   b. Describe some of the equipment or vehicles (etc.) used in this career.
   c. Discuss the photo (summary and commentary) and relate it to the slide's topic.

3. Second Subtopic (Third Slide): *Training Needed for This Career* (include informational photo)
   a. Is a college (or graduate) degree necessary for this career? Discuss this topic.
   b. Does this require an academy or vocational school (etc.)? Describe the training.
   c. Discuss the photo (summary and commentary) and relate it to the slide's topic.

4. Third Subtopic (Fourth Slide): *A Day in the Life in This Career* (include informational photo)
   a. Discuss some of this career's daily tasks and some of its "unusual" activities.
   b. Is this career *dangerous? Fun? Exciting? Interesting? Lucrative?* Why? How?
   c. Discuss the photo (summary and commentary) and relate it to the slide's topic.

5. Conclusion (Fifth Slide): *This Is a Fantastic Career* (include informational photo)
   a. Describe your three favorite parts of this career. Also discuss the photo (summary and commentary).
   b. Why do you want this career? (Talk to the class extemporaneously.)
   c. "Thank you for listening. Are there any questions?"

*This page is permitted to copy.*

*Chapter 17*

# Grades Eleven and Twelve: Seventh Writing Project

## *The Informative Research Project:* "The History behind *The Crucible*" (Part One)

Main Standard 11–12.7:

Conduct short as well as more sustained research projects to answer a question (including a self-generated question) or solve a problem; narrow or broaden the inquiry when appropriate; synthesize multiple sources on the subject, demonstrating understanding of the subject under investigation.

*Author's Notes: This is a prereading project in which students will perform historical research in preparation for reading Arthur Miller's play* The Crucible. *Alternate topics include performing research on such plays as* Death of a Salesman *(Arthur Miller),* Fences *(August Wilson), and* A Raisin in the Sun *(Lorraine Hansberry). Students will write this in the third person. There are no sub-standards here.*

### THREE VERY DIFFERENT PROJECTS

This current standard is the first in a group of three standards called "Research to Build and Present Knowledge." This means that *research* will be a primary focus of the next three projects—but it won't be the only one. We are going to bundle the next three standards together and have our students write three different papers on Arthur Miller's marvelous play *The Crucible*. Please understand that these three papers do not represent three successive drafts of one final shining masterwork. They will be three individual products that utilize *The Crucible* as a vehicle to provide a learning experience that will be effective, engaging, and remarkably complete.

If we look at this current standard, we can see that it is rooted in *inquiry*. The students will gather research in order to answer the following question: *What are the underlying historical forces that shaped Arthur Miller's play* The Crucible? By understanding the history hidden behind the play, students will gain a knowledge of important historical events and will better understand the play and its deep meanings.

In this project, we are going to do something quite unusual. As we teach our students how to perform research, we are going to look ahead to Standard Eight and *import its requirements into this current project*. Standard Eight asks students to gather high-quality sources of information and to use them skillfully in a research paper. This fits in beautifully with the spirit of this current standard, so that's what we're going to do here.

## THE VISIBLE AND THE INVISIBLE

As stated earlier, this is a prereading project that will prepare students to read *The Crucible*, a highly significant play by Arthur Miller (1915–2005). And why *The Crucible*? This play was chosen for a number of reasons, but—to put it simply—it's a great play (deservedly winning the Tony Award in 1953; "Winners"). High school students understand the play and enjoy reading it, and they grasp intuitively its themes of rumors, accusations, and dominance hierarchy. Taught well, it's always a hit in high school classrooms.

*The Crucible* can certainly be read (and viewed) without any preparation, imparting a wonderfully eldritch atmosphere to autumn classrooms. However, it is also exquisitely (and quietly) informed by several important chapters in American history. It contains two major historical threads—one *visible*, the other *invisible*—and these must be understood if we (and our students) are to learn all the lessons this play has to offer.

The *visible* history in the play is the (largely true) story of the Salem Witch Trials (Massachusetts, 1692) and the social epidemic of hysteria that surrounded the trials. It is a complex story, and it offers us lessons in human psychology, groupthink, and the danger of rampant rumors. Under this visible layer of history is the simmering cauldron of the *Cold War* and the resulting epidemic of hysteria that resulted in *McCarthyism*. Indeed, *The Crucible* is an allegory for McCarthyism, and students must understand this if they are to truly understand the play and pluck all the ripe fruits of knowledge and wisdom that it has to offer.

The three subtopics of this research paper will therefore focus on the *Salem Witch Trials*, the *Cold War*, and *McCarthyism*. Here is a brief outline of this project:

1. Introduction
2. First Subtopic: *The Salem Witch Trials*
3. Second Subtopic: *The Cold War*
4. Third Subtopic: *McCarthyism*
5. Conclusion

## INTRODUCE THE PROJECT

As you introduce this project to students, tell them that they are about to read a terrific play. It is extremely entertaining, but it also teaches viewers important lessons from history. Tell them also that in order to *understand* this play, they need to learn about *three major historical themes* that run throughout it. Next, give your students brief "teasers" of these themes, which will provide them with historical orientation:

1. *The Salem Witch Trials* (1692): In Salem, Massachusetts, many people were accused of practicing witchcraft. Before the deadly ordeal ended, a total of twenty people (male and female) had been executed.
2. *The Cold War* (1947–1991): After World War II, the United States and the USSR waged a *war of ideas* that can loosely be described as *capitalism* versus *communism*. It resulted in many large and unpleasant events (including several wars) that changed human history.
3. *McCarthyism* (1950–1954): When a fear of communism spread throughout America, Senator Joseph McCarthy began accusing prominent Americans (such as Arthur Miller) of being communist. In doing this, he severely damaged the lives of many American citizens.

When students understand these basics, explain that the dramatized story of the *Salem Witch Trials* also tells the (allegorical) story of *McCarthyism*. In many respects, these two historical events are very similar.

## LET'S GET STARTED

When the students understand the play's deep connection to history—and the pedagogical *purpose* of this project—it's time to begin the research process. First, tell them that all of their research will be on the *databases*.

The databases remain the students' *best resource* for locating academic research, and they are also a very effective *real-world* approach to conducting academic research. The universities and colleges your students attend will provide databases to students, which renders this project an effective (and realistic) gateway into writing and research for college.

As you teach the databases, be very clear in your expectations and give students simple, tangible goals. It is extremely important that students understand the task and what you expect them to do. Stress that this is a *research* project and that they are going to research three topics: *the Salem Witch Trials, the Cold War, McCarthyism*. Their goal is to find *one article on each topic*, for a total of three articles (students can also find additional articles if necessary). This is a simple, doable, and effective mode of research.

And how will the students learn to use the databases? *You will teach them.* Begin this process by giving your classes a large-screen demonstration. As you do this, keep your explanations simple and direct, and be sure to teach the following ten items:

1. Databases are places to acquire research sources, in the form of brief articles.
2. For this project, students will do *all* of their research on the databases.
3. How to locate and access the databases (provide all necessary passwords. Remember that databases may be accessible through the school library or may be available through the local public library).
4. *Types* of databases. Databases tend to be categorized (and organized) by subject, such as *science, math, literature, art, controversial issues, encyclopedias*, et cetera.
5. How to perform searches on individual databases. (As you demonstrate this, keep it realistic and relevant, and perform research on the *Salem Witch Trials, the Cold War,* and *McCarthyism*. Review Boolean limiters, using quotation marks, such as "salem witch trials" and "cold war.")
6. For this project, strongly suggest that students use the *encyclopedia databases*.
7. How to choose relevant articles from among their hits (look closely at the titles and read the summary or abstract *carefully*).
8. How to *read* relevant articles. Students will search for the information contained on *Outline 11–12.7*. They can also explore *related links* embedded in the articles.
9. How to print articles out (to be annotated later) or how students can *email* articles to themselves.
10. How to locate the article's (premade) bibliographic entry, which is often indicated by a button labeled "*Cite*" (students can simply copy the entry

and then paste it into their bibliographies; MLA style is always a good choice here).

When you finish demonstrating the databases, give all students a copy of *Outline 11–12.7* and go over each component of the assignment. When students understand the project and its requirements, get them on computers (perhaps in your school's computer lab or library or with portable devices on their desks). When they are ready, walk them through the process of accessing and using databases, and give them time to explore and ask questions. The databases are fairly simple to use, but their capabilities are myriad, and learning them takes time and practice.

## WHAT KIND OF PAPER IS THIS?

As students begin finding and reading their research, make sure they understand the essential nature of this writing assignment and what is expected of them. This project (you'll tell them) is a bit different from the others we've done. It is an *informative* research project, designed to impart factual information to readers. (In actuality, it is a *prereading* project intended to impart knowledge to the *writers*.) Although it embodies a *just-the-facts* approach, the conclusion will contain elements of *reflection* (more on that later).

For each of the three subtopics, students will write approximately one-to-two pages. To do this, they will read each article, flagging important passages for later transcription onto electronic documents. Review with students the three ways to use research:

- *Direct Quotation:* Students will quote sentences verbatim from sources, placing these in quotation marks and supplying in-text citations.
- *Paraphrase:* Students will translate quotations into their own words, substantially altering the linguistic structure and style of the quotes. These will be about the same length as the original. These will require in-text citations.
- *Summary:* Students will convert long sections of research into shorter sections. For example, students may condense an entire page into a single paragraph (or even a single sentence). Summaries require in-text citations.

As you review the ways to use research, tell students they can use all three techniques, but *their subtopics should be composed mostly of summaries.* This is a new type of writing, and you must teach it to students. In previous writing assignments, we taught students the five-step process to using research: (1) *introduce the quote*; (2) *provide the quote*; (3) *include the in-text citation*; (4) *explain the quote*; and (5) *comment on the quote*. We will *not* be doing that here, because the informative writing in this assignment requires a different approach.

This current writing assignment is not persuasive, interpretive, or personal. It is *informational* in nature, which means that students will provide information without evaluating or interpreting it. This is an important form of writing, and it should be done artfully and with skill. This process will begin with students reading their articles and (with the help of the *Outline*) flagging the salient portions to include in their projects. After that, students will begin composing their narratives onto an electronic document. But, what exactly will they do?

As stated earlier, each subtopic will be composed mostly of a *summary* (in students' own words) drawn largely from a single article. As students write, they will compress large chunks of information into shorter narratives that are dense, meaningful, and clearly written. This is more challenging than it sounds, and it takes practice. Students must write simply and economically for the goal of imparting basic information to readers. It is essentially a three-step process, and it looks like this:

1. Provide a summary of the ideas in the article (in their own words).
2. *Explain* the ideas drawn from the article (this is recommended, but may not be necessary).
3. Provide an in-text citation. If *one* article is being summarized, students will provide *one* in-text citation, at the end of the summary. If the articles have page numbers (which is not likely on the databases), the students will include multiple in-text citations that include page numbers.

When students complete their summaries, encourage them to revise and edit. As they do this, they must pay attention to clarity, organization, and readability, and they must consider the following: *Is it clearly written? Does it make sense? Is it accurate? Does it flow smoothly from one idea to another? Does it require transitional sentences? Does it feel unified? Is there anything in there that can be deleted or shortened? Do the words and style differ significantly from the original?* (Because they *should*.) *Does it say what the student wants it to say?*

This project will provide very valuable learning to students. It will teach them how to present information clearly and succinctly and will prepare them for the experience of reading (and understanding) *The Crucible*. Below, you will find samples of how these summaries might look. These are original to this book, created from articles in encyclopedia databases. Feel free to share them with students as brief exemplars:

### The Salem Witch Trials

The Salem witchcraft trials took place in 1692, in Salem, Massachusetts, a place where residents believed deeply in the reality of witches and witchcraft. The witchcraft panic began when several girls in the village began to act strangely. They became ill, had fits, and claimed to see ghosts and witches. The doctor who examined them concluded that the illness was supernatural in nature. Allegations of witchcraft began to spread, and people began accusing their neighbors of being witches.

As a result, the colonial government commenced the Salem Witch Trials. This deadly ordeal lasted about a year, until the citizens turned against it and the colony's leading ministers helped stop it. In 1693, the trials ended. Nonetheless, it left twenty people dead. Fourteen women and five men had been executed, and one man had been tortured to death (Morris).

### The Cold War

The "Cold War" (1947–1991) is the conflict that developed between the United States and the Soviet Union (and their allies) after World War II. It was not waged with bullets and bombs, but with ideas and propaganda. The Soviets wanted to spread communism throughout the world, and the United States wanted to prevent communism from spreading. This ideological conflict sparked events such as the Cuban Missile Crisis (1962) and the Vietnam War (1964–1975).

The Cold War continued through the 1970s and 1980s, when both sides increased their military power. In the late 1980s, the Cold War began to deescalate. Soviet leader Mikhail Gorbachev began to "reform" the Soviet Union, which eventually weakened the Soviet Communist Party. In 1991, the Soviet Union collapsed and was replaced by a new Russia that had a democratically elected leader who was opposed to communism. This marked the end of the Cold War (*Britannica School*, "Cold War").

### McCarthyism

"McCarthyism" (1950–1954) is a term for widespread accusations of communism in the United States during the Cold War. The word came from the name of Senator *Joseph R. McCarthy*, who made many charges that certain prominent people were secret communists. It began in 1950, when

McCarthy claimed that communists had infiltrated the government. He also blamed many of the nation's problems on the secret presence of Communists in America.

The resulting accusations and investigations spread quickly and damaged many people. For example, "Librarians, college professors, entertainers, journalists, clergy, and others came under suspicion. Some firms *blacklisted* (refused to hire) people accused of Communist associations." McCarthyism gradually declined after 1954, when McCarthy was condemned by the Senate for conduct unbecoming a senator (Reeves).

As a reaction to the Cold War hysteria he witnessed, Arthur Miller wrote *The Crucible* (1953). He chose the Salem Witch Trials as his subject, because they represented "a series of persecutions that he considered an echo of the McCarthyism of his day, when investigations of alleged subversive activities were widespread." In 1956, Miller himself was accused of being a communist and was called to testify before the House Un-American Activities Committee. There, "he refused to name people he had seen 10 years earlier at an alleged communist writers' meeting. He was convicted of contempt but appealed and won" (*Britannica School*, "Arthur Miller"). Whereas *The Crucible* is a clear case of *art imitating life*, Miller's accusation and conviction is a highly ironic case of *life imitating art*.

## A CLOSER LOOK AT THIS PROJECT

If you look at *Outline 11–12.7*, you'll see that this project is carefully choreographed. It has been designed to prepare students for reading *The Crucible* and to understand the historical circumstances percolating through this great play. As students begin composing their projects, tell them to stick closely to the organization and ideas contained in the *Outline*. However, tell them to regard the *Outline* as an informed guide rather than an absolute monarch, and encourage them to exercise *choice* in their compositions. The *Outline* is like a map through a landscape of learning—students should understand its features but should choose their own journeys. Here is the assignment in detail; please share it with students.

### Introduction: Overview and background

Students will introduce this project simply and truthfully as preparation for reading the *Crucible*. Next, they will provide a brief overview of Arthur Miller's life (a few sentences describing his birth, career, and passing will suffice (students can get this information from the *biography* databases).

Students will conclude this section by mentioning the three subtopics they will discuss.

## 2. First Subtopic: *Salem Witch Trials*

Students will begin with a brief overview of the Salem Witch Trials. Next, they will describe the Trials in some detail. *Where did they take place? How did they start? Who were the major players involved? What occurred during the trials?* Help the reader to understand these bizarre events. After that, students will discuss the aftermath of the trials, describing the victims and their demise. They will conclude this section by describing how this deadly chapter in American history ended.

## 3. Second Subtopic: *The Cold War*

Students will begin with a brief overview of the Cold War (this overview must include references to the United States and the Soviet Union and possibly also to capitalism and communism). Students will discuss some of the major events of the Cold War, such as the *Korean War, Cuban Missile Crisis, Berlin Wall, Space Race, War in Vietnam, major players in the Cold War*, et cetera. They will conclude this section by discussing the conclusion of the Cold War. *How did it end? What historical figures were instrumental in ending the Cold War?*

## 4. Third Subtopic: *McCarthyism*

Students will begin this section with a biographical overview of Senator Joseph McCarthy. *When was he born? What did he do? When did he die?* They will then transition to a brief discussion of *McCarthyism* that demonstrates clarity and basic understanding of this topic. *What is McCarthyism? When (and how) did it begin? When (and how) did it end?* Students will conclude this section by briefly discussing Arthur Miller's accusation (and conviction) of being a communist.

## 5. Conclusion: Summary and reflection

This section is the only part of this project that requires some reflective interpretation. Here, students will reflect on the three subtopics discussed above. For each, they will provide a brief description of the topic, and they will reflect on the lessons that can be learned from each (perhaps relating them to human nature). For example, the *Salem Witch Trials* can teach us that ideas (good and bad) are contagious and that human beings can be swept into a mindless herd mentality. From the *Cold War*, we can learn to focus on the things that *unite* human beings rather than the things that separate us. From *McCarthyism*, we can learn that baseless accusations can be very dangerous—and can take on a mind of their own and a sweeping, dangerous momentum.

## WE ARE READY TO READ A MASTERPIECE

This project is very important in the writing program articulated in this book. It is a remarkably *complete* learning experience, bestowing on our students a deceptively large breadth of academic gifts. We taught our students how to perform historical research in the databases and how to use their sources to compose an *informative essay* that contains elements of reflection. We also introduced our students to several important (and intriguing) periods in world history. Knowledge of these is extremely important in our students' development as writers, and it will do much to prepare them for the rigors of writing and research in college.

However, the most exciting component of this project is its prereading relation to *The Crucible*. This composition has prepared our students to approach, understand, and enjoy one of America's greatest plays. Try to teach it in October, and be sure to read the whole thing out loud, right there in the classroom, with your students taking parts. And remember to turn the lights out, because your students—and *you*—are about to fall under the spell of a literary masterpiece.

Eleventh and Twelfth Grade, Seventh Writing Project: *Outline 11–12.7*
The Informative Research Project: "The History behind *The Crucible*"
Name_____ Date_____
Title _____

Mention *The Crucible* and its author; also mention the historical nature of this project.

1. Introduction (can be more than one paragraph; write this last)
   a. Introduce this project as preparation for reading the play the *Crucible*.
   b. Provide a quick overview of Arthur Miller's life (brief biography).
   c. Provide a brief overview of the three subtopics you will discuss.

2. First Subtopic: *Salem Witch Trials*
   a. What were the Salem Witch Trials? (provide a brief overview)
   b. When, where, and how did the trials start? (etc.)
   c. How many "witches" were executed? What finally ended the trials? (etc.)

3. Second Subtopic: *The Cold War*
   a. What is the Cold War? (provide a brief overview; mention the USA and USSR)
   b. Discuss Cold War events such as the *Cuban Missile Crisis*, *Berlin Wall*, et cetera.
   c. When and how did it end? (discuss the end of the Cold War)

4. Third Subtopic: *McCarthyism*
   a. Who was Senator Joseph McCarthy? (brief biography)
   b. What is *McCarthyism*?
   c. Discuss Arthur Miller's accusation of being communist.

5. Conclusion: Summary and Reflection
   a. What lessons can we learn from the Salem Witch Trials?
   b. What lessons can we learn from the Cold War?
   c. What lessons can we learn from McCarthyism?

*This page is permitted to copy.*

*Chapter 18*

# Grades Eleven and Twelve: Eighth Writing Project

## *Literary Analysis:* "Interpreting *The Crucible*" (Part Two)

Main Standard 11–12.8:

Gather relevant information from multiple authoritative print and digital sources, using advanced searches effectively; assess the strengths and limitations of each source in terms of the task, purpose, and audience; integrate information into the text selectively to maintain the flow of ideas, avoiding plagiarism and overreliance on any one source and following a standard format for citation.

*Author's Notes: After reading* The Crucible *closely and carefully, students will perform literary analysis on characters, events, and plot structure. Students will write this in the third person; there are no sub-standards here.*

### ORIGINAL LITERARY ANALYSIS

This is the second project in a trio of assignments on Arthur Miller's play *The Crucible*. The previous assignment was a prereading project in which students performed research on three major historical themes running throughout this great play: the *Salem Witch Trials*, the *Cold War*, and *McCarthyism*. Having done that, they are now ready to read this play with understanding and enjoyment.

A quick look at the standard above reveals that it is rooted in performing and utilizing *research*. However, you will recall that we imported these requirements into the previous project, where they helped teach our students the basics of research and informative writing. In this current project, we will interpret Standard Eight (embracing its spirit of research) and offer our students a terrific assignment that grows naturally from the previous project and builds on the knowledge gained there.

Rather than performing research on outside (secondary) research sources, our students will treat *The Crucible* as a *primary source* literary document and will perform "research" within the pages of the text. With our guidance and assistance, students will compose original *literary analyses*, unlocking and revealing the deep secrets this play has to offer.

As you teach this project, remember that your students are budding scholars and that we're still introducing them to the process of literary analysis. This is very challenging for young students, so we're going to keep it simple and give our students lots of structure. The literary analysis in this project will be *evaluative* in nature, and we are going to ask students to make judgments in order to determine *the most important elements in this play*. As students compose their analyses of various dramatic elements, they will follow (once again) the paradigm of *description* followed by *analysis* (often described as *summary and commentary*).

As you explain this to students, emphasize that there are no definitively right or wrong answers here. The goal is for students to decide upon important elements and then present and analyze their choices logically and clearly (thus *process* will be more important than *product*). In the three subtopics, students' analyses will focus on *character*, *action*, and *plot structure*. Here is a brief outline of this project:

1. Introduction
2. First Subtopic: *The Most Important Character in This Play*
3. Second Subtopic: *The Most Important Scene in This Play*
4. Third Subtopic: *The Most Important Grail in This Play* (there are several)
5. Conclusion

## DRAMATIC CONTEXT AND THEATRICAL ELEMENTS

Now that students understand the historical background of this play, explain its dramatic and social context. In 1692, Salem (Massachusetts) was a vibrant town populated by a strict religious sect (called *Puritans* [Gomez-Galisteo]) who were governed by a very severe *theocracy* (Miller 146). And what is a theocracy? Explain to your students that it is a form of government that combines the prevailing religious institution (the "church") with the established legal institution. These two institutions formed a monolithic establishment that cast a large shadow over the daily lives of Salem citizens. It expected strict compliance in matters legal *and* religious, and it often perceived no difference between the two.

When your students understand the religious and legal background of this play, it's time to begin the rapturous experience of *reading* it. Read *the entire play* out loud in class, with your students (and you) playing verbal roles. Encourage them to "ham it up" and to inject mannerisms and character into their voices, because this play is great fun. The characters are lively and authentic, the dialogue is marvelous, and it's filled with moments of humor as well as tension. It's a terrific play for this age group.

Also, be sure to teach your students *how to read a play*. In many respects, reading a play is like reading a novel or a short story. It is supported by two enormous load-bearing pillars: *character* and *plot*. In this project, our students will be examining (and analyzing) both of these very deeply. As you discuss the process of literary analysis, remind your students that every work of literature (if it is to be called *literature*) functions on two levels: the *visible* and the *invisible*.

The *visible* layer is the story taking place. It is the tale being told; it's what we read and see and hear and enjoy. The *invisible* layer is the deeper meaning we find in the text through the process of analysis. *What messages does the author wish to convey? What ideas and themes are being examined? What lessons can we learn from the text? What is this text* really *about?* Both of these—the *visible* and the *invisible*—are important, and they are the two major components of all literary analysis (*What is happening?* and *What does it mean?*). They are also the main focus of this project.

And now, hand each student a copy of *Outline 11–12.8*, because we're going to take a close look at each component of this project.

## 1. Introduction: *Inform readers that you will discuss the following* (write this last)

Here, students will provide an overview of this writing assignment. They will inform readers that they will be discussing the most important character, scene, and grail in *The Crucible*. This will be at least one paragraph long. As always, students will write this last.

## 2. First Subtopic: *The Most Important Character in This Play*

As students choose characters to analyze, tell them that literary characters (like real human beings) reveal themselves through what they *say* and what they *do* (therefore we must closely examine their *words* and *actions*). Characters are also revealed (to a lesser extent) through what *other characters say about* them. (However, we can only accept these secondhand revelations when *we trust the character who is speaking*.) Just like real people, dramatic characters sometimes speak the truth, and they sometimes lie—often for personal gain (a transaction seen repeatedly in *The Crucible*).

Miller was a dramatic genius, and he was a master of the rule "Show, Don't Tell." The characters' words *tell* us something. However—and often more important—they also *show* us something about the characters. What (and *how*) do their words *show* us? Instruct your students to read their chosen character's lines closely and critically. To do this, they should ask themselves questions, such as these: *What do these lines suggest about the character? Is this character lying or telling the truth? Does this character have some sort of agenda, such as power, revenge, or personal gain? Is this character interested in helping others, or is this character motivated by selfish interests? In general, is this character good, evil, or somewhere in between? Does this character grow, evolve, or change throughout the narrative? If so, is it for better or worse?* Et cetera.

Now, let's talk about how students will compose the first subtopic. If you look at *Outline 11–12.8*, you'll see that students are required to do three things: *name and describe the character, provide the character's most important line(s), describe what the dialogue reveals about the character.* Here is a model response to share with students:

> The most important character in this play is Giles Corey. Although not the "star" of the play, he leaps off the pages (and into our hearts) because of his innate humor and his deep humanity. He is eighty-three years old and still quite physically powerful (25). A perennial favorite among theater-goers, he is the comedic center of this play, and his lines never fail to evoke laughter, as well as pathos.
>
> As the play opens, Miller places us in the home of Reverend Parris. There, we find Betty (Parris's ten-year-old daughter) very sick and lying inert in bed (3). Various characters enter to speak with Parris, including Rebecca Nurse (the play's moral center) and (shortly after) Giles Corey. When Rebecca sees Giles enter, the two have the following delightful exchange (25):
>
> REBECCA: There is hard sickness here, Giles Corey, so please to keep the quiet.
>
> GILES: I've not said a word. No one here can testify I've said a word. Is she going to fly again? I hear she flies.
>
> Rebecca knows Giles well and quickly alerts us to his talkative nature. Hearing that, Giles denies it and then immediately *confirms* it by jabbering a wild rumor he heard about Betty flying through the air. It's a brief exchange,

but it shows us a great deal about Giles's personality. He is colorful, lovable, and quite irritating. He is also argumentative and easily offended, and he can be rather litigious (hinted at by his use of the word "testify").

However, let's take a close look at Giles's line about Betty Parris flying. Although Giles is honest and truthful (he is not seeking earthly gain and does not wish to capitalize on the misfortune of others), he can be gullible and naive, and he loves to hear a good story—believable or not. However, Giles's most dominant personality characteristic (revealed in many of his lines) is that he simply *talks too much*. Eventually, it will cost him his life.

## 3. Second Subtopic: *The Most Important Scene in This Play*

As you introduce the second subtopic to students, explain the word *scene* to them, because (in this play) it's a bit fuzzy. The subtitle for *The Crucible* is *A Play in Four Acts*. Indeed, it is clearly broken into four large acts but lacks the smaller *scene breaks* we see in all of Shakespeare's plays. So, how shall we identify "scenes" in *The Crucible*?

In general, a scene in *The Crucible* is a brief segment of the plot in which something specific takes place. It may occur in a single setting between two people, or it may be a clearly defined *event* that involves a group of people. In well-constructed plays, all scenes serve three essential purposes: *they advance the plot, they shed light on the themes being explored*, and *they reveal character*. If you look at *Outline 11–12.8*, you'll see that the second subtopic requires students to do three things: *choose and describe the most important scene in the play, analyze its importance*, and *discuss what it reveals about the characters in it*.

As students begin this component, tell them to think about the story and see if they can remember a *turning point*—a place where something changed the trajectory of the story or changed the circumstances (or life) of an important character. This is challenging, so tell them to look at the *closings* of all four acts. (When Miller closes an act, something very important usually happens.) Tell them also to look closely at the scenes occurring in *Act Three*—it is a masterwork of dramatic composition.

In Act Three, we find crucial events, such as John Proctor publicly confessing to adultery; Elizabeth Proctor unwittingly denying John's confession; Mary Warren confessing to lying—and then *reversing* her confession (after the girls accuse *her* of witchcraft); and Mary Warren accusing John Proctor of practicing witchcraft (which results in Proctor getting arrested). Each one of these scenes alters the trajectory of the plot—and the characters' lives—and reveals something about the characters involved. Here is a model response. Note the elements of *description* and *analysis*, and please share it with students:

The most important scene in *The Crucible* is John Proctor's courtroom confession of committing adultery with Abigail. When Mary Warren admitted that she and the other girls were lying about seeing supernatural visions, the girls (led by Abigail) responded by accusing Mary of bewitching *them*. To discredit Abigail, Proctor admits to committing adultery with her—which Abigail strongly denies.

In the following courtroom examination, Elizabeth Proctor (unaware of John's confession) states that John did *not* commit adultery. In the eyes of the court, this immediately establishes John as a liar and elevates Abigail's position as a purveyor of truth and goodness. Buoyed by their success, the girls continue accusing Mary Warren of practicing witchcraft, until Mary saves herself by accusing Proctor of being "the Devil's man" (118).

This scene is extremely important in several respects. First, it represents a public destruction of Proctor's integrity and reliability and leads directly to his arrest, imprisonment, and execution. It's also significant because it elevates the girls' status and veracity in the eyes of the court. Because of their convincing theatrics, the girls have become compelling links between the natural and supernatural worlds, and they have gained great social and legal power.

This scene also reveals a great deal about all the characters involved, stripping away false veneers and revealing the truth of their souls and motivations. For example, Proctor's confession demonstrates his courage and unselfishness. He sacrifices his reputation in order to discredit Abigail and to save others. The falsehood told by Elizabeth demonstrates courage on her part and the great love (and forgiveness) she feels for Proctor.

Mary Warren's confession establishes her as a dramatic foil to Proctor. By reversing her confession and accusing Proctor of witchcraft, she emerges as a liar and a coward who is willing to sacrifice others in order to save herself. Similarly, the girls' continued lies and accusations firmly establish them as evil and selfish. They seek only to protect themselves and to wield their newfound power and remain unaffected by the lives they destroy and the deaths they cause.

## 4. Third Subtopic: *The Most Important Grail in This Play* (there are several)

In previous chapters of this book, we have discussed plot structure in terms of the One-Story approach (containing the elements *grail*, *conflict*, and *resolution*). In this subtopic, the students must identify the most important grail in the story (there are several, because different characters have different motivations) and then discuss why they chose it. This will require students to look very closely at the text and to develop (and exhibit) a deep understanding of the play's plot structure and characters.

As you teach this subtopic to your students, explain that *The Crucible* follows the One-Story approach but does so with complexity and nuance. This is challenging stuff, so let's give our students structure and organization as they approach this subtopic. First, explain that there are three "worlds" in *The*

*Crucible*, and each world is represented by a major character. Here they are, along with their individual grails, conflicts, and resolutions:

The *Innocent Accused*, represented by John Proctor

- *Grail*: Proctor yearns for *self-redemption*.
- *Conflict*: Proctor's tormenting conscience will not allow him to forgive himself.
- *Resolution*: Proctor chooses death rather than providing a false confession.

The *Villainous Accusers*, represented by Abigail Williams

- *Grail*: Abigail wants a romantic relationship with John Proctor.
- *Conflict*: Proctor is married and deeply regrets his affair with Abigail.
- *Resolution*: Proctor is condemned to death, and Abigail absconds with Parris's money.

The *Court*, represented by Judge Danforth

- *Grail*: Danforth wants to enact earthly and divine justice.
- *Conflict*: The trial is based on falsehoods and incidents that never occurred.
- *Resolution*: Twenty innocent people are executed.

The grails pursued by those characters are crucial to the plot and shed light on the characters' true motivations and the purity (or corruption) of their hearts. To compose this subtopic, *your students will choose a grail from among those three characters*.

Now, let's talk about how students will compose the third subtopic. If you look at *Outline 11–12.8*, you'll see that students are required to do three things: *describe the grail, conflict, and resolution they have chosen*; *discuss why the grail is so important*; and *evaluate the resolution*. Here is a model response to share with students.

> In many ways, this is John Proctor's play. He is powerful and honest and quickly captivates audiences with his charisma and likability. Nonetheless, he is also deeply flawed and has committed the sin of adultery with Abigail Williams. In doing so, Proctor violates his own high standards of honesty and integrity, and he spends the entirety of the play seeking *self-redemption*. This is his grail.
>
> In his tortured quest, we are given a glimpse of Proctor's innermost heart, and there we find purity, honesty, and goodness. Proctor's search for self-redemption is the most noble of all the grails sought during the play's action. It is also the most important, because it displays to audiences the complexities of the human

heart—full of tragedy and triumph—and surely this display is the highest goal of dramatic art.

Nonetheless, this road toward redemption will not be easy for Proctor. His finely tuned conscience torments him in the privacy of his thoughts. The sight of Elizabeth (his wife) is a living reminder of the damage and pain caused by his adultery. Abigail serves as a living, strutting symbol of his scarlet sin. These three elements combine to represent the formidable conflict that John must overcome if he is to ever forgive himself and restore his self-respect.

Eventually, John does achieve some measure of redemption. Toward the end of the play, he seeks to save his life by providing the court with a false confession. Nonetheless, he quickly recants his confession and tears the document to pieces. In doing this, Proctor willingly accepts *death* rather than providing the court with the falsehood it demanded. It is a bittersweet resolution to his journey. Through this act of scorching honesty, Proctor has voluntarily chosen death, but has also committed an act of pure redemption. This represents (at least) a partial attainment of his grail, providing Proctor with—as he describes it—"some shred of goodness" (144).

## 5. Conclusion: *Tragedy* and *Triumph*

This conclusion will have a "grownup" feel to it, and it will be one or more paragraphs long. Rather than simply providing a summary, students will evaluate the play in terms of the tragic and triumphant elements it contains, providing answers to the following questions: *How is this play a tragedy?* and *How is this play a triumph?* As you teach this, explain to students that, on the surface, the play is clearly (and technically) a *tragedy*, because it ends with the deaths of beloved characters John Proctor and Rebecca Nurse.

Nonetheless, it also contains elements of triumph and hope. By accepting death, Proctor has achieved a degree of redemption. Miller confirms this with Elizabeth's final statement in the play (which is also the play's final line of dialogue): "He have his goodness now. God forbid I take it from him!" (145). This exercise will help students to consider *The Crucible* in its full complexity. Like the characters we meet in this play, the themes and topics it explores are full of nuance and chromatic gradients.

Students will conclude this project by discussing something it taught them about human nature. As you teach this, offer students these leading questions: *From reading this play, what did you learn about human behavior? What motivates people to act the way they do? Why are people so susceptible to rumors? Why do herd mentalities develop? How difficult is it to oppose a dominant group? What are some positive and negative traits of human nature—and which traits tend to be dominant in most people?* This will be challenging for students, so tell them to keep it simple and do their best with it.

## CAN YOU DIG IT?

Let's think for a moment about what our students have accomplished. They have learned about the historical background of *The Crucible* (the Salem Witch Trials, the basics of communism, and the specter of McCarthyism), and they have looked deeply into (and analyzed) the text of this play. These are noteworthy achievements and have provided our students with a terrific multifaceted learning experience.

However, there is one more project left in our tripartite examination of *The Crucible*, and it will be the most fun yet. This project will be *creative* in nature and will allow our students to utilize their abundant new knowledge and play with the ideas, scenes, and characters reverberating in their minds and their imaginations. They are about to dig up (literally!) undiscovered documents that shed light on the historical underpinnings of this play, along with the fascinating characters who reside in it.

Eleventh and Twelfth Grade, Eighth Writing Project: *Outline 11–12.8*
Literary Analysis: "Interpreting *The Crucible*"

Name_____ Date_____
Title _____

Mention *The Crucible* and its author; also mention the main focus of this project.

1. Introduction: *Inform readers that you will discuss the following* (write this last)
   a. The most important *character* in this play
   b. The most important *scene* in this play
   c. The most important *grail* in this play (there are several)

2. First Subtopic: *The Most Important Character in This Play*
   a. Name and describe the most important character in this play.
   b. What is (are) this character's most important line(s)?
   c. What does this line (or these lines) reveal about this character?

3. Second Subtopic: *The Most Important Scene in This Play*
   a. Describe the most important scene in this play.
   b. Why is it important? How does it substantially impact the play's plot?
   c. What does it reveal about the play's *character(s)*?

4. Third Subtopic: *The Most Important Grail in This Play* (there are several)
   a. Describe the grail, conflict, and resolution you want to discuss.
   b. Why is this grail important? What does it reveal about the character?
   c. Discuss the resolution. Is the grail attained? Is it happy or sad?

5. Conclusion: *Tragedy and Triumph*
   a. How is this play a *tragedy*? (John Proctor—and others—are hanged at the conclusion.)
   b. In what ways is this play a *triumph*? (Again, think about John Proctor.)
   c. Briefly discuss something *The Crucible* taught you about *human nature*.

*This page is permitted to copy.*

*Chapter 19*

# Grades Eleven and Twelve: Ninth Writing Project

## *The Creative Project:* "Unearthing *The Crucible"* (Part Three)

Main Standard 11–12.9:
Draw evidence from literary or informational texts to support analysis, reflection, and research.

*Author's Notes: Students will compose three reflective documents that shed light on* The Crucible *and the Salem Witch Trials. These will include a brief court transcript, a letter from Abigail to Proctor, and a letter of response from Proctor to Abigail. This will be written in the first person.*

\*Sub-Standard A:
Apply *grades 11–12 Reading standards* to literature (e.g., "Demonstrate knowledge of eighteenth-, nineteenth-, and early-twentieth-century foundational works of American literature, including how two or more texts from the same period treat similar themes or topics").

*Author's Notes: Students will compose three brief, creative texts that grow out of* The Crucible. *These will be imaginative suppositions regarding the fates of John Proctor and Abigail Williams.*

Sub-Standard B:
Apply *grades 11–12 Reading standards* to literary nonfiction (e.g., "Delineate and evaluate the reasoning in seminal U.S. texts, including the application of constitutional principles and use of legal reasoning [e.g., in U.S. Supreme Court case majority opinions and dissents] and the premises,

purposes, and arguments in works of public advocacy [e.g., *The Federalist*, presidential addresses]").

*Author's Notes: This sub-standard will not be a major focus in this project.*

## IMAGINE AN ALTERNATE VERSION

This is the final assignment in our triumvirate of projects on *The Crucible*. Our students have been working very hard, so it's time to give them a break with a project that will be fun and creative. Standard Nine calls for a project that's rooted in "analysis, reflection, and research." Our students have already performed *research* and *analysis* on *The Crucible*, so it's time to *reflect* on this play and the characters in it.

If we look at Sub-standard A, we see that it asks students to apply the *Grade 11–12 Reading* standards to their writing. If we distill the example it provides (the ninth reading standard) into simplicity, the sub-standard essentially asks for students to do this: *describe how different works of American literature discuss similar concepts*. This is a well-formulated approach to learning, but we are going to improve on it (while nonetheless adhering to the *spirit* of the standard). Rather than have students read these works of literature, we are going to have students *write* them.

In this project, students will use their knowledge and imaginations to compose fictional narratives about certain "undiscovered" events that took place during and after the events of *The Crucible*. To do this, they will reflect upon their knowledge of history, the text, and the characters. By intertwining their knowledge (historical and literary) with their imaginations, students will make imaginative inferences about the two most interesting characters in the play: *John Proctor* and *Abigail Williams*. They will compose a brief "missing scene" between the two, and they will provide first-person narratives that describe the tragic lives of Proctor and Abigail after *The Crucible* ended. In doing this, students will offer an *alternate version* of the play and of history. In a sense, they will be composing *historical fiction*.

## SETTING THE STAGE

Let's talk for a moment about the history of Proctor, Elizabeth, and Abigail after the curtain dropped like a mourning veil. In Miller's text, Abigail escaped from Salem. She robbed Parris (taking all of his money) and ran away with Mercy Lewis (126). John Proctor was executed, and (when the play concluded) Elizabeth Proctor was still alive. Remember also that Elizabeth was expecting a child, and the Proctors had several children at home.

If we read Miller's coda after the play's conclusion (146), he writes that the *historical* Elizabeth Proctor survived the witchhunt and that she "married again, four years after Proctor's death." He also writes, "Legend has it that Abigail turned up later as a prostitute in Boston." Those are the facts and suppositions, dramatically and historically speaking. Explain these to students and then explain that they are about to rewrite history.

## ANOTHER LOOK AT PROCTOR AND ABIGAIL

For this project, we are going to imagine an "alternate history" for *The Crucible* in which our students will present (and examine) the characters of Proctor and Abigail under different circumstances. *Will they change? Will they grow? Will they behave differently? What do their futures hold?* These questions are creative and speculative in nature, and there are no definitively right or wrong responses here. Here are these characters in their new situations; please share this with your students:

### John Proctor

In this alternate version, *Elizabeth Proctor is put to death, and John Proctor's life is spared* (when he provides a false confession). However, the theocratic bureaucrats and bullies remain furious at Proctor, and they punish him severely. They take his property (a lawful possibility suggested by Elizabeth's description of Giles's death on page 135), and they remove Proctor's children, giving them to families in the village. Proctor is forbidden to contact his children until they turn twenty-one, and he is forever banished from Salem. He is left with *nothing*.

Eventually, Proctor makes his way to Plymouth, Massachusetts (a distance of about sixty miles). Once there, Proctor acquires a small parcel of land and starts a modest farm. Living in solitude, he works his farm, keeps to himself, and engages with others as little as possible. He is haunted by the torments of the past—especially his affair with Abigail, the fate of Elizabeth, and the false confession he gave the court. An oppressive and inescapable sense of regret suffocates his spirit, clinging to him like a cloak of despair. He has become a living ghost.

## Abigail Williams

Abigail has moved to Boston and works as a housekeeper for a modestly successful couple who have three children. She is a competent (but unenthusiastic) housekeeper. To get hired for this job, Abigail lied about her past. No one knows about her connection to the Salem Witch Trials, and she is terrified that her true identity will one day be discovered. Other than the fear of getting caught, she has very few regrets—and very few friends.

Abigail is still deeply in love with John Proctor. She thinks of him constantly and harbors a secret fantasy that, someday, she will find him and marry him. One day, Abigail learns (purely by accident) that John is living on a small farm in Plymouth (a distance of about forty miles from Boston). She is bursting with excitement and decides that she *must* contact him, as soon as she possibly can.

### LET'S DIG A LITTLE DEEPER

We are going to frame this project very creatively and colorfully, and do something very unusual. Tell your students that they are about to become *archaeologists*. And what is an archaeologist? It's someone who studies the "ancient and recent human past through material remains" ("What Is Archaeology?"). Explain it to students like this:

> *You are an archaeologist! You are working in Salem, Massachusetts, trying to unearth artifacts and evidence about the Salem Witch Trials. To do this, you are performing archaeological digs in certain places significant to Salem in the late 1600s. Rain or shine, warm or cold, you're in the field, with dirty clothes and worn maps, and weathered shovel in hand. It is slow, difficult work, and you have not found anything significant yet.* A button. The rusted head of an axe. A cup that once held cider. *These are interesting, and all of them will find their way into the local museum. But still, you have found nothing pertaining to the Witch Trials, and you are growing discouraged.*
>
> *One afternoon in late October—it is cold and rainy—you decide to terminate the search and label it "unsuccessful." It's time to go. The last thing you pack into the car is the metal detector.* One last try wouldn't hurt, right? *You turn it on and walk through the rain, waving it over the ground and hoping to hear its alarm. Nothing. The whisper of silence and October rain. You venture over to a bit of desolate land that previous archaeologists have labeled "barren." It's a rocky, lonely place, surely uninviting for early American settlers. You turn to go, and suddenly—the metal detector's alarm shrieks, and it sounds like the echo of a scream, three-hundred years ago.*
>
> *After sprinting from the car with your shovel, you begin to dig, and you hit something metallic. It is a metal strongbox buried in the earth long ago. It is*

*rusted and dirty, but still quite sound. You are jubilant to find it unlocked, and when you open the lid, your hands begin to tremble:* it contains three original documents related to the Salem Witch Trials. *You bring the box and its precious contents to the car to keep them out of the rain. You begin reading the documents (all are on parchment), and it is like a voyage into the past.* Here are the contents of the strongbox:

- A court transcript in which Abigail questions Proctor
- A letter from Abigail to Proctor
- A letter from Proctor to Abigail

These are the documents that you are going to write.

## LET'S GET STARTED

After explaining the framework of this project, hand out *Outline 11–12.9* and go over each component with your students. Here is the project in detail:

### 1. Introduction

You'll start this project by briefly describing how you discovered these documents. Next, provide an overview of each document and describe how this find sheds new light on the characters and events of *The Crucible*. Write this in the persona of an archaeologist sharing this discovery with the world. This will be several paragraphs long.

### 2. First Subtopic: *Excerpt of a Court Transcript: Abigail Asks Proctor Three Questions*

Here, we discover that Judge Danforth allowed Abigail to ask John Proctor three questions in the courtroom (these questions are contained on the *Outline*). Danforth has informed Proctor that Abigail is an official representative of the court and an anointed emissary of God. As such, any direct attacks on Abigail will be considered a work of the devil. In her new role, Abigail's private and personal goal is not to assist with the proceedings but to taunt Proctor and to discredit his wife, Elizabeth. As Abigail asks him the questions, a court reporter takes down each word spoken, also recording the (potentially revelatory) actions and body language of the speakers.

Although framed as a court transcript, students will compose this as a "missing scene" in the play. They will format this as a playwright does (shown below), providing the speaker's name, lines spoken, and the physical gestures of the characters (*in italics*). As students compose this, they should *show* us the characters' personalities through the things they say. They can also include (if appropriate) the verbal indicators of archaic speech, just as Miller did. Here is an example to share with your students:

> ABIGAIL WILLIAMS (*with a slight smirk on her face*): John—I mean, 'Mr. Proctor'—do you repent of the terrible things you have done?
>
> JOHN PROCTOR (*attempting to control his fury*): Abby—*'Miss Williams'*—I *heartily* repent of the sins I have committed, and my conscience will stab me with them for the rest of my days. (*Pause. Thinking*) I took . . . *someone* into my home . . . and then turned from my dear wife, and gave in to fleshly sin. Before this court, and before God, I willingly admit this and ring the death knell of mine honor. (*Pause. Raising his voice to a controlled shout*) But this *other person* did embrace the sin! She bears great responsibility for the unspeakable acts committed in the darkness of night! And now, *she* refuses to admit it, and seeks the ruin of others . . . including my dear wife Elizabeth. You know this to be true! (*Leaning toward Abigail and shouting*) *Don't* you, Abby! (*Glaring at Abigail and shaking with rage*)

## 3. Second Subtopic: *Letter from Abigail to John Proctor* (five years later: August 1697)

As stated above, Abigail is working as a housekeeper in Boston. When Abigail discovers that John is living in Plymouth, she writes him a letter. In this letter, Abigail describes how she escaped from Salem and informs Proctor about her current situation. She concludes the letter by telling him that she still loves him and wants to marry him (these three components are detailed on the *Outline*).

As students begin writing this letter, they must keep in mind the description of Abigail's current situation (see "Abigail Williams," above). They will include a date (it is August 1697). Students will format this subtopic in the form of a letter and will include date of composition, salutation, text, closing, and signature. They can also get creative with the letter, including lies told by Abigail (this is certainly in-character for her; the example below contains several outrageous fabrications). Students can also hand-write the letter, print it in a script font, or age the document so that it looks older. They can also include the verbal indicators of archaic speech we saw in *The Crucible*. Here is a brief example to share with your students:

*August 13, 1697*

*Dear John,*

*How I have missed you! I trust you miss me also. I do apologize for leaving Salem so quickly, without bidding you farewell. I just felt I have outgrown Salem, and I wanted to work in Boston. Mr. Parris, he plan my departure, and he give me gold for travel. It were a good man, Mr. Parris. I work as a house manager for a very good family in Boston. I have achieved a successful station in life, and I make my way in the world. I am still beautiful. There are many prominent gentlemen in the city who seek for my hand in marriage. But I love another, and I am saving myself only for him.*

*Yours forever,*
*Abigail*

Please note that the above example has been greatly compressed, for the sake of brevity. Students' letters should be quite detailed and imaginative.

## 4. Third Subtopic: *Letter from Proctor to Abigail* (nearly three months later: October 1697)

As students begin composing this subtopic, they should consult the description of John's current situation above (titled "John Proctor"). In this component, Proctor will write a letter of response to Abigail's unwelcome correspondence. After describing where he is, and what he has been doing, he will question how Abigail found him. Next, he will describe the great damage that Abigail caused to him, to others, and to the town of Salem. Proctor will conclude his letter by telling Abigail never to contact him again. Assuming that she has lied about her past, he may attach a threat to expose her role in the Salem Witch Trials.

Just as they did in the previous subtopic, students will present this in the form of a proper letter, including date, salutation, text, closing, and signature. They can again present this letter creatively, handwriting it or formatting it in a font *different from Abigail's*. They should include Proctor's character and mannerisms (he tends to be quite caustic and derisive), and they should try to include the indicators of archaic speech. Here is a brief (compressed) example to share with your students:

*October 31, 1697*

*Abigail Williams,*

*It is an unwelcome marvel that you contact me. How did you discover me? I work a small and unprosperous farm in Plymouth. I keep a quiet way and yearn for the company of no one. That you dare write me is a wonder I cannot fathom. Why do you seek my attention? I live with the torment of mine own error, yet your conscience seem to bear no burden of sin. Guilt and shame are my constant companions. But you—you seem to bear no weight for the awful sins of your past. Do you not understand what you did?*

*My mind misgive that you live in secrecy, and your employer know not of your past. Perhaps I will contact your employer and neighbors and describe your role in the Salem witch trials. I will think on this. Do not ever contact me, ever again. If you do, the results will not be in your favor.*

*May God have mercy on you.*

*Mr. John Proctor*

Again, please note that the above example has been greatly compressed, for the sake of brevity.

## 5. Conclusion (scholarly conclusions about the three documents you discovered)

Students will write the conclusion in the persona of an archaeologist. In it, they will reflect on the three documents, looking closely at the things they wrote, commenting on Proctor and Abigail (and their venomous relationship), and making inferences about the characters' futures. *What does the court transcript reveal about each character? Has either character grown or changed? What do the letters reveal about each character? From reading these three documents, what can you infer about their futures? What do you suppose happened to each character after the letters were composed, sent, and read?*

This conclusion will give students an opportunity to analyze their own writing and to reflect on the meaning they built into their narratives. This will be several paragraphs long.

## WHAT'S NEXT?

This creative assignment concludes our trio of projects on *The Crucible*. These three assignments have presented a remarkably complete and varied learning experience for our students, all unified by one marvelous play. Let's think for a moment about all that our students have accomplished. They have learned the history behind (and within) this remarkable play; they have analyzed the text of this play deeply and, in the guise and garb of archaeologists, they have composed three original documents that germinated in the text and flowered in their imaginations.

These three projects have been a terrific learning experience for our students, and they have also brought us to the final writing project of the year. In keeping with the adventurous spirit of archaeology, our students are about to take a wistful journey into the past—and a hopeful glimpse into an unwritten future.

Eleventh and Twelfth Grade, Ninth Writing Project: *Outline 11–12.9*
The Creative Project: "Unearthing *The Crucible*"

Name_____ Date_____
Title _____

Mention title and author of play; mention also the focus of the project.

1. Introduction (write this as an archaeologist, and write it last)
   a. Describe how you discovered three documents buried in Salem.
   b. Briefly describe each document.
   c. Mention that these documents shed light on the characters and events of *The Crucible*.

2. First Subtopic: *Excerpt of a Court Transcript: Abigail Asks Proctor Three Questions*
   a. "Earlier today, your wife lied in court. Did the devil make her lie?"
   b. "Do you admit to practicing witchcraft and casting a spell on me?"
   c. "Do you repent of the terrible things you have done?"

3. Second Subtopic: *Letter from Abigail to John Proctor* (five years later: August 1697)
   a. Abigail tells Proctor how she escaped with Parris's money (and Mercy Lewis).
   b. She tells him where she is and what she's been doing (she's a housekeeper in Boston).
   c. She confesses her continued love for Proctor and expresses a desire to marry him.

4. Third Subtopic: *Letter from Proctor to Abigail* (three months later: November 1697)
   a. Proctor describes where he is and what he's doing (he's a farmer in Plymouth, MA).
   b. He describes the damage that Abigail caused (to him, to others, to the town).
   c. He tells Abigail that he never wants to see her again and never to contact him again.

5. Conclusion (write this as an archaeologist and offer conclusions about the documents you discovered)
   a. What do they show us about Abigail?
   b. What do they show us about Proctor?
   c. Make inferences about the characters' futures, *after* the letters were sent (and read).

*This page is permitted to copy.*

*Chapter 20*

# Grades Eleven and Twelve: Tenth Writing Project

## *The Reflective Project:* "Creating a Time Capsule"

Main Standard 11–12.10:
Write routinely over extended time frames (time for research, reflection, and revision) and shorter time frames (a single sitting or a day or two) for a range of tasks, purposes, and audiences.

*Author's Notes: Students will reflect on the past year (or two years) of writing by creating a time capsule. After choosing the contents of the time capsule, students will write about their choices and themselves. This will be five-to-unlimited pages long and will be written in the first person. There are no sub-standards here.*

### LONG RANGE REFLECTION THROUGH A TIME CAPSULE

Well, we have reached the final project of the year. For our twelfth graders, it's the final project of this writing program. This is a bittersweet moment, but it's also the perfect time for students to look back and reflect on all they have learned and all the growth they have achieved writing in our classrooms. So, we'll give them a quirky, fun, and unique reflective project in which students revisit their earlier assignments and consider all they have achieved. They can also reflect on the people they have grown into—and the ones they will become.

This standard is the only one in a "group" called "Range of Writing." It encourages students to compose a variety of writing assignments in which they incorporate "research, reflection, and revision." Because this is the final assignment of the year, and we've done lots of research and revision, we are going to give students a highly variegated assignment that focuses on the process of *reflection*. This will be a terrific opportunity for students to review their writing journey and to revisit the things they wrote—and we are going to do this through the device of a *time capsule*. This is an unspoken metaphor for the passing of time and will make a wonderful follow-up to the previous project. Remember the metal box unearthed in Salem by our budding archaeologists? That was a time capsule.

## WHAT EXACTLY IS A TIME CAPSULE?

Begin this project by telling your students about time capsules. They won't truly know what these are, or what their purpose is, so you should present this concept with clarity and passion. *Time capsules,* you'll tell them, *are like a time machine. They give us contact with people and with worlds that have passed from the earth, and they give us a glimpse into what it was like to be alive, in a particular place, a long time ago.* Emphasize to your students that time capsules are real, they exist in the world, and there are many different kinds of them.

Very often "time capsules are collections of items that are buried underground, likely in a container to protect the contents, with instructions to open the time capsule on a certain date" (White). Right now—this very second—there are time capsules sleeping in the earth and in sealed chambers, waiting to be opened and awakened, in a distant future that we can't even imagine.

Time capsules are the patient and poetic inhabitants of time, and they are also the object of serious study. There is a very high-level scholarly organization called the International Time Capsule Society (ITCS). This was created in 1990 "to promote the careful study of time capsules. It strives to document all types of time capsules throughout the world and to make this information accessible to the public" (The International Time Capsule Society, "About Us").

As you teach your students about time capsules, teach them not just the form of the time capsule but the *concept* as well. Most time capsules are carefully constructed, but some are *unintentional*. For example, old books and movies are de facto time capsules. *People* are time capsules, and the contents are their memories. Caves (such as Lascaux, France), decorated with prehistoric cave paintings, are time capsules. Sites of ancient civilizations (such as Pompeii, Italy) are time capsules. And remember that box of photos and crayon drawings that you discovered one day while cleaning out a closet? That's a time capsule too, revealing and preserving who *you* were in kindergarten. All of those are unintentional time capsules, providing primary-source glimpses into the people and events of the past.

And now, let's talk about the *ingredients* of a time capsule. First, it's in some sort of container. This container can be a weather-tight packing tube, a room, a vault, or a simple box (etc.). It can even be an electronic time capsule, stored online, or in a computer file (The International Time Capsule Society, "How to Make a Time Capsule"). The time capsule has clearly defined boundaries and must be sealable. It usually represents a group, location, organization, or individual, capturing who they were at a specific moment in time.

It should have identifying information on the outside, including a name for the time capsule, information about the people who assembled the time capsule, the date of sealing, and the specific date for the capsule to be opened. When it is opened (many years later), it is like receiving a package delivered from a time machine, or a late-night whisper from the past, gently echoing through the memories of time.

## OUR VERY OWN TIME CAPSULES

For this project, each student will create an actual time capsule, not a theoretical one. It is going to be a physical object that students take home and put away, to be opened by a future version of themselves. Although time capsules have traditionally been buried in the earth, we will not do that here. For this project, students have a choice of containers. However, a cardboard box (such as a shoe box) will work very well.

And what will they put into the time capsule? All of the portfolios generated during this writing program (including this current project). These portfolios contain more than assignments completed. They represent the learning and the growth that students have achieved while working with you and writing in your classroom, and they capture who the student is at a particular point in time. Students will also include *at least one artifact* (up to three). These artifacts must be somehow significant to students, and they must reveal something about who the students are *now*. This time capsule project is a terrific (and very meaningful) way to conclude this writing program, and it will be assembled while completing this current assignment. Here is a brief overview of this project:

1. Introduction
2. First Subtopic: *Email: Response to Your Last-Year Self*

3. Second Subtopic: *Include at least one item you own that is important to you*
4. Third Subtopic: *A letter to your future self*
5. Conclusion

And now, let's talk about logistics.

If students are in eleventh grade, they will create a time capsule, but they will not seal it *yet*. Eleventh graders will do this project once again, a year from now, when they are seniors. At that time, they will place into it all the writing portfolios they have completed, along with new artifacts. If your seniors did *not* create a capsule in the eleventh grade, they will do it now, at the end of twelfth grade. When the time capsule is complete, they will seal it to be opened at a later date, during a time unimaginable for young students.

## HOW WILL WE DO THIS?

When students understand the concept of time capsules and the basic goal of this project, motivate them by explaining the project like this:

> *You are each about to create a time capsule! This will encapsulate your learning and your growth over the last few years, and it will preserve the person you are at this moment. These time capsules will be very special, and you will open them a long time from now, when you are a vastly different person. We are not going to bury our time capsules. Your time capsule will be a box (like a shoe box), and the contents will be the writing you generated during this program and some objects that have meaning for you—along with anything else you want to put in there.*
>
> *When all of the contents are assembled and placed in the box, you are going to label it on the outside. On this label, you will write your name and the name you have chosen for your time capsule. You will also write the date you sealed the time capsule and the specific date for it to be opened. No peeking before that date, or else you break the spell of time! After you label your capsule, we will have a sealing ceremony together, in this classroom. To seal it, we will use clear packing tape. And then you will take your time capsule home and put it away somewhere safe. Don't lose it, and don't forget about it.*
>
> *When will your time capsule be opened? That is up to you to choose! But it must be a specific date, and it must be a substantial amount of time—at least ten years. You may wish to open your time capsule ten, twenty, or thirty years from today. You may wish to open your time capsule on your thirtieth, or fortieth, or fiftieth birthday. (Your thirtieth birthday is a terrific option, but this remains your choice!). When you open your time capsule, it will be a visit from your former self, and you can take pride in who you were then and how much you have grown. So, get ready for the adventure of making a time capsule!*

## TIME FOR A QUICK REVIEW

Before beginning the actual writing of this project, review with your students some writing techniques suited to this time capsule project. In particular, you should go over the following four writing techniques:

1. *Show, Don't Tell*: This is a very important rule for writers because it animates their writing in the minds of readers. When writers *show* us a person or event taking place, they create a three-dimensional image in our minds that helps us to understand and imagine the action being described.
2. *Imagery*: Remind students to include *all five senses* in their descriptions. How does something *look, sound, feel, taste,* and *smell*? Two senses work well in each description, and writers should include no more than three.
3. *Summary and Commentary*: As students discuss the contents of their time capsules, they will liberally employ the paradigm of *summary and commentary*. They will discuss each item included, and they will explain the *meaning* associated with each one. All of these discussions should focus on the learning and growth they achieved during this writing program and on the people they are *today*.
4. *Description, Reflection, Insight (D-R-I, sounds like "dry")*: This is similar to the summary and commentary process, but takes it one step further. In these three steps, writers will begin with a description of a person, event, or item. After that, they will reflect on what it means to them and to their lives. Finally, they will describe what they learned from the thing being discussed, in the hopes that readers can learn it also.

Here is an example of a passage (original to this book) that would be quite at-home in a time capsule. In this passage, the writer discusses an artifact (a baseball) and the great meaning attached to it. Note that this excerpt includes all four writing techniques described above. Please share this with your students and encourage them to identify places where the writing techniques emerge in the piece:

\*\*\*

## GAME BALL

I included an old baseball in my time capsule. It's scuffed and dirty, and it means a great deal to me. A long time ago, I played little league baseball. I was very strong, but I was a mediocre baseball player. During one game, when I got up to bat, I swung very hard, and I connected with the ball. *"POK!"* the ball said. I watched it soar far over the outfielders' heads while they sprinted after it. I ran the bases as fast as I could, finally landing on third base *(a triple!)*, while everyone in the bleachers cheered for me. *My ball hit the fence!* It was nearly a homerun, and I was beyond thrilled.

After we won the game and my coach was talking to the team, he said (quite suddenly), "I have the game ball here, and I want to give it to Timmy, for hitting the fence." When he smiled at me and handed me the ball, I couldn't believe it. I was literally speechless and could not whisper the words *Thank you*. I cradled the ball on my lap in both my hands and bent my head down to look at it.

But I wasn't really looking at the ball. I tilted my head down because the extraordinary joy had filled my eyes with unexpected tears, and I didn't want anyone to see me cry. I was still wearing my orange baseball cap, and, with my head tilted down, the bill of the hat blocked my face. And this, I thought, would ensure the privacy of my emotion. A single tear dropped onto the ball, and I quickly wiped it away. The gift was so sudden and shocking, and it filled me with such unexpected elation that all I could do was weep with silent, magnificent joy.

That was the only game ball I ever won, and it's still one of the best things that ever happened to me. I still think about it from time to time (here I am, telling you about it so many years later), because it's important. It reminds me to approach life with an open heart and an open mind, to swing for the fences, and to embrace the unexpected miracles that life sends us every once in a while. These miracles are quite rare, but they are given to us—I believe—to remind us that our joys and our tears are necessary as we move through our lives and through our years. These unexpected miracles are part of the baffling and blissful and beautiful experience of being alive and being human . . . and they matter. *A lot.*

\*\*\*

## CREATING A TIME CAPSULE

The first step to creating this time capsule is assembling all writing generated during this program. We will begin this process through locating writing portfolios from previous years. So, if students have generated portfolios from earlier grades, ask them to bring those portfolios to class. If students are currently in eleventh or twelfth grade, give them a new folder and have them label it prominently (and simply) with something like "Eleventh (or Twelfth) Grade Writing Portfolio." Next, have them place their nine completed writing assignments from this year into their new portfolio (in chronological order). This way, all of your students' writing is present for them to revisit and consider.

And now, let's take a close look at the components of this assignment.

### 1. Introduction

Students will introduce their time capsules by briefly describing what they're doing. In their descriptions, they will provide the name of the capsule, and they'll inform readers that this is an actual time capsule to be opened by the student in the future. They will also provide an "inventory" of items in the capsule, mentioning each element included there. They will conclude the introduction by stating the time, date, and place that the time capsule was sealed. Students will write this last.

### 2. First Subtopic: *Email: Response to Your Last-Year Self*

In this section, students will evaluate their growth over the past year. If you recall, the final (reflective) writing projects of grades nine and ten (described in chapter 10 of this book, Third Subtopic) required students to write *emails to their future selves* (which are their *current selves*, right now). In these emails, they articulated goals for the future, gave advice to their future selves, and described themselves as they were, *in that moment*, a year ago. Now, the students are going to find those emails, read them, and respond (respectively) to each component of those emails. In a sense, those emails are miniature time capsules.

To do this, students will write actual emails to their earlier selves. First, they will look at the goals they projected a year ago and evaluate whether or not they achieved them. Next, they will evaluate their growth as writers, students, and people over the past year. *How (and how much) have they grown and improved?* Finally, they will compose a brief anecdote describing who they are, *right now*. After students send these emails to their last-year selves, they will *print them out* to be included with this current project.[1]

## 3. Second Subtopic: *Include at least one item you own that is important to you*

Here, students will include at least one object they own (up to three objects). The object placed into the time capsule must belong to the student, and it must have some emotional or memorial significance attached to it. For each object placed into the time capsule, the students will name it, describe it, and discuss it. As they do this, they will follow the summary and commentary model, describing their histories with these objects and their emotional attachments to them.

And what might students place in their time capsules? Anything, as long as it's meaningful to the student. Possible choices will include *photographs, books, souvenirs from vacations, mementos from childhood, awards, and letters or gifts from someone special* (etc.). Exhort students to choose their objects carefully, and remind them to exercise caution, because these artifacts will be sealed inside a time capsule. Although students will continue to own these objects, they will not have access to them for a very long time.

## 4. Third Subtopic: *A letter to you, when you open the time capsule*

In this section, students will write letters to their future selves. They will structure these as traditional letters, including the date the time capsule was sealed, salutation (e.g., "Dear Timmy in the Future"), text of the letter, closing (e.g., "I look forward to meeting you"), and handwritten signature (e.g., "*Timmy in Twelfth Grade*"). A script font also works very well here.

Students will begin these letters by describing who they are *today*. These descriptions will be optimistic, and students will focus on their good qualities and things they like about themselves. Next, students will write about the person they hope to become in the future. *What values do they hope to find in their future selves? Will they be hardworking? Educated? Friendly? Honest? Kind? Generous? Family-oriented? What kind of person will they grow into? What version of themselves would make them proud?*

Finally, they will describe three goals they hope to accomplish before they open the time capsule. For example, *What career do they hope to attain? Where do they want to live? Do they want to travel? Do they hope to be married? Have children? Become wealthy? What dreams do they have that might blossom to fruition while the time capsule sleeps?*

## 5. Conclusion: Last Words about This Writing Program

Students will conclude this project, the time capsule, the year of writing, and (if they're seniors) the entire program by reflecting on what this experience has meant to them as writers and human beings and how it has helped them grow into the people they are today. They'll begin by describing their favorite part of the program and what they'll miss about it. *Is there a favorite moment that stands out in their minds? Were there any "breakthrough" moments? What lessons did they learn, beyond the lessons of writing? Will they miss the stimulating environment, the challenges, the people involved?* They can structure this section like a story if they want.

Next, students will discuss some ways they have grown during this program. *How did it help them to grow as writers, as students, and as people? Did it help them to think about the world, and about themselves, in different terms? How have their attitudes toward writing grown and changed as a result of this program? How did the writing they composed (and the thinking they did) help them to grow and mature?*

Finally, students will say farewell to this program. They will *thank it* for helping them learn to write, for teaching them life lessons, and for assisting them as they grew and matured during these formative years. *How did this program impact their lives? How might they be different people without all the writing, thinking, and growth this program fostered?*

And then they will say good-bye.

## A SEALING CEREMONY

When all writing is completed, graded, and handed back, have your seniors prepare for the "sealing ceremony" (The International Time Capsule Society, "How to Make a Time Capsule"). For the final class of the year, have them bring to class all the ingredients of their time capsules—boxes, portfolios, emails, and artifacts (and anything else they want to place in there).

When they (and their time capsules) are assembled in your classroom, it's time for the sealing ceremony. Turn off the lights and bid all present to approach this ceremony with a tranquil spirit. Begin the ceremony with a single solemn chime of a bell (for this sound effect, see the video at *Primitive Relaxing Music* in References). Give each student a handout you've prepared that will become the official seal of their time capsules (perhaps structured like an official certificate, proudly announcing "Time Capsule" and featuring a mysterious *clock* emblem).

On this paper, they will write their full names, the name they gave to the time capsule, the date of sealing (the current date), and the date the time capsule is to be opened. For the date of opening, the students can choose any date they want (it should be somehow significant to them), but their thirtieth birthday is always a good choice. It will seem impossibly distant to them, but it gives them time to venture into the world and do great things.

Finally, secure the capsules and affix the seal across the opening of the box (all of this can be done with clear packing tape). When this is complete, announce, *"Your time capsules are now sealed. Their clocks have begun ticking."* And close the ceremony with another single chime of a bell—and listen as it slowly fades into the past.

\*\*\*

## GOODBYE

And this concludes the high school writing program! The time capsule project is a wonderful metaphor on which to wrap up the year and mark your students' experience of learning and growing in your classroom. It represents the passing of time, and it also preserves the memories and the essence of your students during this wonderfully formative period of their lives. And, when they open their time capsules in a dozen summers or so, they'll examine the contents in there—the papers, the letters, the artifacts, and the silent, sleeping memories it awakens—and they'll remember who they were back then.

During this encounter with their younger selves, they'll marvel at how far they've come and how much they've grown. And they'll also remember *you*, the teacher who taught them how to write and how to consider the world in new and different terms. And they'll smile wistfully as they think about all the gifts you gave them and how these gifts helped them to grow and to compose their own unfinished stories, long after they left your classroom.

Eleventh and Twelfth Grade, Tenth Writing Project: *Outline 11–12.10*
The Reflective Project: "Creating a Time Capsule"

Name_____ Date_____

Title _____

This is the name of your time capsule.

1. Introduction: *Creating a Time Capsule That Presents* You *as You Are Today* (write this last)
   a. Describe this project (creating a time capsule to be opened in the future).
   b. Mention the items you are including.
   c. State the recipient (*you!*) and the date you sealed it.

2. First Subtopic: *Email: Response to Your Last-Year Self* (and print it out)
   a. Did you achieve the goals you described in last year's email? Discuss.
   b. How much have you grown over the past year, as a writer and as a person?
   c. Write a brief anecdote that describes and defines who you are *today*.

3. Second Subtopic: *An Item That Is Important to You* (include up to three)
   a. Name the item and describe it. What is it?
   b. Discuss your history with this item and the emotional connection you have with it.
   c. What does this item reveal about you as a person?

4. Third Subtopic: *A Letter to Your Future Self* (to be read by you when you open the time capsule)
   a. Describe the person you are right now (focus on your good qualities).
   b. Describe the person you hope to become in the future—the adult you will grow into.
   c. State at least three goals for the future and how you will achieve them (before you open the time capsule).

5. Conclusion: *Last Words about This Writing Program*
   a. What was your favorite part of it? What will you miss about it?
   b. Discuss some ways that you have grown during the program.
   c. Thank the program for helping you write and grow—and then say good-bye to it.

*This page is permitted to copy.*

# Conclusion
## *A Call for Change*

One of the joys of my life has been teaching students the basics and beauties of literature and writing, and I have done this in various formats. Throughout my years in academia, I have held various positions, including assistant director of a university writing center, adjunct professor of writing and literature, teacher of high school English, high school library media specialist, and director of a high school library writing center. I adore classroom and library instruction, and I also love teaching students in the format of the one-on-one writer's conference. This is a specialized form of tutoring that—done correctly—provides the finest and most effective writing instruction possible.

During all that time and through all those experiences, I have come to understand something undeniable: overwhelmingly, *our students can't write* (this is true up to—and often including—*graduate school*). This is an enormous problem educationally and culturally, and for a long time I have been wondering about a rather simple thing: *as an educator, how can I help to correct this?*

A few years ago, I created the *School Library Writing Center*, and I wrote two books on it that span the educational journey from kindergarten through twelfth grade (see titles in References). Next, I decided to create two writing programs that would run in tandem, one after the other, and I wrote books about both. The first program would run in junior high school (see my book *Let's Create Writers: Writing Lessons for Grades Seven and Eight*). The second writing program would run in high school, and you are reading that book right now.

## WHAT IS CAUSING THIS PROBLEM?

After considering this problem through the lens of my teaching experience, I quickly perceived one of the main causes. In the contemporary academy—in particular, on the high school level—*writing is being assigned, but not truly taught*. I have been saying this for years, and recently I found a nearly identical sentiment echoed in a scholarly article. The authors state: "American schools haven't been teaching students how to write. Teachers may have assigned writing, but they haven't explicitly taught it in a careful sequence of logical steps" (Hochman and Wexler 31).

Writing projects are *assigned* to students, but the skill of writing is not being *taught* to students in the depth or degree it needs. Consider this: if a student wants to play a sport, the school district offers about twelve hours of coaching and rigorous practice each week. How much specialized writing instruction (as opposed to literature instruction) do students receive each week? Based on my own experience and observations, probably no more than a few minutes.

Here, I want to state something very clearly: *I am not blaming classroom teachers or school districts*. These individuals and organizations are extremely dedicated, care deeply about students, and are doing magnificent work. This deficiency is *not their fault*. I am considering the larger educational environment, and I am calling for a change in the contemporary school culture and curriculum. Read on.

## WHAT DO HIGH SCHOOL STUDENTS NEED?

Although I understand this problem quite well, I wanted a glimpse of it from the students' perspective, so I contacted a half dozen of former students whom I had tutored in the school library writing center I created. These students are all recently graduated and are excited to tell their tales. And now, meet my former students: *Brandon, Denise, Jade, Jennifer, Olivia,* and *Reece*. They are all intelligent and kind, and it was my privilege to teach them the beauties of writing and literature.

I sent each student a brief questionnaire in which I asked three questions and requested truthful responses of any length they chose—and they complied graciously. Here are the questions I asked:

1. What was difficult about writing in (and for) high school?
2. What would have made it easier to write in high school?
3. How did I help you learn to write in high school?

As I looked through the students' responses, I noticed several similar concerns regarding what was difficult and what was (and would have been) helpful. When answering the first question (the difficulties of writing in high school), five of the six students agreed that writing was not truly taught to them in high school. Here are their responses:

- Denise: *I wish in high school we were taught more about the reasoning behind certain things in writing, besides being expected to know it. As students, we were just "expected" to know things.*
- Olivia: *No one taught me how to organize and properly develop a good essay.*
- Brandon: *The most difficult thing for me about writing in high school was the lack of preparation I felt when beginning every written assignment. I felt like every time I had to write an essay I just did not know how to start or what I was supposed to be doing.*
- Reece: *In middle school, teachers held the students' hands through the writing process. By high school, students are flying solo and are faced with a daunting assignment often worth a decent chunk of their grade for the semester.*
- Jennifer: *I think the main challenge I faced was the pressure and very little guidance. By the time you reach high school, you are expected to know how to write. Not only are you supposed to know how to write, but you are supposed to be a strong writer. There is little support for the students who fall through the cracks and now need support.*

As you can see, there is nearly universal consensus among these students. If we look closely at their descriptions, we find a tale of students arriving at high school unprepared for the rigors of secondary-level writing—and then *never being taught how to write*. This is a recipe for unrealized potential, and it ensures that students show up to college unprepared to write in that environment also. Did you ever wonder why virtually every college and university in existence has a thriving writing center? It's because the students who arrive at college were never truly taught how to write. In college, that becomes a problem with serious repercussions.

## WHERE DO I BEGIN?

My two remaining questions concerned what *would have been* helpful for the students, and how I helped them in my teaching. Here, nearly all of the students voiced concerns about how to structure and organize an academic paper. These are essential foundational issues. They need to be taught clearly and then reinforced through repetition, because students cannot write a competent paper without them. In three of these students, this manifested as not knowing how to *begin* a writing assignment. Here is what they said:

- Brandon: *The largest impact you had on me was teaching me to look at an assignment and find the place to start instead of just staring at it completely overwhelmed.*
- Reece: *I think it was difficult to know where to begin.*
- Olivia: *Students like me have a hard time getting started on writing assignments. I often just don't know where to start.*

Not knowing where (or how) to start writing is a form of writer's block. This results from not knowing what to write, which stems directly from not knowing *how* to write. Here is the good news: *all of this can be remedied.* In the writing methods provided in this book, one of the mainstays is the five-part outline. Once students develop a clear and simple outline, they have a tangible place to start writing. This leads us to another cornerstone of this program: *write the introduction last.* When our writers create their outlines, the contents of their essays are mapped out *physically and visibly*, and the starting point reveals itself: *begin with writing the first subtopic.* The outline process works beautifully, and three students commented on its effectiveness.

- Jennifer: *You always asked me to slow down and write an outline. This made me think about what I was doing, and it made me organize my thoughts. Then, I began to develop the outline and form an essay and generate well-written papers. This process is something I still use today.*
- Olivia: *Writing the outline helped me get my ideas in order before I started writing the essay. Outlines help students stay focused on the main topic of the essay and help them include the requirements of the assignment. Nowadays, I never start writing an essay without writing an outline first.*
- Jade: *The outline process you taught provides a framework to structure your thoughts upon, which helps with the organization of your writing. The better organized the writing, the clearer the paper is.*

## HOW CAN WE FIX THIS PROBLEM?

First, let's start by defining this problem in great clarity. I will present it in two parts:

1. Students arrive at high school not knowing how to write.

2. In high school, students are not properly *taught* how to write.

When presented in those terms, it's a rather simple dilemma. But why is this occurring? *Why are students not being taught to write?*

This situation is caused by the fact that the ongoing pedagogical culture and curriculum in high school contain an implicit assumption that high school students (in general) possess proficient writing skills, when they do not. Because of this unspoken assumption, pure writing instruction is missing from the curriculum. Because of this absence, teachers are not teaching writing in the depth, manner, and abundance in which it needs to be taught. The end result is that students in high school are not adequately taught how to write.

I'm aware that writing *is* taught in schools, in various incarnations, such as Advanced Placement (AP) courses, honors courses, and International Baccalaureate (IB) programs. I have personally taught AP courses and honors courses, and I have mentored IB students as they composed their Extended Essays. These students' writing skills tend to be better than average (although proficiency levels vary greatly), and the writing instruction they receive is generally very good.

Nonetheless, these high-level courses function as oases in an educational desert and thus impact a limited population. Exclusive by nature, they are not mandatory for all students, in all grades, on all levels. So, the blight continues, and the great majority of our students pass through high school without truly learning how to write.

## A CALL FOR CHANGE

One of the purposes of this book (and especially this conclusion) is to *raise awareness of this problem*. Our students cannot write, and my personal experience has verified this (in spectacular fashion) over and over. I realize this is due to a variety of factors (many of which exist beyond the academy), but educators are in a position to help correct this problem. *So, what should we do?* To put it simply, we must change the way writing is (not) taught in high school, because our current methods are simply not working.

To begin, I encourage teachers of high school English, writing, and humanities to begin teaching the methods, techniques, and projects contained in this book. They are extremely effective. Everything in this volume is accessible to high school students and is designed to help them understand (and enjoy) the writing process and to *complete* the writing assignments they begin. And now, we arrive at the highest and most important purpose of this book: I am calling for the contemporary academy (which means every secondary school in the

United States) to *implement academic courses that are exclusively devoted to teaching students how to write.*

Please note that I am not arguing for the removal of courses such as AP, IB, or honors. These remain valuable educational assets. I am arguing for the creation and implementation of *new courses* singularly devoted to the art and science of *writing*. These courses will not be electives. They will become a permanent part of the mainstream curriculum (across the United States) and will provide highly focused writing instruction for *every secondary student in the nation* regardless of grade level or existing forms of academic stratification.

These writing courses will start in ninth grade, and extend upward through all four years of high school.[1] Allow me to emphasize this crucial requirement: in the writing program I'm articulating here, *every secondary student in the nation will take a writing course, every year in high school, for a total of four ascending writing courses*. In these courses, students will receive *pure writing instruction* unfiltered through any particular pedagogic lens that might narrow the students' approach to (and view of) writing.

This will ensure that, in every year of secondary school, our students receive a challenging and stimulating encounter with *writing* in a form that is engaging and comprehensible. And what shall we name these courses? As always, we'll keep things simple:

- Writing 9
- Writing 10
- Writing 11
- Writing 12

At this point, you may be wondering a simple question: *Who will compose this new writing curriculum, and what will it look like?* Fear not. I have already written the curriculum, and you are holding it in your hands right now. It is this book. This curriculum is full and complete, and is now waiting to be implemented. As you (the new teacher of *Writing*) learn the composition system I have created—and grow to understand its deep structures—you are encouraged to contribute to the curriculum, developing your own original writing assignments emanating from the model I provided here. This will assist with differentiation and with avoiding potential repetition among the grades.

Logistically speaking, what will this course look like? The structure is simple and logical. For each grade in this book, there are ten writing projects described. There are also ten months in the school year. This means that students will complete *one writing project each month*. This is an extremely reasonable rate, and will allow students to absorb the methods, techniques, and writing process contained in each chapter. It will also provide students time to *complete assignments*. Further, the civilized pacing of this course allows for trips to the library or computer lab, where students can *write in class* (an indispensable opportunity for growth), ask questions, and overcome the eternal specter of procrastination.

As students compose each project, they will receive writing instruction tailored to that particular assignment. This instruction includes writing methods and techniques that will periodically repeat throughout the program, thereby reinforcing the skills and knowledge previously taught to the students. When students complete this program, they will be highly proficient writers, ready for the rigors of writing in college and the workplace.

## LET'S START THIS *TODAY*

I am now going to make a prediction. I believe that within one generation, we will see high-quality writing courses created and implemented in virtually every secondary school in the nation. *But why wait that long?* If we delay, we produce another generation of students who enter the adult world without the ability to write well. Let's begin these changes *today*. I urge every teacher and administrator who is reading this book to argue for, propose, and create a four-year writing program that functions in your school and in your district.[2] *How will you do this?*

I can't possibly anticipate every contingency that might occur, but in general, I can offer these steps: First, propose this program to building administration and get their approval. Next, ask your building administrators to propose the program to district administration. Finally, urge your district administration to propose this program to the board of education—where it has a very good chance of being approved.

I am optimistic about the ultimate approval of this program, because it represents the addition of courses essential to the curriculum—and to our students' education. It is entirely feasible, and by writing this book, I have done all the preliminary groundwork. When we do create and implement these courses, we will be changing students' lives forever, enabling them to function proficiently in the worlds of college and career.

Perhaps more important, we will give them enduring gifts of perception and enlightenment. These will reverberate quietly throughout their lives, illuminating their minds with clarity and insight and whispering songs about the miraculous experience of being alive. And these will be loyal and helpful companions for our students, striding with them as they write and grow into all their bright and beautiful tomorrows.

# Notes

## INTRODUCTION

1. Portions of this introduction were previously published in the author's book *Let's Create Writers: Writing Lessons for Grades Seven and Eight* (Lanham, MD: Rowman & Littlefield, 2021).

2. The author has written previously (and extensively) about the five-part outline. See his books *Create Your School Library Writing Center, Grades K–6* (Santa Barbara, CA: Libraries Unlimited, 2017); *Create Your School Library Writing Center, Grades 7–12* (Santa Barbara, CA: Libraries Unlimited, 2016); and *Let's Create Writers: Writing Lessons for Grades Seven and Eight* (Lanham, MD: Rowman & Littlefield, 2021).

## CHAPTER 6

1. Portions of this chapter were originally published in the author's book *Let's Create Writers: Writing Lessons for Grades Seven and Eight* (Lanham, MD: Rowman & Littlefield, 2021), ch. 6.

## CHAPTER 8

1. Portions of this section were originally published in the author's book *Let's Create Writers: Writing Lessons for Grades Seven and Eight* (Lanham, MD: Rowman & Littlefield, 2021), ch. 8.

## CHAPTER 12

1. If you are showing the video in a group presentation, consider showing it on a site that removes potentially offensive clutter. Two excellent sites for this are SafeShare and ViewPure. For URLs, see References.

## CHAPTER 14

1. In most cases, the in-text citation includes the subject's *last name* only. In this case, the subject's *first* name has been included to distinguish him from the author (they share the same last name).

## CHAPTER 16

1. "Fire Truck." Photograph by Bob Hennelly, *The Chief*, 20 March 2018, accessed 5 September 2021, https://thechiefleader.com/news/news_of_the_week/fdny-cuts-staff-again-at-10-engine-companies/article_54a5e614-292f-11e8-b702-5ba233b52c53.html.

## CHAPTER 20

1. If students did not email themselves last year, you can offer them an alternative subtopic in which students choose and discuss their *favorite writing assignment* of the program. To do this, students can use the pattern described in chapter 10 of this book (First Subtopic).

## CONCLUSION

1. Ideally, middle schools will also implement courses devoted to *writing*. For the middle school writing curriculum, see the author's book *Let's Create Writers: Writing Lessons for Grades Seven and Eight* (Lanham, MD: Rowman & Littlefield, 2021).

2. As you create this new writing program, you are encouraged also to create a *writing center* that will collaborate symbiotically with your new writing program. The blueprint for this writing center is contained in the author's book *Create Your School Library Writing Center: Grades 7–12* (Santa Barbara, CA: Libraries Unlimited, 2016).

# References

"About JSTOR." *JSTOR*. Last modified 2021. Accessed 3 July 2021. https://about.jstor.org/.

Anderson, Monica, and Jingjing Jiang. "Teens, Social Media and Technology 2018." Pew Research Center. 31 May 2018. Accessed 19 July 2021. https://www.pewresearch.org/internet/2018/05/31/teens-social-media-technology-2018/.

Baum, L. Frank. *The Wizard of Oz*. Illustrated by W. W. Denslow. New York: Barnes & Noble, 2013.

Book Creator. "Book Creator Tutorial for Students." YouTube, 1 May 2020, 7:04. Accessed 3 June 2020. https://www.youtube.com/watch?v=vMYLaGD9Xjs.

"Book Creator: Bring Creativity to Your Classroom." Book Creator. Tools for Schools, Inc. Accessed 7 June 2021. https://bookcreator.com/.

Book Creator. "Home." YouTube Channel. Accessed 12 June 2021. https://www.youtube.com/user/bookcreatorapp.

"Boolean Operators and Nesting." Library of Congress. Accessed 4 July 2021. https://catalog.loc.gov/vwebv/ui/en_US/htdocs/help/searchBoolean.html.

Brandon. Email interview by the author. New York. 14 May 2021.

Britannica School. "Arthur Miller." Accessed 5 September 2021. https://school-eb-xaaa.orc.scoolaid.net/levels/high/article/Arthur-Miller/52708.

Britannica School. "Cold War." Accessed 5 September 2021. https://school-eb-xaaa.orc.scoolaid.net/levels/high/article/Cold-War/24721.

Coyle, Daniel. *The Talent Code: Greatness Isn't Born, It's Grown. Here's How*. New York: Bantam Books, 2009.

Denise. Email interview by the author. New York. 10 May 2021.

"English Language Arts Standards, Anchor Standards, College and Career Readiness Anchor Standards for Writing." Common Core State Standards Initiative. 2021. Accessed 12 August 2021. http://www.corestandards.org/ELA-Literacy/CCRA/W/.

"English Language Arts Standards, Language, Grade 9–10." Common Core State Standards Initiative. 2021. Accessed 29 May 2021. http://www.corestandards.org/ELA-Literacy/L/9-10/.

"English Language Arts Standards, Language, Grade 11–12." Common Core State Standards Initiative. 2021. Accessed 21 August 2021. http://www.corestandards.org/ELA-Literacy/L/11-12/.

"English Language Arts Standards, Reading, Grade 9–10." Common Core State Standards Initiative. 2021. Accessed 18 August 2021. http://www.corestandards.org/ELA-Literacy/RL/9-10/.

"English Language Arts Standards, Reading, Grade 11–12." Common Core State Standards Initiative. 2021. Accessed 12 August 2021. http://www.corestandards.org/ELA-Literacy/RL/11-12/.

"English Language Arts Standards, Writing, Grade 9–10." Common Core State Standards Initiative. 2021. Accessed 2 March 2021. http://www.corestandards.org/ELA-Literacy/W/9-10/.

"English Language Arts Standards, Writing, Grade 11–12." Common Core State Standards Initiative. 2021. Accessed 26 July 2021. http://www.corestandards.org/ELA-Literacy/W/11-12/.

"Firefighter: Get Hired." JoinFDNY. Accessed 5 August 2021. https://www.joinfdny.com/careers/firefighter/.

Frank, Anne. *The Diary of a Young Girl*. Translated by B. M. Mooyaart-Doubleday. New York: Bantam Books, 1993.

Gomez-Galisteo, Carmen. "Salem Witch Trials: Puritanism, Material Wealth, and Local Disputes." *American History, ABC-CLIO*, 2021. Accessed 12 September 2021. https://americanhistory-abc-clio-xaaa.orc.scoolaid.net/Search/Display/2247627.

Hochman, Judith C., and Natalie Wexler. "One Sentence at a Time: The Need for Explicit Instruction in Teaching Students to Write Well." *American Educator* 41, no. 2 (July 2017): 30–37. https://www.proquest.com/scholarly-journals/one-sentence-at-time-need-explicit-instruction/docview/1941335894/se-2?accountid=699.

Horan, John. Telephone interview by the author. New York. 15 August 2021.

Horan, Timothy. *Create Your School Library Writing Center: Grades K–6*. Santa Barbara, CA: Libraries Unlimited, 2017.

Horan, Timothy. *Create Your School Library Writing Center: Grades 7–12*. Santa Barbara, CA: Libraries Unlimited, 2016.

Horan, Timothy. *Let's Create Writers: Writing Lessons for Grades Seven and Eight*. Lanham, MD: Rowman & Littlefield, 2021.

Horan, Timothy. "Mindset in Your Library: Teaching Young People to Learn and Grow." *VOYA: Voice of Youth Advocates* 42, no. 1 (April 2019): 20–23.

Hurley, Katie. "Teenage Cell Phone Addiction: Are You Worried about Your Child?" Psycom.net. 16 November 2020. Accessed 12 July 2021. www.psycom.net/cell-phone-internet-addiction.

IBorganization. "What Is the Extended Essay?" International Baccalaureate, 2021. Accessed 6 November 2021. https://www.ibo.org/programmes/diploma-programme/curriculum/extended-essay/what-is-the-extended-essay/.

The International Time Capsule Society. "About Us." ITCS. 2020. Accessed 17 October 2021. https://www.itcsoc.org/about.

The International Time Capsule Society. "How to Make a Time Capsule." ITCS. 2020. Accessed 19 October 2021. https://www.itcsoc.org/how-to-make-time-capsule.

Jade. Email interview by the author. New York. 15 May 2021.

Jennifer. Interview by the author. New York. 3 May 2021.

Join FDNY. "FDNY Fire Academy: An Overview of the FDNY Fire Academy's Physical Fitness Standards." YouTube Video, 6:19, 29 January 2015. Accessed 16 August 2021. https://www.youtube.com/watch?v=NxgAy6Fp_Ao.

Kemp, Dan. "Add a Photo from the Image Search." Book Creator. Accessed 12 June 2021. https://intercom.help/bookcreator/en/articles/2398641-add-a-photo-from-the-image-search.

Kemp, Dan. "Publishing Your Book Online with Book Creator." Book Creator. Last modified May 2020. Accessed 15 June 2021. https://intercom.help/bookcreator/en/articles/2398637-publishing-your-book-online-with-book-creator.

Kordich, Catherine J. "How to Write about *Of Mice and Men*." *Bloom's How to Write about John Steinbeck*. Chelsea House, 2017. Accessed 2 July 2021. online.infobase.com/Auth/Index?aid=16254&itemid=WE54&articleId=45746.

"Limit Your Device Not Your Life: Discover Change That Lasts." reSTART. 2019. Accessed 18 July 2021. https://www.netaddictionrecovery.com/.

Miller, Arthur. *The Crucible: A Play in Four Acts*. New York: Penguin Books, 1982.

Morris, M. Michelle. "Salem Witchcraft Trials." *World Book Student*. World Book, 2021. https://worldbookonline-xaaa.orc.scoolaid.net/student/article?id=ar485960. Accessed 4 September 2021.

"Myths vs. Facts." Common Core State Standards Initiative. 2021. Accessed 12 November 2021. http://www.corestandards.org/about-the-standards/myths-vs-facts/.

Olivia. Email interview by the author. New York. 28 May 2021.

Owens, Louis. "Deadly Kids, Stinking Dogs, and Heroes: The Best Laid Plans in Steinbeck's *Of Mice and Men*." *Western American Literature* 37, no. 3 (Fall 2002): 319–33. Quoted in *Children's Literature Review*, edited by Jelena Krstovic, Vol. 172. Detroit, MI: Gale, 2012. Gale Literature Resource Center. Accessed 2 July 2021. https://link-gale-xaaa.orc.scoolaid.net/apps/doc/H1420107877/LitRC?u=nysl_li_esuff&sid=bookmark-LitRC&xid=c5e8cccb.

"Photos for Class." Photos for Class. Last modified 2021. Accessed 8 May 2021. https://www.photosforclass.com/.

"Pics4Learning." Tech4Learning. Last modified 2021. Accessed 8 May 2021. https://www.pics4learning.com/.

Primitive Relaxing Music. "1 Hour Mindfulness Meditation Bell, Bell Sound." YouTube, 28 April 2017, 1:00:49. Accessed 30 October 2021. https://www.youtube.com/watch?v=mE5-7-7mqB0&t=249s.

Reece. Email interview by the author. New York. 17 May 2021.

Reeves, Thomas C. "McCarthyism." *World Book Student*. World Book, 2021. https://worldbookonline-xaaa.orc.scoolaid.net/student/article?id=ar350785. Accessed 5 September 2021.

Rideout, Victoria, and Michael Robb. "The Common Sense Census: Media Use by Tweens and Teens," 2019. San Francisco, CA: Common Sense Media. 2019-census-8-to-18-key-findings-updated.pdf (commonsensemedia.org).

SafeShare. "Share YouTube and Vimeo Videos Safely and without Distractions." SafeShare. Accessed 24 July 2021. https://safeshare.tv/.

Steinbeck, John. *Of Mice and Men*. New York: Penguin Books, 1993.

"Studying at the Fire Academy." JoinFDNY. 15 February 2017. Accessed 15 August 2021. https://www.joinfdny.com/fdny-fire-academy/.

"Stunning Free Images & Royalty Free Stock." Pixabay. Accessed 12 June 2021. https://pixabay.com/.

Super Schoolhouse. "Google Slides for Kids – Episode 1." YouTube Video, 7:07, 27 November 2019. Accessed 23 August 2021. https://www.youtube.com/watch?v=lfpneIqnXTE.

TEDx Talks. "Quit Social Media." YouTube Video, 13:50, 19 September 2016. Accessed 15 July 2021. https://www.youtube.com/watch?v=3E7hkPZ-HTk&t=6s.

ViewPure. "Watch Purified YouTube Videos." ViewPure. 2021. Accessed 14 July 2021. http://www.viewpure.com/.

"What Is Archaeology?" Society for American Archaeology. Accessed 3 October 2021. https://www.saa.org/about-archaeology/what-is-archaeology.

White, David. "Time Capsules: Buried Reminders for Future Discovery." 2014. Accessed 16 October 2021. https://explore.proquest.com/sirsdiscoverer/document/2250236416?accountid=699.

"Winners." Tony Awards. 2021. Accessed 8 November 2021. https://www.tonyawards.com/winners/year/1953/category/any/show/any/.

# Index

academic argument, 11; elements of, 106–7
academic databases, 74–76; and bibliography, 79–80; use of, 165–67
academic language, 53
academic voice, 10, 22, 104, 114
accuracy of information, 137
*add comment* function, 51
analysis, 176; in argumentative essay, 13–14; in informative essay, 24–25; literary, 63–72, 175–84; on quote, 78
anecdotes, 44, 100
argumentative essays, 10, 103–11; format and organization of, 16–17; personal, 9–18; qualifications in, 107–8
artifacts, for time capsule, 197–98, 202
audience, 6–7
autobiography, fictional, 29–37

biased information, 137
bibliography, 79–80, 116–17, 166–67; for internet research, 137; for interviews, 137
blacklist, 170
blogs, versus diaries, 85
Book Creator, 56–58; illustrations in, 59–61
Boolean limiters, 75–76, 136–37

BOWA method, 137

capitalism, 165
careers: goals for, 25, 202; ideal, 134–35, 140–41; log entries on, 143–52; oral presentations on, 153–62; resources on, 135–36
cell phones: addiction to, 115, 119; use of, 105, 107–8
characters, 30, 33–34, 123; in creative essay, 147–48; creative project on, 83–91; most important, 177–79
choice: in argumentative essay, 108; in creative project, 86, 88–89; in personal essay, 135; in reflective project, 94
citations, 68, 76, 166–68, 216n1 (chap. 14); for internet research, 137–38; for interviews, 137–38; in-text, 116–17; for quotes, 118
clarity, 40–42
close reading, 63, 67
Cold War, 164–65, 169
collaboration, on e-books, 58
commentary, 14, 176, 199; in informative essay, 24–25; on quote, 78; in reflective essay, 43
Common Core Writing Standards, 2–3, 103–5, 185

communism, 165, 169–70
conclusion, 17, 27, 45–46, 104, 114, 124, 192
conditions, 15
Conflict, 6, 30–31, 36, 128
counterarguments, 14–15, 17, 106–7, 109
court transcripts, 189–90
cover, of e-book, 57
creative compositions, 10; essay, 143–52; literature-inspired, 83–91, 185–93

*The Crucible* (Miller), 163–73, 175–93

Cuban Missile Crisis, 169

databases, academic, 74–76; and bibliography, 79–80; use of, 165–67
definition of terms, 106, 109; in argumentative essay, 13, 17; journal versus diary, 95
deleting, 52
description, 14, 44, 68, 176, 199
development of ideas, 40, 43
dialogue, 30, 33–34; and character, 33; in creative essay, 147–48; format of, 34; in interview, 96; in short story, 123, 126–27
diary entries, 143; format of, 85–86; versus journal entry, 95; literature-inspired, 83–91; nature of, 84–85
distribution, of writing, 39–40
drafts: first, 39–47, 63–72; second, 49–54; third, 55–62
drama, writing on, 163–73, 175–93; missing scenes, 189–90
dreams: in *Of Mice and Men*, 64, 66–67, 69–70
DRI (description, reflection, insight), 43, 199

e-books, 55–62
editing, 49–54, 120; versus revision, 50; tips for, 52–54

Eleventh Grade, length guidelines for, 3
Eleventh/Twelfth Grade program, 103–205; Project 1, 103–11; Project 2, 113–22; Project 3, 123–31; Project 4, 133–42; Project 5, 143–52; Project 6, 153–62; Project 7, 163–73; Project 8, 175–84; Project 9, 185–93; Project 10, 195–205
email, 99–100, 197, 201–2; format of, 94, 97
emotion, in reflective essay, 44
essays: argumentative, 9–18, 103–11; creative, 143–52; e-book, 55–62; first draft, 39–47; informative, 21–28, 113–22; reflective, 39–47, 49–62; revising and editing, 49–54
evidence, 13–14, 104, 106
examples, 26, 109; research for, 117
explicit instruction, need for, 208–9, 211

fiction, 29–37
first draft: of literary research paper, 63–72; of reflective essay, 39–47
first-person narration, 83, 93, 123–24
Five-Part Outline, 4–5
focus, 40, 42–43; and revision, 52
foreshadowing, 34
format: of argumentative essay, 16–17; of court transcript, 189–90; of dialogue, 34; of diary entries, 85–86; of e-books, 55; of email, 94, 97; of informative essay, 113; of interview, 94, 96; of journal entry, 94–95; of letters, 190–92; of slides, 155
Frank, Anne, 84–85
free-write periods, 125, 134–35, 145
future self: email to, 97, 99–100; ideal career of, 133–42; letter to, 197, 202

Google, 75; Docs, 55, 160; Slides, 154–55
Gorbachev, Mikhail, 169
Grail, 6, 30–31, 36, 66, 127–28, 180–82
grammar, 53
graphics, 23

green lights, in revision, 51–52
guidance, need for, 208–9, 211

headings, 23, 26, 120–21

ideas: development of, 25, 40, 43; importance of, 42
illustrations: for e-book, 56, 59–61; for informative essay, 113, 119–21; for slide presentation, 156
imagery, 34–35, 44, 124, 126, 146–47, 199
information, evaluation of, 137
informative essays, 10, 21–28, 113–22; purpose of, 116; structure of, 26–27
informative oral presentations, 153–62
informative research project, 163–73
insight, 40, 43–45, 199
internal monologue, 95
International Time Capsule Society, 196
internet, 75, 135; location and evaluation of resources on, 136–38
interpretation, 14, 175–84
interview, 98–99; for career essay, 136; format of, 94, 96
introduction, 177; of argumentative essay, 16–17; of short story, 129; writing last, 5, 210

journal entry, 98; versus diary entry, 95; format of, 94–95
JSTOR, 75

Language Standards, 49
letters: fictional, 190–92; to future self, 197, 202
library, of e-books, 57–58, 61
listening, and revision, 50–51
literary analysis, 63–72, 175–84
literary criticism, 73–81
literary research paper: first draft, 63–72; second draft, 73–81; third draft, 83–91
log entries, 143–52

loneliness: in *Of Mice and Men,* 64, 66–67, 69–70

main character, 33
McCarthy, Joseph, 165, 169–70
McCarthyism, 164–65, 169–70
Miller, Arthur, 163–73, 175–93

narratives, 123–31; techniques in, 123
Ninth Grade, length guidelines for, 3
Ninth/Tenth Grade program, 9–102; Project 1, 9–18; Project 2, 21–28; Project 3, 29–37; Project 4, 39–47; Project 5, 49–54; Project 6, 55–62; Project 7, 63–72; Project 8, 73–81; Project 9, 83–91; Project 10, 93–102
nonfiction, literary, reading standards on, 185
note-taking, 67

objectives, 1
*Of Mice and Men* (Steinbeck), 63–81, 83–91
old information, 137
One-Story Approach, 5–6, 123, 127–28, 149, 180
optimism, 97
oral presentations, 153–62
organization: of argumentative essay, 16–17; of informative essay, 23–24; of reflective essay, 40
outlines: argumentative essay, 19, 111; creative coda, 91, 194; creative essay, 152; e-book, 62; end-of-year reflection, 102; Five-Part, 4–5; importance of, 210; informative essay, 28, 122; informative oral presentation, 162; informative research project, 173; literary analysis, 72, 184; personal essay, 142; reflective essay, 47, 54, 62; secondary sources, 81; short story, 38, 132; slide presentation as, 155; time capsule, 205

paraphrasing, 74, 118, 167
pencils: for annotating, 76; for editing, 51
personal essays: argumentative, 9–18; informative, 21–28; reflective, 39–47, 49–62; research, 133–42
philosophy, of research, 64–65
plagiarism, 65, 118
plot, 30
poetry, journal entry and, 95
polishing, 120
portfolios, 101; for time capsule, 197–98
prereading project, 163, 167
prevision, 51
primary sources, 73–74, 176
primary text, and research, 65
prior knowledge, 125–27
privacy issues: diaries and, 85; e-books and, 58
Problem-and-Solution method, 148–49
production, of writing, 39–40
projects: length of, 3; number of, 3
proofreading, 52
publication: of e-books, 61; of oral presentations, 153–54
public speaking: oral presentations, 153–62; support for, 161
purpose, 6–7; of argumentative essay, 10; of informative essay, 23

qualifications, 107–8
qualifying argument, 15
question, research, 65, 163
quotation marks, used as Boolean limiters, 75–76, 136–37
quotes: analyzing, 67–68; integrating into essay, 76–79; literary, 67–68, 76–79; research, 117–19, 139–40, 167

range of writing, 93, 196
realistic fiction, 143–52
red lights, in revision, 51–52

reflection, 40, 43, 45, 93, 199; and creative composition, 83–91, 185–93; and time capsule, 195–205
reflective essays: e-book, 55–62; end-of-year, 93–102; first draft, 39–47; revising and editing, 49–54
reflective short story, 123–31; rules for, 128–29; structure of, 129–30
rehearsals, for oral presentation, 161
rereading: partner for, 53; and revision, 51
research, 22, 63–64; integrating into essay, 76–79; resource types, 135–36; secondary sources in, 73–81; uses of, 118–19
research projects: coda to, 83–91; informative, 113–22; literary, 63–81, 83–91; personal, 133–42; process for, 116–20
Resolution, 6, 30–31, 36, 128
revision, 49–54, 120; versus editing, 50; and listening, 50–51
rewriting, 49
rule of three, 4

Salem Witch Trials, 164–65, 169–70
scenes, dramatic, 179–80
searches: in academic databases, 75–76, 166; for illustrations, 60; on open internet, 136–38
secondary sources, 73–81
second draft: of literary research paper, 73–81; of reflective essay, 49–54
selection, 23–24
senses, and imagery, 34, 44, 124, 126, 146–47, 199
sequencing, in short story, 124
setting, 129
short story, 29–37; journal entry and, 95; reflective, 123–31
Show, Don't Tell rule, 30, 35, 123, 126, 146–47, 178, 199
simplicity, 41
situation, 129
skill development, issues in, 208

slide presentation, 153–62, 157*f*; format of, 155; technology for, 153–55; tips for, 153–62
Soviet Union, 165
spell check, issues with, 53
standards. *See* Common Core Writing Standards
starting, tips for, 209–10; argumentative essay, 15–16; creative essay, 144–45; historical research, 165–67; informative essay, 25; oral presentation, 160
Steinbeck, John, 63–81, 83–91
stories, 29–37, 123–31; journal entry and, 95; Problem-and-Solution method for, 148–49; realistic fiction, 143–52; in reflective essays, 44
stream of consciousness, 95
students, needs of, 208–9
subtopics, 4
summary, 14, 176, 199; in informative essay, 24–25; in informative research project, 167–68; in reflective essay, 43

t-chart, 16, 108, 125
technology: for e-books, 55–62; for group viewing, 216n1 (chap. 12); for oral presentation, 153–55
Tenth Grade: length guidelines for, 3. *See also* Ninth/Tenth Grade program
texts, types and purposes of, 10–11, 104–5
themes, literary, 66–67, 177
theocracy, 176–77
thesis, 12–13, 106
thesis statement, 11–12; placement of, 12
third draft: of literary research paper, 83–91; of reflective essay, 55–62
third-person narrator, 30–33; limited, 32; omniscient, 32–33
time capsules, 101, 195–205; ingredients of, 197; nature of, 196–97; sealing ceremony for, 203–4
title, necessity of, 5, 26
topic: of argumentative essay, 11; importance of, 42; of informative essay, 115
tragedy, 182
transcription, 117
transitional elements, 10, 104, 114
triumph, 182
Twelfth Grade: length guidelines for, 3. *See also* Eleventh/Twelfth Grade program

United States, 169

videos, 135–36
Vietnam War, 169
villain, 33
voice, academic, 10, 22, 104, 114

websites, 135; location and evaluation of, 136–38
Wikipedia, 75
workplace log entries, 143–52
writer's block, 4, 12, 26, 210
writing: issues in, 207–9; production and distribution of, 39–40; recommendations for, 210–13
writing center, 216n2
writing program, 1–7, 203, 211–13
writing techniques, 145–48, 199; favorite, 99; review of, 125–27